ABERRANT BELIEFS AND REASONING

An aberrant belief is extreme or unusual in nature. In the most serious cases these beliefs cause emotional distress in those who hold them, and typify the core symptoms of psychological disorders. Each of the chapters in this volume seeks to examine the role that biases in reasoning can play in the formation of aberrant beliefs.

The chapters consider several conjectures about the role of reasoning in aberrant belief, including the role of the jumping to conclusion bias in delusional beliefs, the probabilistic bias in paranormal beliefs, the role of danger-confirming reasoning in phobias, and the controversial notion that people with schizophrenia do not succumb to specific forms of reasoning bias. There are also chapters evaluating different theoretical perspectives, and suggestions for future research.

Aberrant Beliefs and Reasoning is the first volume presenting an overview of contemporary research in this growing subject area. It will be essential reading for academics and students in the fields of human reasoning, cognitive psychology and philosophy, and will also be of great interest to clinicians and psychiatrists.

Niall Galbraith is Senior Lecturer in Psychology at the University of Wolverhampton, UK. His research interests encompass delusional thinking, schizotypy, attitudes toward psychological disorders and help-seeking.

D1638432

Current Issues in Thinking and Reasoning
Series Editor: Linden Ball

Current Issues in Thinking and Reasoning is a series of edited books which will reflect the state of the art in areas of current and emerging interest in the psychological study of thinking processes.

Each volume will be tightly focussed on a particular topic and will consist of from seven to ten chapters contributed by international experts. The editors of individual volumes will be leading figures in their areas and will provide an introductory overview.

Example topics include thinking and working memory, visual imagery in problem solving, evolutionary approaches to thinking, cognitive processes in planning, creative thinking, decision making processes, pathologies of thinking, individual differences, neuropsychological approaches and applications of thinking research.

Emotion and Reasoning
Edited by Isabelle Blanchette

New Approaches in Reasoning Research
Edited by Wim De Neys and Magda Osman

The Developmental Psychology of Reasoning and Decision-Making
Edited by Henry Markovits

Aberrant Beliefs and Reasoning
Edited by Niall Galbraith

Reasoning as Memory
Edited by Aidan Feeney and Valerie A. Thompson

ABERRANT BELIEFS AND REASONING

Edited by Niall Galbraith

Psychology Press
Taylor & Francis Group

LONDON AND NEW YORK

First published 2015
by Psychology Press
27 Church Road, Hove, East Sussex BN3 2FA

and by Psychology Press
711 Third Avenue, New York, NY 10017

Psychology Press is an imprint of the Taylor & Francis Group, an informa business

British Library Cataloguing in Publication Data
A catalogue record for this book is available from the British Library

Library of Congress Cataloging-in-Publication Data
    Aberrant beliefs and reasoning / edited by Niall Galbraith.
    pages cm.—(Current issues in thinking and reasoning)
    Includes bibliographical references and index.
    1. Delusions. 2. Reasoning (Psychology) I. Galbraith, Niall.
    RC553.D35A24 2015
    616.89—dc23
    2014012804

ISBN: 978–1–84872–341–2 (hbk)
ISBN: 978–1–84872–342–9 (pbk)
ISBN: 978–1–31579–786–1 (ebk)

Typeset in Bembo
by Swales & Willis, Exeter, Devon

Printed and bound in Great Britain by
TJ International Ltd, Padstow, Cornwall

CONTENTS

List of illustrations   *vii*
List of contributors   *viii*
Preface   *x*

Introduction: the role of reasoning in aberrant beliefs   1
Niall Galbraith

1   A psychological model of delusional belief: integrating reasoning
    biases with perceptual, self-concept and emotional factors   7
    Niall Galbraith and Ken Manktelow

2   Prediction-error and two-factor theories of delusion formation:
    competitors or allies?   34
    Kengo Miyazono, Lisa Bortolotti and Matthew R. Broome

3   Reasoning and delusions: do people with delusions really
    jump to conclusions?   55
    Robert Dudley, Kate Cavanagh, Kate Daley and Stephen Smith

4   Affect, dual processes and some pertinent questions about
    delusional reasoning   80
    Stephanie Rhodes and Claire Jones

5   Reasoning in schizophrenia   99
    Amelia Gangemi and Valentina Cardella

6   Paranormal believers' proneness to probabilistic reasoning biases:
a review of the empirical literature   114
Paul Rogers

7   Danger-confirming reasoning and the persistence of phobic
beliefs   132
Peter J. de Jong

8   Non-pharmacological treatment targeting cognitive biases
underlying delusions in schizophrenia: metacognitive training
and therapy   154
*Ryan Balzan, Todd S. Woodward, Mahesh Menon and
Steffen Moritz*

Index   *171*

ILLUSTRATIONS

Figures

3.1 The beads task 57

3.2 VAS ratings for the three groups for the first four beads drawn on the salient task 71

7.1 Main elements of a dual system, multi-process model of anxiety vulnerability 133

7.2 Square root normalized mean median RT (ms) on neutral, threat, and safety syllogisms, varying over validity and believability 143

7.3 Square-rooted RTs (ms) on the four conditions of the social anxiety convictions domain for the lowest (BFNE = 1) and the highest (BFNE = 42) socially fearful participants 145

8.1 "Frog" stimuli set for "fragmentation exercise" in the JTC module 158

8.2 Example of a "BADE exercise" from the Changing Beliefs module 159

8.3 "Kiosk scene" from the Memory and Overconfidence module 161

8.4 Participants are asked to determine what the character may think about another person 162

Table

3.1 Variation in responses across studies 59

CONTRIBUTORS

Ryan Balzan, Flinders University, Australia

Lisa Bortolotti, University of Birmingham, UK

Matthew R. Broome, University of Oxford, UK

Valentina Cardella, University of Messina, Italy

Kate Cavanagh, University of Sussex, UK

Kate Daley, Newcastle University, UK

Peter J. de Jong, University of Groningen, Netherlands

Robert Dudley, Newcastle University, UK

Niall Galbraith, University of Wolverhampton, UK

Amelia Gangemi, University of Messina, Italy

Claire Jones, University of Wolverhampton, UK

Ken Manktelow, University of Wolverhampton, UK

Mahesh Menon, University of British Columbia, Canada

Kengo Miyazono, University of Birmingham, UK

Steffen Moritz, Universitätsklinikum Hamburg-Eppendorf, Germany

Stephanie Rhodes, University of Wolverhampton, UK

Paul Rogers, University of Central Lancashire, UK

Stephen Smith, Newcastle University, UK

Todd S. Woodward, University of British Columbia, Canada; and British Columbia Mental Health and Addictions Research Institute, Canada

PREFACE

Something interesting happened in the psychology of reasoning in the late 1990s and, looking around, we can see it happening in other areas too. For a long time, possibly since the dawn of the cognitive era in psychology 40 years before, researchers had been largely content with the classic hypothesis-testing experimental setup, whereby you give some materials to a group of 'subjects', as we used to say, in a factorial design, and compute the significance of any observed differences between the groups. These computations preferably, if you wanted to publish in the best journals, involved parametric statistics, those that take account of averages and variances.

But an average can conceal as much as it reveals, because in any distribution of scores, the people scoring high or low, or in the middle, might be doing so for a reason that the experiment is not addressing: they might be different sorts of people. Somehow, then, the individual person had got lost along the way. Consider the lodestar of reasoning research: the Wason selection task. It has been known since its earliest times that around 90% of participants, as we now say, fail to select the solution sanctioned by standard logic, a figure that has stayed stable ever since (Manktelow, 2012). The interesting thing that happened in the psychology of reasoning was that Stanovich and West (1998, 2000; Stanovich, 1999) asked: what is it about the logical 10%? What have they got that the rest of us lack?

High intelligence turned out to be the answer, depressingly for someone who was completely baffled by another of Wason's problems, the THOG problem (Wason & Brooks, 1979), on first encountering it. But not the whole answer. Stanovich has gone on to show that other dimensions of individual difference also predict reasoning performance: dimensions of personality. To think your way through reasoning problems, you need not only the appropriate skills, or mindware as Stanovich calls them, but the propensity to use them appropriately. People differ in this, and so they differ in their ability to think rationally; some people cannot see below the problem's surface, and so give the immediate, intuitive response, the System 1 response in the terms of dual system theory (Evans, 2010; Kahneman, 2011; Stanovich, 2011). But some find it easier to park these initial heuristic impressions and work through the problem's implications, using System 2, and some are much better than others at seeing the need to do this in the first place.

Thus there are documented individual differences in the ability to think rationally, just as there are in intelligence, but intelligence and rationality are readily separable – we all know people who are clever but not in the least bit streetwise. Which brings us to the concerns of this book, which are with the kinds of reasoning associated with one form of extreme irrationality, the one associated with aberrant beliefs. Aberrant beliefs take various forms, as you will see from the chapters presented here: phobic beliefs, belief in the paranormal and, most studied of all, delusional beliefs.

Research into aberrant beliefs and reasoning ran parallel to the research on individual differences outlined above, but it is a property of parallel lines not to touch. Except that now they do, and one of the goals of the present volume is to describe aspects of this convergence. One vehicle for it has been the acceptance of the continuity model of mentality (Claridge, 1988), the notion that there are measurable degrees of thinking tendencies which in their extreme forms would be classed as clinical disorders: paranoia, for instance. We are all sensitive to being watched, talked about or conspired against, to some degree, at some times, but only when your normal functioning is interfered with do you have a clinical condition.

Fortunately, there is now a battery of measures of subclinical delusional ideation, paranormal beliefs and so on, which have opened up numerous routes into the kinds of research areas that are portrayed here. The sense is of a field that is already substantial and gathering pace, which has produced important outcomes of both scientific and human significance, and can only produce more in the future. This is a good time to take stock of what has been done so far, and where the signposts are pointing.

Ken Manktelow
University of Wolverhampton

References

Claridge, G. S. (1988). Schizotypy and schizophrenia. In P. Bebbington & P. McGuffin (Eds.), *Schizophrenia: the Major Issues*. Oxford: Heinemann Professional.

Evans, J. St. B. T. (2010). *Thinking Twice: Two Minds in One Brain*. Oxford: Oxford University Press.

Kahneman, D. (2011). *Thinking, Fast and Slow*. Harmondsworth: Penguin.

Manktelow, K. I. (2012). *Thinking and Reasoning*. Hove: Psychology Press.

Stanovich, K. E. (1999). *Who is Rational? Studies of Individual Differences in Reasoning*. Mahwah, NJ: Lawrence Erlbaum Associates.

Stanovich, K. E. (2011). *Rationality and the Reflective Mind*. Oxford: Oxford University Press.

Stanovich, K. E., & West, R. F. (1998). Cognitive ability and variation in selection task performance. *Thinking and Reasoning, 4,* 193–230.

Stanovich, K. E., & West, R. F. (2000). Individual differences in reasoning: Implications for the rationality debate? *Behavioral and Brain Sciences, 23,* 645–726.

Wason, P. C., & Brooks, P. J. (1979). THOG: The anatomy of a problem. *Psychological Research, 41,* 79–90.

INTRODUCTION

The role of reasoning in aberrant beliefs

Niall Galbraith

The title of this text contains the term 'aberrant beliefs', which we define as beliefs which are extreme or unusual in nature, or which (in the most serious cases) may cause emotional distress or social turmoil to the individuals who hold them. Thus the types of belief which are explored in this book are mostly those which typify core symptoms of psychological disorders: in particular, delusions and phobia. In addition to delusional and phobic beliefs, this book also explores paranormal belief and there is some controversy in claiming that paranormal ideas are aberrant. Paranormal beliefs are common, do not necessarily reflect psychological disorder and are not necessarily associated with extreme distress or with social turmoil. Despite this, there is some evidence that paranormal beliefs may predict psychotic disorder (Cella, Vellante & Preti, 2012; Thalbourne, 1994), even though such beliefs often manifest in a non-clinical form (Genovese, 2005; Schofield & Claridge, 2007). Furthermore, paranormal beliefs can overlap with delusional themes and may occupy a place on the psychosis continuum (Goulding, 2005). One must be careful not to pathologise paranormal belief per se, but the theoretical overlap between common paranormal belief and delusions suggests that the study of the former may provide valuable insights into the latter and perhaps into psychological disorder.

The question of whether reasoning plays a role in aberrant beliefs has become increasingly important for psychology, psychiatry and philosophy. The popularity of this idea is usually credited to Beck (e.g. Beck, 1976; Beck & Clark, 1997), who championed the role of thought processes in the development and maintenance of depression and anxiety. Specifically, Beck argued that psychological disorders could be understood and treated once the therapist identified the faulty inferences and beliefs which were contributing to the cause and maintenance of the disorder. Since the emergence of Beck's cognitive theory of anxiety and depression, research into reasoning and psychopathology has intensified considerably. A large volume of research literature has been generated on reasoning in relation to delusional and paranormal beliefs as well as anxiety and phobia.

The bulk of the chapters in this volume focus on reasoning in delusional beliefs. The study of reasoning biases in people with delusions began with the proposal by von Domarus (1944) that schizophrenic thinking was underpinned by reasoning which was illogical. Subsequently, however, due to repeated failures to uphold this hypothesis (e.g. Williams, 1964) and the growing realisation that human reasoning itself was often at odds with formal logic (Manktelow & Over, 1987; Wason, 1968; Wason & Evans, 1975), the study of delusional reasoning biases fell out of favour. However, in the late 1980s, researchers began again to examine the area, perhaps with the implicit understanding that, although normative systems such as logic may serve as a benchmark for describing what the deluded do and do not do when they reason (e.g. Bayes' Theorem, see Garety & Hemsley, 1994), mere deviation from a normative system should not be taken as a starting point for pathological thinking. Instead studies began to report on the differences between patient and control groups on a range of reasoning tasks: Brennan and Hemsley (1984) demonstrated that paranoid patients were prone to illusory correlations, and Huq, Garety & Hemsley (1988) found evidence for a jump-to-conclusions (JTC) reasoning bias in patients with delusions. The implication of these findings was that delusional patients may display biases in reasoning which could contribute to the formation and/or maintenance of delusional beliefs.

Over the next two and a half decades, the study of delusional reasoning grew. The field has been advanced by research groups all over the world. In the UK, Rob Dudley has produced a number of definitive papers on the jump-to-conclusions bias. The group led by Philippa Garety and Daniel Freeman has published prolifically on the JTC bias as well as on a range of other psychological factors in delusions, culminating in the threat anticipation model of paranoia (Freeman, 2007; Freeman, Garety, Kuipers, Fowler & Bebbington, 2002).

From outside the UK, the partnership between Steffen Moritz (from Germany) and Todd Woodward (from Canada) has led to new perspectives on the JTC bias. One of their important contributions is the notion that people with delusions have a liberal acceptance threshold for implausible ideas or for weak evidence (e.g. Moritz, Woodward & Lambert, 2007). They have also produced a number of influential papers outlining findings of a bias against disconfirmatory evidence (BADE; Woodward, Buchy, Moritz & Liotti, 2007). More recently, they have used their empirical work to develop a promising method for training people with psychological disorders to modify unhealthy reasoning (Moritz, Veckenstedt, Randjbar, Vitzthum & Woodward, 2011).

Another influential research team, based mainly in Australia and led by Max Coltheart, Robyn Langdon, Ryan McKay and colleagues, has developed the two-factor theory (Coltheart, Menzies & Sutton, 2010; Davies & Coltheart, 2000) of delusional belief. Factor 1 is a neuropsychological deficit leading to anomalous perceptions. The resultant explanation for these unusual perceptions may develop into a delusion if a second factor is also present: namely a deficit in belief revision.

The two-factor theory has so far been applied almost exclusively to monothematic delusions – that is, beliefs with a singular theme, such as the Capgras (a loved one is believed to be an impostor) or Cotard (the individual believes they are dead or dying) syndromes.

We begin this monograph with the chapter by myself and Ken Manktelow. We offer a theoretical review of the empirical research on reasoning biases in delusional belief. Our aim is to explore whether such reasoning biases can be integrated with other psychological factors in delusions. In doing this, we present a more comprehensive theory of delusions, which attempts to account for the four stages in delusion formation/maintenance: emergence of the delusional idea; consideration of the tentative delusional hypothesis; selection of evidence and full acceptance; maintenance of the belief.

In Chapter 2, Kengo Miyazono, Lisa Bortolotti and Matthew Broome analyse the apparent impasse between the two-factor theory of Max Coltheart and colleagues (e.g. Davies, Coltheart, Langdon & Breen, 2001; Coltheart, 2007; Coltheart, Menzies & Sutton, 2010) and the prediction-error theory put forward by Corlett and others (Corlett, Taylor, Wang, Fletcher & Krystal, 2010; Fletcher & Frith, 2009). The two-factor theory has stimulated a great deal of research but has been challenged by proponents of the prediction-error theory (Corlett, Taylor, Wang, Fletcher & Krystal, 2010; Fletcher & Frith, 2009). The prediction-error theory contends that a single process underlies both hallucinatuions and delusions. This process is an excessive or unwarranted prediction error signal, in other words the erroneous detection of a mismatch between what is expected and what is observed. Miyazono, Bortolotti and Broome question whether these two theories may have more in common than in contrast and whether they may indeed be reconciled. Miyazono *et al.* critically disect the two theories in order to reveal unique perspectives and new arguments.

Following on from this, in Chapter 3, Rob Dudley, Kate Cavanagh, Kate Daley and Stephen Smith offer an in-depth review of the literature on the jump-to-conclusions bias. Dudley has produced a number of influential research papers on the jump-to-conclusions bias (e.g. Dudley, John, Young & Over, 1997a, 1997b; Dudley & Over, 2003; Dudley *et al.*, 2013) They cast a critical eye over this research field as they ask fundamental questions about the state of knowledge and speculate on future directions for what has become the most widely researched and most reliably replicated reasoning bias in those with delusional beliefs. Chapter 4 by Stephanie Rhodes and Claire Jones asks fundamental questions about the definition of delusions, about the crucial role of affect in delusional reasoning and also about the relevance of dual-process theories of reasoning in relation to delusional thinking. Chapter 5 presents a truly unique perspective on delusions and reasoning by Amelia Gangemi and Valentina Cardella. They advance the argument which contrasts with the now discredited historical view that people with schizophrenia are illogical (Arieti, 1964). They argue that careful analysis of the evidence suggests that such individuals are excessively logical and that their difficulty may stem from an over-reliance on logical reasoning and a deficiency in belief flexibility. The view that people with delusions do *not* have a general deficit in reasoning has been around for some time (e.g. Dudley & Over, 2003), but Gangemi and Cardella's chapter has the potential to change the way we conceptualise the subtle reasoning biases that they *do* exhibit.

In Chapter 6, we move away from delusions to paranormal beliefs. The interest in reasoning style as a psychological factor in paranormal belief began to take hold in the 1980s (e.g. Alcock & Otis, 1980; Blackmore & Troscianko, 1985; Wierzbicki, 1985). As with the literature on delusional beliefs, the research field has subsequently blossomed and a large volume of empirical studies on reasoning and other psychological factors in paranormal beliefs now exists. The relevance of this work to that of the preceding sections on delusions is considerable. Paranormal belief may be conceived as a delusional theme and may fall on the delusional continuum (Peters, Joseph, Day & Garety, 2004) and there is evidence that believers in the paranormal are more likely to hold delusional ideas (Hergovich, Schott & Arendasy, 2008). As with delusional belief, there is an abundance of research evidence suggesting that believers in the paranormal are prone to probabilistic biases. A review of this literature is now warranted. Paul Rogers explores this research and evaluates the argument that probabilistic biases in paranormal believers may be indicative not of a wholesale deficit in reason, but rather of a misperception of randomness.

In Chapter 7, Peter J. de Jong provides a review of research into the thinking which underpins phobic danger-beliefs. Following the work of Beck and colleagues (e.g. Beck, Emery & Greenberg, 1985), de Jong has for many years been a leading authority on reasoning in anxiety and phobia, and his work has come to define the field (e.g. de Jong, Mayer & van den Hout, 1997; Smeets, de Jong & Mayer, 2000; Vroling & de Jong, 2009). He presents a dual-process approach involving a reflexive system, which activates threat-related associations and emotions and a rule-based system involving reasoning. The chapter presents an argument for how the rule-based system will tend to confirm and therefore strengthen phobic beliefs, thus perpetuating avoidance of the phobic stimulus. As with the chapter on paranormal belief, this research is also theoretically interrelated to delusional reasoning (Dudley & Over, 2003), especially given the prominent role that anxiety plays in paranoia (see Fowler *et al.*, 2006). This chapter concludes with recommendations for future research priorities and the therapeutic applications of this empirical work. This discussion leads logically to our final chapter, in which Ryan Balzan, Todd Woodward, Mahesh Menon and Steffen Moritz present their metacognitive training (MCT) programme for delusions. Their programme helps clients with delusions to recognise and modify the biased thinking which underlies their beliefs. Balzan *et al.*'s chapter describes this programme and subsequently outlines its theoretical foundation in the cognitive and social biases which characterise delusions. They finish with a look at the efficacy of the MCT programme as an intervention for patients with delusions. This final chapter then provides a fitting testament to the applied value of the empirical research into beliefs and reasoning which has flourished over the past 25 years or so.

References

Alcock, J. E., & Otis, L. P. (1980). Critical thinking and belief in the paranormal. *Psychological Reports, 46*(2), 479–482.

Arieti, A. (1964). *Interpretazione della schizofrenia*. Milano: Feltrinelli.

Beck, A. T. (1976). *Cognitive Therapy and the Emotional Disorders*. New York: IUP.

Beck, A. T., & Clark, D. A. (1997). An information processing model of anxiety: Automatic and strategic processes. *Behaviour Research and Therapy, 35*, 49–58.

Beck, A. T., Emery, G., & Greenberg, R. L. (1985). *Anxiety Disorders and Phobias: A Cognitive Perspective*. New York: Basic Books.

Blackmore, S., & Trościanko, T. (1985). Belief in the paranormal: Probability judgements, illusory control, and the 'chance baseline shift'. *British Journal of Psychology, 76*(4), 459–468.

Brennan, J. H., & Hemsley, D. R. (1984). Illusory correlations in paranoid and non-paranoid schizophrenia. *British Journal of Clinical Psychology, 23*, 225–226.

Cella, M., Vellante, M., & Preti, A. (2012). How psychotic-like are paranormal beliefs? *Journal of Behavior Therapy and Experimental Psychiatry, 43*(3), 897–900.

Coltheart, M. (2007). The 33rd Sir Frederick Barlett Lecture: Cognitive neuropsychiatry and delusional belief. *The Quarterly Journal of Experimental Psychology, 60*(8), 1041–1062.

Coltheart, M., Menzies, P., & Sutton, J. (2010). Abductive inference and delusional belief. *Cognitive Neuropsychiatry, 15*(1/2/3), 261–287.

Corlett, P., Taylor, J., Wang, X.-J., Fletcher, P., & Krystal, J. (2010). Toward a neurobiology of delusions. *Progress in Neurobiology, 92*, 345–369.

Davies, M., & Coltheart, M. (2000). Introduction: Pathologies of belief. *Mind and Language, 15*, 1–46.

Davies, M., Coltheart, M., Langdon, R., & Breen, N. (2001). Monothematic delusions: Toward a two-factor account. *Philosophy, Psychiatry, & Psychology, 8*, 133–158.

de Jong, P. J., Mayer, B., & van den Hout, M. (1997). Conditional reasoning and phobic fear: Evidence for a fear-confirming reasoning pattern. *Behaviour Research and Therapy, 35*(6), 507–516.

Dudley, R., Daley, K., Nicholson, M., Shaftoe, D., Spencer, H., Cavanagh, K., & Freeston, M. (2013). 'Jumping to conclusions' in first-episode psychosis: A longitudinal study. *British Journal of Clinical Psychology, 52*(4), 380–393.

Dudley, R. E. J., John, C. H., Young, A., & Over, D. E. (1997a). Normal and abnormal reasoning in people with delusions. *British Journal of Clinical Psychology, 36*, 243–258.

Dudley, R. E. J., John, C. H., Young, A., & Over, D. E. (1997b). The effect of self-referent material on the reasoning of people with delusions. *British Journal of Clinical Psychology, 36*, 575–584.

Dudley, R. E. J., & Over, D. E. (2003). People with delusions jump to conclusions: A theoretical account of research findings on the reasoning of people with delusions. *Clinical Psychology and Psychotherapy, 10*, 263–274.

Fletcher, P., & Frith, C. (2009). Perceiving is believing: A Bayesian approach to explaining the positive symptoms of schizophrenia. *Nature Reviews Neuroscience, 10*, 48–58.

Fowler, D., Freeman, D., Smith, B., Kuipers, E., Bebbington, P., Bashforth, H., . . . & Garety, P. (2006). The Brief Core Schema Scales (BCSS): Psychometric properties and associations with paranoia and grandiosity in non-clinical and psychosis samples. *Psychological Medicine, 36*(6), 749–760.

Freeman, D. (2007). Suspicious minds: The psychology of persecutory delusions. *Clinical Psychology Review, 27*, 425–457.

Freeman, D., Garety, P. A., Kuipers, E., Fowler, D., & Bebbington, P. E. (2002). A cognitive model of persecutory delusions. *British Journal of Clinical Psychology, 41*, 331–347.

Garety, P. A., & Hemsley, D. R. (1994). *Delusions: Investigations into the Psychology of Delusional Reasoning*. Oxford: Oxford University Press.

Genovese, J. E. (2005). Paranormal beliefs, schizotypy, and thinking styles among teachers and future teachers. *Personality and Individual Differences, 39*(1), 93–102.

Goulding, A. (2005). Healthy schizotypy in a population of paranormal believers and experients. *Personality and Individual Differences, 38*(5), 1069–1083.

Hergovich, A., Schott, R., & Arendasy, M. (2008). On the relationship between paranormal belief and schizotypy among adolescents. *Personality and Individual Differences, 45*(2), 119–125.

Huq, S. F., Garety, P. A., & Hemsley, D. R. (1988). Probabilistic judgements in deluded and non-deluded subjects. *Quarterly Journal of Experimental Psychology: Human Learning and Memory, 40A*, 801–812.

Manktelow, K. I., & Over, D. E. (1987). Reasoning and rationality. *Mind & Language, 2*(3), 199–219.

Moritz, S., Veckenstedt, R., Randjbar, S., Vitzthum, F., & Woodward, T. S. (2011). Antipsychotic treatment beyond antipsychotics: Metacognitive intervention for schizophrenia patients improves delusional symptoms. *Psychological Medicine, 41*(9), 1823–1832.

Moritz, S., Woodward, T. S., & Lambert, M. (2007). Under what circumstances do patients with schizophrenia jump to conclusions? A liberal acceptance account. *British Journal of Clinical Psychology, 46*, 127–137.

Peters, E., Joseph, S., Day, S., & Garety, P. (2004). Measuring delusional ideation. *Schizophrenia Bulletin, 30*(4), 1005–1022.

Schofield, K., & Claridge, G. (2007). Paranormal experiences and mental health: Schizotypy as an underlying factor. *Personality and Individual Differences, 43*(7), 1908–1916.

Smeets, G., de Jong, P. J., & Mayer, B. (2000). If you suffer from a headache, then you have a brain tumour: Domain-specific reasoning 'bias' and hypochondriasis. *Behaviour Research and Therapy, 38*(8), 763–776.

Thalbourne, M. A. (1994). Belief in the paranormal and its relationship to schizophrenia – relevant measures: A confirmatory study. *British Journal of Clinical Psychology, 33*(1), 78–80.

von Domarus, E. (1944). The specific laws of logic in schizophrenia. In J. Kasanin (Ed.), *Language and Thought in Schizophrenia*. Berkeley, CA: University of California Press.

Vroling, M. S., & de Jong, P. J. (2009). Deductive reasoning and social anxiety: Evidence for a fear-confirming belief bias. *Cognitive Therapy and Research, 33*(6), 633–644.

Wason, P. C. (1968). Reasoning about a rule. *The Quarterly Journal of Experimental Psychology, 20*(3), 273–281.

Wason, P. C., & Evans, J. St. B. T. (1975). Dual processes in reasoning? *Cognition, 3*, 141–154.

Wierzbicki, M. (1985). Reasoning errors and belief in the paranormal. *The Journal of Social Psychology, 125*(4), 489–494.

Williams, E. B. (1964). Deductive reasoning in schizophrenia. *Journal of Abnormal and Social Psychology, 69*, 47–61.

Woodward, T. S., Buchy, L., Moritz, S., & Liotti, M. (2007). A bias against disconfirmatory evidence is associated with delusion proneness in a nonclinical sample. *Schizophrenia Bulletin, 33*, 1023–1028.

1

A PSYCHOLOGICAL MODEL OF DELUSIONAL BELIEF

Integrating reasoning biases with perceptual, self-concept and emotional factors

Niall Galbraith and Ken Manktelow

This chapter attempts to integrate the research on reasoning biases in delusional thinking with other psychological theories of delusion, encompassing the self-concept, perceptions, affect and cognition. The first section will reflect briefly on the nature of delusions and will make a proposal for what a complete theory of delusion formation/maintenance should be able to account for. This will be followed by an outline of psychological theories of delusions, culminating in an in–depth review of the role of reasoning biases in delusional beliefs. The literature on reasoning biases in delusions has afforded a range of theories and a major focus will be on integrating these theories along with other psychological explanations into a coherent model of delusion formation/maintenance. Following this, recommendations for future research will be proposed.

Delusional beliefs

Delusions have been described as the sine qua non of psychosis (e.g. Kemp, Chua, McKenna & David, 1997). They are beliefs which, according to the DSM-5 (APA, 2013) are fixed and resistant to change in the face of conflicting evidence. Delusions are also multidimensional and may be assessed in terms of the degree of distress they bring to the believer, level of preoccupation, degree of conviction and action (Garety & Freeman, 1999). Delusions are most commonly thought of as a symptom of schizophrenia (Tandon & Maj, 2008); however they may also feature in a range of other conditions (e.g. depression; Johnson, Horwath & Weissman, 1991).

Although delusions are normally associated with illness, there is an abundance of literature suggesting that delusions and other features of psychosis can be measured on a continuum ranging from the general population through to the clinical population (Freeman, Pugh, Vorontsova, Antley & Slater, 2010; van

Os, Linscott, Myin–Germeys, Delespaul & Krabbendam, 2009). The subclinical range of psychotic-like behaviours and experiences is known as schizotypy, and is regarded by many as a multidimensional personality trait (Claridge & Beech, 1995). It is also argued that, although high levels of schizotypy do not equate to mental illness, they may represent a proneness to psychotic breakdown (Claridge & Beech, 1995).

What should a complete theory of delusion formation and maintenance be able to account for?

Consistent with theoretical accounts of delusions (e.g. Coltheart, Menzies & Sutton, 2010; Fine, Gardner, Craigie & Gold, 2007; Freeman, 2007), we identify four major stages of delusion formation/maintenance.

1. Emergence of the delusional idea

There must be a precipitating factor to provide the genesis for the delusional hypothesis. What factors bring about the need for a delusional explanation and why does this delusional hypothesis emerge?

2. Consideration and tentative acceptance of the delusional hypothesis

The delusional hypothesis must then be considered as a viable candidate for belief. Why does a person with delusions not immediately reject an implausible hypothesis as a non-starter for belief?

3. Selection of evidence and full acceptance of the delusional hypothesis

Once the delusional hypothesis has been granted consideration as a potential candidate for belief, in what way is evidence gathered and selected to either 1) support the hypothesis so that it becomes a consolidated belief, or 2) disconfirm the hypothesis so that it is discarded and not adopted as a belief?

4. Maintenance of the belief

Once the belief has been established, how is it maintained and preserved over time?

This chapter will explore the extent to which reasoning biases, in harmony with other psychological factors, can account for these stages in delusional belief. The following section will outline the most influential psychological theories of delusions, encompassing a range of cognitive, perceptual and emotional processes, before a more in-depth review of delusional reasoning is undertaken.

Psychological theories of delusions

Aberrant perceptions

Maher (1974, 2005) posits that delusions are formed from patients' attempts to explain anomalous perceptual experiences. Crucially, Maher initially argued that it is not faulty reasoning which leads to delusional beliefs but rather faulty perceptions which taint the normal reasoning process. The notion that unusual perceptual experiences can stimulate delusional-type beliefs has empirical support. For example, hypnotically induced deafness (Zimbardo, Andersen & Kabat, 1981) or natural hearing loss in the elderly (e.g. Cooper, Kay, Curry, Garside & Roth, 1974) can lead to paranoid beliefs in non-patients. Furthermore, delusions and hallucinations commonly co-exist in psychotic patients (Peralta & Cuesta, 1999) and people who are delusion-prone show a reduced ability to predict sensory outcomes from self-generated actions (Teufel, Kingdon, Ingram, Wolpert & Fletcher, 2010).

In spite of the support for Maher's position, others have failed to replicate the relationship between hearing impairment and delusions (Cohen, Magai, Yaffe & Walcott-Brown, 2004; Östling & Skoog, 2002). Indeed Maher (1999) moved away from a purely perceptual account, later proposing an additional probabilistic reasoning impairment in addition to faulty perceptual processes. Maher's theory has been extended by Coltheart and colleagues, who propose a two-factor model (e.g. Davies & Coltheart, 2000; Coltheart, Langdon & McKay, 2011). Perceptual anomalies constitute the first factor; the second factor is a deficit in the mechanism of belief revision, which prevents the individual from rejecting the implausible ideas which arise from the perceptual anomaly.

Affect and schemas

Freeman and colleagues' threat anticipation model (e.g. Freeman, 2007; Freeman, Garety, Kuipers, Fowler & Bebbington, 2002) also acknowledges that hallucinations are central to (particularly persecutory) delusions, but contends that other factors combine in the formation of delusions. In addition to internal hallucinatory experiences, external events such as interactions with other people and negative environmental occurrences may also be precipitating factors in the genesis of delusional ideas. Anxiety strongly predicts delusions in both clinical and non-clinical samples (e.g. Fowler et al., 2006; Freeman et al., 2005; Martin & Penn, 2001) and negative schemas about the self (e.g. I am weak, unloved, vulnerable, etc.) and others (e.g. others are hostile, untrustworthy, nasty, etc.) have strong relationships with paranoia (Fowler et al., 2006; Smith et al., 2006). Other affective states such as worry (Freeman et al., 2013) and depression (e.g. Galbraith et al., 2014) may also exacerbate paranoia. The combination of anxiety and negative schemas is central to the threat anticipation model. In line with Beck's schema-based cognitive model of anxiety (e.g. Clark & Beck, 2010), the threat anticipation model proposes that negative schemas lead to a biased construal of the self, the world and other people.

In addition, anxiety leads to a hyper-vigilance for threat. Negative schemas and anxiety combine then, to leave the individual feeling both personally vulnerable and at risk from malicious others (Fowler *et al.*, 2006). If hallucinations occur in such individuals, their putative causal hypotheses for these experiences may be coloured by negative schemas and anxiety, and thus hallucinations are attributed to sinister causes. Biased data-gathering (Freeman, Pugh & Garety, 2008) or self-referent reasoning (Galbraith, Manktelow & Morris, 2008) may then consolidate these putative delusional hypotheses.

Bentall and colleagues (e.g. Kinderman & Bentall, 1996, 1997) have proposed that persecutory delusions are characterised by a bias to blame other people (as opposed to situational factors or oneself) for negative events. Such a tendency may prime one to formulate persecutory ideas, in which other people are to blame when bad things happen to the self. Bentall and colleagues argue that this bias has a defensive function, as persecutory beliefs may block out negative self-representations and therefore protect fragile self-esteem. Despite empirical support, there have also been failures to replicate the attributional bias in paranoid individuals (e.g. Lincoln, Mehl, Exner, Lindenmeyer & Rief, 2010; Martin & Penn, 2001; Young & Bentall, 1997b). Freeman (2007) contends that a more parsimonious position would be that people with persecutory delusions may sometimes make external attributions but that this need not reflect a defensive process or an external personalising bias. Indeed some evidence from non-clinical studies (e.g. Galbraith *et al.*, 2014) and from clinical studies (e.g. Barrowclough *et al.*, 2003) supports the view that paranoia is more likely to be negatively related to self-esteem and positively related to depression, thus reflecting a non-defensive account.

Conversely, grandiose beliefs may be strongly linked with positive affect. For example, (Smith *et al.*, 2006) found that such beliefs were associated with strong positive-self schemas but also negative-other schemas. This combination of schemas may increase one's perceived social standing relative to others (Smith *et al.*, 2006). Contrastingly, others have found grandiose delusions as characterised by less negative schemas, both for the self and for others (Garety *et al.*, 2013). Furthermore, people with grandiose delusions may have a cognitive style which predisposes them to misinterpret both internal and external events as personally relevant and in a way which amplifies positive affect (Knowles, McCarthy-Jones & Rowse, 2011; Mansell, Morrison, Reid, Lowens & Tai, 2007). As Knowles *et al.* (2007) point out, research which focuses specifically on grandiose delusions is relatively scant, and therefore conclusions about the psychological underpinnings of these beliefs cannot be as confident as those on paranoid ideas, for example.

Theory of mind

Frith (1992) argues that delusions of persecution, reference and misidentification are due to an inability to represent the thoughts, attitudes, beliefs and intentions of others – that is, a poor theory of mind (ToM). A number of studies have reported links between delusions and ToM (e.g. Corcoran, Cahill & Frith, 1997; Gooding

& Pflum, 2011; Taylor & Kinderman, 2002). However, many studies have failed to observe associations between ToM and delusions or paranoia (e.g. Blackshaw, Kinderman, Hare & Hatton, 2001; Greig, Bryson & Bell, 2004), or have instead found associations between ToM and other features of psychosis, such as negative symptoms or thought disorder (Kelemen *et al.*, 2005; Pickup & Frith, 2001). The ToM deficit might reflect a generic mental illness factor (Corcoran *et al.*, 1997) or a cognitive deficit (Bora, Yücel & Pantelis, 2009; Langdon *et al.*, 1997). The ToM account is intuitively appealing as it can explain why some people misconstrue the intentions of others (potentially leading to ideas of persecution), but despite some good empirical support, the data are somewhat inconsistent and the deficit may not be specific to delusions.

This section has provided an overview of what are currently the most widely cited psychological theories of delusions. The next section will examine the evidence on delusional reasoning.

Reasoning in delusions

The following section will review literature on delusional reasoning biases. In this context, the term 'bias' is taken to mean a systematic tendency to respond or behave in a manner which differs from some reference group. The reference group is typically either psychiatric or non-psychiatric controls or, in the case of non-clinical studies, people from the general population who themselves do not score highly on measures of subclinical delusional belief.

The jump-to-conclusions bias

By the 1980s, research into reasoning in schizophrenia had fallen out of favour, particularly after Williams (1964) had refuted von Domarus's (1944) claims that schizophrenia was underpinned by a deductive reasoning bias. The idea that reasoning played a role in delusional belief was re-ignited by Huq, Garety and Hemsley's (1988) seminal study. They used Phillips and Edwards' (1966) 'beads task', in which participants decided whether a sequence of beads (drawn one at a time) was being taken from a jar containing mostly pink beads or a jar containing mostly green beads (ratio 85:15). Based on the number of beads drawn before making a decision (the 'draws to decision' [DTD] version of the task), they found that patients with delusions made decisions after seeing, on average, 2.22 beads (non-psychiatric controls averaged 3.6). In addition to measuring draws to decision, Huq *et al.* (1988) also found that, after the first bead was drawn, patients with delusions also made more confident probability estimates about which jar the beads were being taken from. The implication was that perhaps people with delusions have a systematic tendency to jump to conclusions (JTC), thus making hasty decisions on the basis of relatively little evidence compared to people without delusions. Such a tendency may leave people more prone to formulating unsound beliefs – beliefs based upon an impoverished set of evidence. Indeed there is some clinical validity to this claim, as patients who are unable to generate alternative explanations for their delusion-based experiences also tend to gather less data on difficult versions (ratio 60:40) of the beads task (Freeman *et al.*, 2004).

The JTC bias in people with delusions was replicated (Garety, Hemsley & Wessely, 1991) and has since become a robust experimental paradigm in the literature on delusional reasoning (see Fine *et al.*, 2007). Some studies have applied a different format to the task, known as 'draws to certainty' (DTC) (e.g. Garety *et al.*, 1991; Huq *et al.*, 1988; Peters, Thornton, Siksou, Linney & MacCabe, 2008). Here participants see all beads, but after each bead, they make probability estimates about the likelihood that the beads are being drawn from one jar rather than the other. Two review papers (Garety & Freeman, 1999; Fine *et al.*, 2007) have established that the DTD version of the task is a reliable method for distinguishing between people with and without delusions, but that the DTC format is not. There is some evidence that, in the DTC version of the task, people with delusions over-adjust their probability estimates when the colour of the bead changes (e.g. a black bead is drawn after four preceding orange beads) (e.g. Garety *et al.*, 1991; Langdon, Still, Connors, Ward & Catts, 2014; Moritz & Woodward, 2005). However, this finding has not always been replicated: in their critical review of cognitive theories of delusions, Garety and Freeman (1999) concluded that there was some support for the theory that people with delusions over-adjust their probability estimates in response to disconfirmatory information. In contrast, in their meta-analysis, Fine *et al.* (2007) concluded that there was insufficient support for this claim.

Changes in delusions over time have been shown to lead to changes in the JTC bias (Woodward, Munz, LeClerc & Lecomte, 2009), and maintenance of JTC over time leads to worsening symptoms (Dudley *et al.*, 2013). There is now growing evidence that training in reasoning can improve data-gathering (Ross, Freeman, Dunn & Garety, 2011) and can reduce delusional conviction (Moritz, Veckenstedt, Randjbar, Vitzthum & Woodward, 2011; Waller, Freeman, Jolley, Dunn & Garety, 2011).

A reasoning deficit or a data-gathering bias?

The literature does not appear to suggest that people with delusions have an inability to reason, but instead they may demonstrate a bias in the way evidence is gathered. For example, Dudley, John, Young and Over (1997a) found that when they, the experimenters, determined the amount of evidence that was seen, deluded patients performed similarly to controls, both on statistical judgements and when choosing the jar on the beads task. Patients differed from controls only when they were free to determine the amount of evidence that was seen: here, as in earlier studies, patients requested less evidence before they made their decisions. Patients with delusions did adjust their data-gathering in accordance with changes to the base rate (e.g. 60:40 compared to 85:15) and therefore showed evidence of engaging in reasoning, but they still showed a JTC relative to controls. This finding has been replicated since (Lincoln, Ziegler, Mehl & Rief, 2010). Deluded patients have been found to gather less data on the beads task but reason similarly to controls on the Wason selection task (Linney, Peters & Ayton, 1998; Peters *et al.*, 2008). These studies seem to suggest that people with delusions are not unable to reason or make statistical judgements, but instead that they tend to collect less data or are less able to utilise data when making a decision.

However, as shown by the DTC studies (e.g. Peters *et al.*, 2008), delusional reasoning biases are not only evident on tasks requiring participant-determined data-gathering. People with delusions may also be less adept at using information when reasoning. For example, delusion-prone individuals may be less sensitive to the importance of sample size and sample heterogeneity in statistical judgement (Galbraith, Manktelow & Morris, 2010; Linney *et al.*, 1998).

Data-gathering with realistic tasks

Part of the appeal of the original beads task is that it appears to show a reasoning bias which is unconnected to the themes of delusional beliefs. This suggests a systematic weakness in reasoning which may pre-date delusional beliefs and which may therefore be a causal factor in their formation. The abstract nature of the beads task also presents a problem: does the JTC effect generalise to more realistic situations? In order to address this question, numerous studies have employed more realistic materials. For example, Dudley, John, Young & Over (1997b) replicated the JTC effect with a realistic version of the beads task: statements referring either to the self or to another were used instead of beads. Delusional reasoning has also been examined using hypothesis-testing tasks. John and Dodgson (1994) found that deluded participants requested less information on a version of the 'Twenty Questions Game' before making judgements that were also of poorer quality compared to controls. Ziegler, Rief, Werner, Mehl and Lincoln (2008) report on a new data-gathering problem, in which participants gather increasingly diagnostic data to name a partially displayed letter or number. Compared to the classic beads task, this new task was more strongly related to non-clinical delusional ideation.

Using a visual discrimination task, Young and Bentall (1995) found that people with delusions were less inclined to focus down to a final hypothesis. Also, compared to controls, they were more likely to revise their hypotheses after positive feedback and were more likely to stick to hypotheses following negative feedback. Linney *et al.* (1998) observed that non-clinical participants, high in delusional ideation, made judgements based on particularly limited amounts of information on an adaptation of Wason's 2-4-6 task. These studies are largely consistent with the probabilistic reasoning work, in that they point to a data-gathering bias in deluded/delusion-prone participants. An interesting feature of the hypothesis-testing studies is that they suggest that people with delusions are biased not only to gather less data but also to gather data of poorer quality. Young and Bentall (1995), in line with Hemsley (1988), concluded that people with delusions are less able to make use of sequential information. This idea, however, is not consistent with those studies employing the probability estimates version of the beads task, where patients with delusions have often been found to make few errors and to respond similarly to controls. In this version of the task, the number of trials is predetermined, and the processing of sequential information is therefore crucial if one is to choose the correct jar.

In summary then, the JTC bias represents a potential mechanism for how delusions are formed or maintained. A number of other reasoning biases or anomalies have been implicated in delusional thinking, some of which complement the JTC account. The following section will outline these and will also explore their relation to the JTC literature.

The liberal acceptance bias

Another bias which has been reliably replicated in the literature is the liberal acceptance bias (Moritz & Woodward, 2004; Moritz, Woodward, Jelinek & Klinge, 2008; Moritz, Woodward & Lambert, 2007; Zawadzki et al., 2012). Using the Thematic Aperception Test (TAT; participants were asked to rate the plausibility of various explanations for ambiguous pictorial scenes), Moritz and Woodward (2004) found that patients with schizophrenia were more likely than controls to consider multiple options as plausible and were also more likely to endorse implausible explanations, an effect since replicated on a different task where participants rated the plausibility of various titles for classic paintings (Moritz et al., 2009). This liberal acceptance bias has been further replicated in recognition memory (Moritz et al., 2008), where delusional patients were more likely to be distracted by weak lures compared to controls.

Together, these studies demonstrate that people with delusions have a lowered threshold for accepting implausible evidence – they are more likely to accept as plausible what others would see as implausible. Moritz et al. (2007) subsequently argued that the liberal acceptance bias manifests as an early decision because, with only two jars to choose from, one jar quickly passes the threshold of acceptance, whereas the other jar is deemed as too implausible, even by liberal standards. Interestingly however, Moritz et al. (2007) found that, with multiple alternatives, patients' JTC bias disappeared. They argued that in those with a lower threshold of acceptance, multiple alternatives would be accepted as viable, resulting in confusing ambiguity and uncertainty, not hastiness. Bensi, Giusberti, Nori & Gambetti (2010) corroborated this aspect of the liberal acceptance account: hasty data-gathering in delusion-prone participants was eliminated when the number of alternatives in the beads task was increased from two to three.

There is indeed evidence – for example, in the prepulse inhibition literature – that people with schizophrenia have difficulty in filtering out competing stimuli (e.g. Geyer, Krebs-Thomson, Braff & Swerdlow, 2001; Ziermans, Schothorst, Magnée, van Engeland & Kemner, 2011) and Moritz et al.'s (2007) account is consistent with Young and Bentall's (1995) finding that people with delusions struggle to focus down to a single hypothesis on hypothesis-testing tasks. Conflicting findings have been reported by White and Mansell (2009) though, who report a draws to decision JTC effect not only on the classic two-jar version of the beads task but also on three and four-jar versions (see also Broome *et al.*, 2007). They argue that the discrepancy may be due to Moritz *et al*'s tendency to rely on probability estimates (Moritz *et al.*, 2007) or plausibility estimates (Moritz & Woodward, 2004) rather than DTD. White and Mansell (2009) argue that it is the final decision between competing hypotheses which is crucial, not evaluations of those alternatives. Moritz *et al.*'s (2007) findings also run contrary to those of Ziegler *et al.* (2008), whose letter task presents multiple alternatives for the first several trials and yet yielded increased JTC in delusion-prone participants.

Moritz *et al.* (2007) argue that other biases (such as a bias against disconfirmatory evidence) will combine with liberal acceptance in order to consolidate hypotheses. Additionally, a need for closure may explain how competing hypotheses are finally filtered out (Moritz *et al.*, 2007; Zawadzki *et al.*, 2012). Need for closure (NFC) has been described as a general desire to find a firm answer to a topic and to avoid ambiguity (Kruglanski & Webster, 1996). Therefore, NFC may provide the mechanism by which people with delusions overcome ambiguity and settle upon a single delusional explanation. It may be difficult to reconcile the coexistence of two apparently opposing biases: a propensity to accept multiple alternatives (liberal acceptance) and a propensity to seek out definitive answers (NFC). This aspect of the theory is currently under-developed and would benefit from further research. However, the notion that delusional belief may be explained through a NFC deserves some attention. The following section will evaluate this proposal in more detail.

Need for closure

The NFC construct can be conceived as a trait and a state variable. An individual who is high in NFC is characterised by close-mindedness, decisiveness, a preference for order and an aversion for ambiguity (Webster & Kruglanski, 1994). The construct is typically measured with the Need for Closure Scale (NFCS; Webster & Kruglanski, 1994). A high NFC is appealing as an explanation for delusional thinking as it represents a motivational factor for jumping to conclusions: people with delusions JTC because they crave a decisive solution to the task. In line with this idea, Bentall and Swarbrick (2003) found that both currently deluded and remitted patients showed higher NFC than controls. Similarly, Colbert and Peters (2002) reported higher NFC and a JTC bias in non-clinical but delusion-prone individuals.

Elsewhere however, the evidence is less convincing. Freeman *et al.* (2006) found no direct relationships between NFC and either psychotic symptoms or a JTC bias amongst patients who, in contrast to the NFC hypothesis, describe themselves as indecisive. Although McKay, Langdon and Coltheart (2006) found that both NFC and a JTC bias predicted delusional belief, the NFC and JTC were independent of each other and therefore NFC did not explain the JTC bias. The same authors subsequently reported a further failure to find a relationship between NFC and

JTC, even though patients scored higher on NFC than controls (McKay, Langdon & Coltheart, 2007). A longitudinal study found that patients with delusions scored higher on NFC than controls, but NFC did not distinguish between recovered and non-recovered patients after 12 months (Colbert, Peters & Garety, 2006). Cognitive flexibility, a construct related to NFC, has also been found to be unrelated to JTC in a non-clinical sample (Freeman *et al.*, 2008).

Hence the literature provides inconsistent support for the link between delusional beliefs and NFC, but there is little evidence for the notion that NFC is a motivational factor in JTC. Perhaps this is because the beads task does not typically present highly ambiguous situations: the participant is usually faced with only two options to decide between. NFC may show stronger relationships with modified versions of the beads task which incorporate multiple jars, thus adding to the ambiguity of the problem. However, in a separate non-clinical study, where multiple jars (three and four) were employed, neither NFC nor intolerance of uncertainty (IU) were found to be related to JTC and neither was related to delusional ideation (in the case of IU, after general psychopathology was partialled out) (White & Mansell, 2009).

Bias against disconfirmatory evidence (BADE)

In addition to the liberal acceptance bias, Moritz, Woodward and colleagues have proposed a further mechanism contributing to delusions, namely a bias against disconfirmatory evidence (BADE; Moritz & Woodward, 2006; Woodward, Moritz, Cuttler & Whitman, 2006). Compared to non-delusional patients and non-patient controls, delusional patients were less willing to reduce their plausibility ratings for pictures which, although initially tenable, became increasingly implausible. This behaviour did not appear to represent a general difficulty in processing evidence, as the bias was absent when patients rated new confirmatory evidence for pictures which, although initially untenable, became increasingly credible (Woodward *et al.*, 2006). Subsequent research confirmed that the BADE was a cognitive process distinct from executive functioning, IQ and memory and could also be replicated in high schizotypes (Buchy, Woodward & Liotti, 2007; Woodward, Buchy, Moritz & Liotti, 2007). These findings suggest that delusional or delusion-prone individuals maintain commitment to their initial, strongly held beliefs even in the face of increasingly disconfirmatory evidence, thus presenting a potential mechanism for how beliefs are maintained, or perhaps for how early delusional hypotheses are concretised.

How does the BADE complement the liberal acceptance model? Thus far the research suggests that people with delusions jump to hasty conclusions, perhaps due to a liberal threshold for acceptance of implausible ideas. This may render people with delusions as more likely to accept an initial delusional hypothesis. Once the delusional hypothesis has been entertained as credible, its resistance against incoming disconfirmatory evidence may be provided by a protective BADE. What is not known is whether BADE is 1) due to an inability to recognise that evidence is disconfirmatory or 2) due to an inability to use the evidence in reasoning. Additionally, the liberal acceptance bias may mitigate against any disconfirmatory evidence which does receive attention. This is because, even though disconfirmatory evidence should diminish the potency of the delusional hypothesis, a liberal threshold for acceptance of implausible ideas means that the delusional hypothesis may still seem tenable even when its potency is undermined by new evidence.

Intuitive versus analytical thinking

There is some support for the notion that delusional reasoning is characterised by an over-reliance on intuitive reasoning (instinctive, rapid, non-reflective) and an under-reliance on analytical thinking (deliberative, effortful). Speechley, Whitman & Woodward (2010) offer behavioural evidence for why the JTC bias may be linked to intuitive judgements: according to them, the JTC arises because matches between incoming evidence and the current hypothesis are hypersalient to people with delusions. To investigate this, Speechley *et al.* (2010) created a realistic version of the beads task (with different coloured fish being caught from one of two lakes) with a modified probability estimates format. Instead of requiring participants to state their certainty about which one of the two lakes they believed the fish were being caught from, they asked participants to give probability ratings for both lakes. They found that people with delusions gave higher probability ratings for whichever lake (i.e. the one with mostly black fish or mostly white fish in it) matched the colour of the most recently caught fish. So if a black fish was presented, the delusions group gave higher probability ratings for the lake containing mostly black fish. This trial-by-trial effect was not observed in probability ratings for the non-matching lake; here ratings were comparable with controls. Speechley *et al.* argue that on the 'draws to decision' version of the beads task, the hypersalience of the evidence–hypothesis match may be compelling enough to convince the delusional participant that they have sufficient grounds for making an early judgement, without the need for further evidence. Thus the hypersalience of the evidence–hypothesis match is intuitively appealing enough to override the need for effortful, analytical reasoning.

However, in the probability estimates version of the beads task, people with delusions often over-adjust their probability estimates when the colour of the bead suddenly changes (e.g. Moritz & Woodward, 2005). What is not yet clear is why presentation of new (contradictory) evidence has opposing effects on the BADE task (where people with delusions have been found to resist the evidence) and on the beads task (where people with delusions sometimes over-react to new contradictory evidence). Do people with delusions react more strongly than controls to disconfirmatory evidence, or do they deny it? Speechley *et al.* (2010) offer an answer to this problem. They point out that, in the traditional beads task, there is a single bipolar rating scale with jar A and B at the extremities. New evidence in favour of the previously unsupported jar – for example, jar B – inspires an adjustment in favour of jar B. Due to the use of only a single bipolar scale, an upgrading on the probability of B necessarily means a down-grading of jar A. Speechley *et al.* (2010) argue that this over-adjustment is not in favour of disconfirmatory evidence per se; it merely suggests that people with delusions simply attach greater importance to whichever option is currently supported by the latest unit of data. If a double rating scale is applied in the beads task (as Speechley *et al.*, 2010, did), the over-adjustment in the beads task would only apply to the upward rating of the currently favoured option – that is, to the new incoming data – not to the downward rating of the currently non-matching option. As Speechley *et al.* show, this hypersalience is observed on the very first trial of the beads task and this would typically be classed as JTC. When this process occurs in the middle of the series of trials, it would normally be classed as over-adjustment in response to disconfirmatory evidence. Speechley *et al.* argue that, instead, over-adjustment in people with delusions simply reflects the greater salience for the new hypothesis–evidence match, not a bias towards disconfirmatory evidence as such.

Other studies have provided further support for the hypersalience argument. Patients with delusions and delusion-prone non-patients prefer confirmatory over disconfirmatory evidence (Balzan, Delfabbro, Galletly & Woodward, 2013a), are more susceptible to both illusory correlations and illusions of control (Balzan, Delfabbro, Galletly & Woodward, 2013b) and are more prone to the representativeness and availability heuristics (Balzan, Delfabbro, Galletly & Woodward, 2012). In using the Rational Experiential Inventory (REI; Pacini & Epstein, 1999), Freeman, Evans and Lister (2012) found that experiential (intuitive) thinking was predictive of paranoia and rational thinking was protective against it.

Interestingly, however, although people with delusions have demonstrated over-adjustment of estimates on the beads task in numerous previous studies (e.g. Moritz & Woodward, 2005), the patients with delusions in Speechley *et al*'s (2010) study did not. Therefore, follow-up work is necessary to provide strong evidence that mid-series over-adjustment does indeed relate exclusively to evidence–hypothesis matches and not to evidence–hypothesis non-matches. Additionally, some work still needs to be done to explain why the gradual changes in evidence on the BADE tasks (e.g. Woodward *et al.*, 2006) do not produce a hypersalience of new evidence–hypothesis matches but the sudden change in evidence on the beads task does.

If the hypersalience of evidence–hypothesis matches does underpin JTC, then it suggests an intuitive reasoning strategy, in which decisions are made with little analytical processing of information. Building on this work, Speechley, Woodward and Ngan (2013) draw on dual process theories of reasoning (Evans & Stanovich, 2013; Kahneman, 2003) to argue that a 'dual stream modulation failure' (DSMF) is responsible for delusional thinking. More specifically, they argue that, although our stream 1 processing (intuitive, instinctive, rapid) is responsible for most of our daily decisions, when incoming data is in conflict with background knowledge or belief, the resulting dissonance prompts a recourse to stream 2 processing (deliberative, analytical, effortful) in order to modulate the conflict. Excessively intuitive reasoning in people with delusions, they argue, is due to a conflict modulation failure

(CMF), where the person with delusions is less likely to utilise system 2 to resolve the conflict. They instead fall back on system 1 thinking, meaning that potentially contradictory evidence is not collected and that intuitive, potentially erroneous stream 1 judgements go unchallenged. Employing deductive conditional reasoning problems, where the aim was to assess the logical validity of conclusions, Speechley *et al.* (Speechley *et al.*, 2013; Speechley, Murray, McKay, Munz & Ngan, 2010) report that delusional patients were particularly inferior to controls in their assessments of validity when believability and logical validity conflicted. They argue that this provides support for their DSMF model. Further support comes from White and Mansell's (2009) study, where they found tentative evidence that, in non-clinical participants, people with higher delusional ideation felt more rushed and that the feeling of being rushed during the beads task predicted JTC. These findings suggest that hasty decisions, based upon system 1 processing, may be made because delusional or delusion-prone participants feel an urgency to decide and therefore forego analytical, system 1 reasoning. Alternatively, the tendency to fall back on system 1 thinking may stem from a depletion of attentional resources, brought about by the additional cognitive load of affect-laden thoughts (Christopher & MacDonald, 2005).

Beyond JTC: delusions and other types of reasoning

The studies by Speechley *et al.* (2010, 2013), highlighted in the previous section, indicate that interest in delusions and deductive reasoning has not faded and that such work may still be relevant and fruitful. As already suggested though, early studies on deductive reasoning in psychosis were fraught with methodological problems or theoretical naivety. In more recent work, group differences on deductive reasoning tasks have been observed, particularly those that have examined the effect of affect-laden content. Kemp, Chua, McKenna and David (1997) found that deluded patients were more likely than controls to endorse fallacies on conditional reasoning tasks; this effect was accentuated by the inclusion of emotional content. The deluded group were also more likely to endorse unbelievable conclusions to syllogisms when the content was emotional. Later studies have provided further evidence that logical reasoning is impaired in deluded patients, but only when the problems themselves contain affect-laden content (Goel & Bartolo, 2004; Mujica-Parodi, Greenberg, Bilder & Malaspina, 2001). Mirian, Heinrichs and Vaz (2011) found differences between patients with schizophrenia and controls on syllogisms but the difference disappeared after controlling for IQ, regardless of problem type. Dudley, Young, John and Over (1998) found that participants with delusions performed comparably with controls on the difficult abstract version of Wason's selection task. The delusion group (but not controls) failed to improve their performance on a realistic (drinking age conditional) version of the task. Dudley *et al.* (1998) concluded that people with delusions did not have a generalised deficit in reasoning, but simply reasoned inefficiently: increases in the realism of Wason's selection task did not lead to the same degree of improvement as with controls.

They speculated that this may be due to a limitation of working memory, which cuts short any attempt to reason and results in erroneous responding (see Christopher & MacDonald, 2005). The evidence suggests, therefore, that people with delusions are generally not impaired on deductive reasoning problems, although emotive content may lead to increases in errors.

Moving away from deductive reasoning, Coltheart et al. (2010), extending the earlier work of Maher (e.g. 1992), propose a Bayesian model of abductive inference as part of their two-factor model of delusions (Davies & Coltheart, 2000; McKay, Langdon & Coltheart, 2005). In reasoning, abduction is inferring to the best possible explanation given the available data. Coltheart et al. use the Capgras delusion (the belief that someone well-known to the individual, e.g. a loved one, has been replaced by an impostor) as a case study. With the Capgras delusion, the perceptual data are very powerful. Due to a disconnection between the facial recognition system and the autonomic nervous system, the emotive familiarity associated with recognition of a loved one's face is absent. This experience is more probable under the delusional hypothesis (this person is an imposter), compared to the competing hypothesis (e.g. this person is my wife). In Bayesian terms, this means that there is a large ratio in the likelihood functions of the two competing hypotheses – a ratio in favour of the imposter hypothesis.

Of course in everyday situations, the prior probability of the bizarre imposter hypothesis would be low. In other words, it would be implausible given most people's knowledge of the world. However, when bizarre perceptual anomalies occur, underpinned by neuropsychological impairment, they may be so potent that they overwhelm the influence of previous knowledge (the prior probability), and the delusional hypothesis will still be favoured. Thus the person with the delusion has formed and consolidated the belief via a rational Bayesian analysis using abductive inference: reasoning to the best available explanation. This constitutes factor 1 in the two-factor model (Coltheart et al., 2011). However, the delusional belief will only be maintained if factor 2 is also present.

Factor 2 constitutes the malfunction of the belief revision system which, in most situations, should help to modify current beliefs by processing new contradictory data. Coltheart et al. (2010) argue that new disconfirmatory incoming data (e.g. proof from the loved one that they are who they claim to be), which should adjust the ratio of likelihood in favour of the 'wife' hypothesis, is ignored. This bias away from disconfirmatory evidence is likened to the tenacity shown by scientists who cling to their own theories whilst rejecting conflicting evidence. The two-factor model therefore outlines the neurological basis for perceptual anomalies and how faultless Bayesian reasoning and dogged resistance to incoming counter-evidence, when combined with highly potent perceptual data, may lead to the acceptance of bizarre delusional hypotheses.

Factor 2 is consistent with the BADE findings, where there is resistance to disconfirmatory data even in relation to neutral, non-delusional content (e.g. Woodward et al., 2006). In line with the two-factor account, BADE is seemingly independent of any tendency for hallucinations (i.e. factor 1).

Delusional reasoning and affect

In addition to the conflict modulation failure, Speechley *et al.* (2013) also proposed a second component to their DSMF model: an accentuated emotional modulation process (AEM), whereby the emotional valence of information intensifies reliance upon intuitive, stream 1 processing. However, in their study emotional content did not significantly increase the error rate on belief-validity conflict problems (compared to neutral conflict problems) for either patients with delusions or controls. This null effect is surprising given that numerous previous studies report that emotionally loaded content exacerbates delusional reasoning (Dudley *et al.*, 1997b; Kemp *et al.*, 1997; Mujica-Parodi *et al.*, 2001). Speechley *et al.* (2013) acknowledge that perhaps their emotional problems were insufficiently evocative to elicit the necessary emotional reaction and indeed this may be a problem affecting other studies (e.g. Galbraith *et al.*, 2010; Menon, Pomarol-Clotet, McKenna & McCarthy, 2006; Young and Bentall, 1997a). In their meta-analysis of the JTC literature, Fine *et al.* (2007) establish that emotional materials do not reliably amplify the JTC effect. However, their meta-analysis of emotional content included only three studies and did not include research with non-clinical participants. Using non-clinical participants, Warman and Martin (2006) have shown that emotional content, in the form of negative or positive comments about the self, does indeed predict a JTC bias in delusion-prone individuals. Subsequently, Warman *et al.* found that similarly designed emotional materials led to higher confidence ratings on task performance in both currently deluded and delusion-prone individuals (Warman, Lysaker, Martin, Davis & Haudenschield, 2007).

The evidence that emotional content exacerbates delusional reasoning may be inconsistent. Perhaps it is not that existing reasoning biases are worsened by the sudden emergence of affect-laden materials. Perhaps instead an enduring affective state of mind must be in existence first in order to capitalise upon a reasoning bias. This is what Dudley and Over (2003) propose. They refer to Evans and Over's (1996) concept of epistemic utility. They argue that one aspect of epistemic utility is the value we place upon gaining more truths as opposed to avoiding more falsehoods. They point out that people without delusions have a tendency to try to confirm statements if those statements predict danger (de Jong, Mayer & van den Hout, 1997). For example, with the statement 'if there is smoke, then there is fire', it is sensible to try to find confirmatory evidence. The cost of believing such a claim may help save our lives; the cost of falsely believing that smoke is coming from a fire is insignificant compared to the potential benefit. Dudley and Over (2003) argue that people with delusions have different epistemic utility judgements to people without delusions, in that they place *more* utility upon confirming strategies. In other words, they apply a danger-confirming strategy to situations where it is not warranted – to situations where there is no danger. Dudley and Over (2003) argue, therefore, that people with delusions are biased towards confirmatory evidence.

In line with Dudley and Over's (2003) argument, direct attempts to induce emotion have arguably been more successful – particularly when considering paranoid or persecutory beliefs – than studies which have simply presented reasoning tasks with emotive content. When enduring experimentally induced stress, delusion-prone individuals were more confident in their decisions on the beads task than those who were not delusion-prone, despite both groups requesting similar numbers of beads (Keefe & Warman, 2011). This effect did not emerge in a no-stress condition. Ellett, Freeman and Garety (2008) found that people with persecutory delusions who were exposed to an urban environment recorded an enhanced JTC compared with those exposed to a brief mindfulness intervention. Moritz *et al.* (2009) report that anxiety-provoking music led to an enhanced JTC style of responding in patients with current delusions. Lincoln *et al.* report an important non-clinical experiment in which an elaborate anxiety-inducing intervention exacerbated JTC and state paranoia. They also found that the effect of the anxiety manipulation upon state paranoia could be partially explained by JTC (Lincoln, Lange, Burau, Exner & Moritz, 2010). Although, in contrast to this, So, Freeman and Garety (2008) found no effect on the JTC bias when manipulating stress/relaxation in either delusional patients or non-clinical participants.

The evidence on the effects of manipulating positive mood is mixed. Lee, Barrowclough and Lobban (2011) found that a manipulation to induce positive mood in non-clinical participants led to increased data-gathering on their realistic version of the beads task. This effect was independent of the type of data (e.g. mainly positive comments about the self, mainly negative comments about the self) and independent of delusional ideation score. Research on patients with bipolar disorder shows that induced positive mood leads to increased opposition to advice-giving when making decisions (Mansell & Lam, 2006). The effect of positive mood on reasoning has implications for grandiose delusions, which are highly mood-dependent (Dunayevich & Keck Jr, 2000). Unfortunately, research on grandiose beliefs specifically is scarce, although there is indication that grandiose beliefs are more strongly associated with JTC and belief inflexibility than persecutory delusions are (Garety *et al.*, 2013).

Integrating findings from delusional reasoning studies

Thus far, evidence has been presented for a number of reasoning styles which characterise delusional patients or delusion-prone non-patients. In addition to reasoning, there exist a number of influential theories of delusions which emphasise the importance of other psychological factors. We propose that current theories of reasoning are insufficient to account for the four stages of delusional belief:

1. *Emergence of the delusional idea*
2. *Consideration and tentative acceptance of the delusional hypothesis*
3. *Selection of evidence and full acceptance of the delusional hypothesis*
4. *Maintenance of the belief*

Reasoning may account for some of these stages but not all. In order to construct a comprehensive model of delusional belief, reasoning must be considered in combination with other psychological factors. The final section of this chapter will set out how perceptions, emotions, self-concept, reasoning and other cognitive variables may be combined in such an integrated model.

1. Emergence of the delusional idea

None of the reasoning biases identified here can easily explain why a delusional hypothesis might first materialise as a candidate for belief. The JTC bias cannot influence belief formation until after a hypothesis has emerged (as Fine *et al.*, 2007, have argued). A liberal acceptance bias only features once a delusional hypothesis has presented itself for acceptance. A BADE may only operate once a tentative belief has been formed. Intuitive or system 1 thinking operates in response to an existing hypothesis, either in accepting or in rejecting it. Affect-driven reasoning also comes into play only once a delusional hypothesis is available for consideration. Hence none of the reasoning biases identified in this review can explain the creation of a delusional hypothesis.

Looking beyond reasoning theories, a number of theoretical models of delusions are in agreement about the most probable sources of delusional hypotheses. Freeman's threat anticipation model (Freeman, 2007), Maher's (1999) anomalous perceptions theory and Langdon, Coltheart and colleagues' two-factor model (McKay *et al.*, 2005) all recognise that delusional hypotheses emerge as potential explanations for unusual perceptual experiences. In addition to perceptual experiences, Freeman (2007) also notes the significance of external events as precipitators of delusional ideas, such as conversations with people, other people's facial expressions and other environmental occurrences.

This still does not explain the content of the delusional hypothesis, as perceptual experiences and external events may be interpreted in a number of different ways. Here the importance of negative schemas and negative affect (which are common in people with delusions, e.g. Fowler *et al.*, 2006) becomes apparent. Negative schemas about the self and depressive cognitions may leave the individual feeling personally vulnerable. Negative schemas about other people and anxiety may foster a view of others as malevolent and leave the person with hyper-vigilance for threat. Thus negative schemas and affect may taint the initial interpretation of distressing perceptual experiences and external events in line with feelings of personal vulnerability and fear of others. Cognitive factors, such as a theory of mind deficit or an attributional bias, may contribute towards misinterpretation of external events. The combination of perceptual anomalies, schemas, affect and cognitive bias help explain why initial delusional hypotheses will reflect common delusional themes such as persecution. Similarly, heightened arousal and inflated positive schemas about the self may predispose an individual to interpret internal or external experiences with a grandiose theme.

2. Consideration and tentative acceptance of the delusional hypothesis

The question then arises as to why a delusional hypothesis is not immediately rejected as untenable (see also Fine *et al.*, 2007). The initial delusional hypothesis has to be considered in some way plausible to warrant any further attention. This stage is unlikely to involve extensive evidence gathering, but instead a snap judgement about plausibility. We argue that, at this point, a liberal acceptance bias may explain why delusional hypotheses are not immediately rejected as implausible. This is because those with a liberal acceptance bias have a reduced threshold for plausibility, thus even bizarre ideas are given consideration. People who are not delusion-prone may be more likely to reject initial delusional-type hypotheses without further consideration because their threshold of acceptance is more stringent. A hyper-vigilance for threat may lead one to form delusional hypotheses which have danger-related themes and, as Dudley and Over (2003) suggest, this may stimulate a desire to confirm even an implausible hypothesis. This would complement a liberal acceptance style, making the implausible delusional hypothesis even more likely to be considered as viable, so that a threat-induced, danger-confirming process can begin. Coltheart *et al.*'s (2010) Bayesian model is also consistent with this proposal, in that the potency of the internal event (anomalous perceptions) and its match with the delusional hypothesis may outweigh prior knowledge which would normally drive home the implausibility of the hypothesis.

3. Selection of evidence and full acceptance of the delusional hypothesis

Once the delusional hypothesis has been granted consideration as a potential candidate for belief, an attempt may be made to gather evidence which is relevant to establishing whether the hypothesis should be fully endorsed as a belief. First, the reasoning processes identified in this chapter may combine with other psychological factors to explain the *quality* of evidence that is gathered. For example, hyper-vigilance for threat may bias one towards searching for a particular kind of evidence: that which confirms the danger-related hypothesis. Similarly, excessive positive mood may bias one towards mood-congruent evidence. Heightened emotion may enhance the hypersalience effect as described by Speechley *et al.* (2010). If the putative delusional hypothesis is consistent with one's current mood, then mood-congruent incoming data will also match the delusional hypothesis, will have increased significance for the individual and will be more likely to be processed than mood/hypothesis incongruent (disconfirmatory) evidence. This process would also be complemented by a BADE. Additionally, the liberal acceptance bias may affect the quality of the evidence which is gathered. A liberal threshold for acceptance may mean that evidence with weak and implausible content is considered 'good enough' to support the putative hypothesis.

It is in relation to the *quantity* of evidence which is gathered that the JTC bias may exercise its effect upon belief formation. The presence of a JTC bias means that the amount of evidence that is gathered will be limited, perhaps resulting in a belief which is poorly supported. A liberal acceptance bias may itself underpin the JTC bias, whereby an inadequate *quantity* of evidence is seen as 'good enough' to support the hypothesis. Alternatively, it may be that attempts to gather data for analytical or system 2 thought are cut short in preference for intuitive, system 1 thinking. This may constitute a failure to engage system 2 thinking because incoming disconfirmatory data conflicts with the delusional hypothesis. This failure and thus a reliance on hasty intuitive judgements may be exacerbated by affect, which itself consumes valuable cognitive resources, making system 2 thought more difficult. Additionally, negative affect may stimulate the confirmatory style of reasoning outlined by Dudley and Over (2003), a further mechanism by which data-gathering may be cut short or narrowed.

4. Maintenance of the belief

How may delusional reasoning biases contribute to delusion maintenance? Following the formation of the belief, there may be periodic instances where additional data-gathering of data pertaining to the belief is conducted. This may be in response to challenges from others or in response to new information. Here the same processes identified in stage 3 will continue to influence the quality and quantity of any new evidence which is gathered. Mood-congruent, confirmatory and potentially implausible evidence may be preferred and the quantity of evidence may be limited, meaning the belief is less likely to be weakened. In line with Coltheart *et al.* (2010) and Maher (1992), the significance and primacy of any precipitating anomalous perception will outweigh new contradictory evidence. Furthermore, delusions will tend to form as explanations for puzzling or distressing anomalous perceptions (Maher, 1992) or external events (Freeman, 2007), and any coherent explanation for such events (even a troubling one) will be preferred to no explanation. As a result, subsequent evidence which undermines the delusional explanation may be ignored to resolve cognitive dissonance. Furthermore, in Speechley *et al.*'s (2013) terms, the normal recourse to system 2 thinking to resolve contradictory evidence may be restricted, meaning increased reliance upon the mood-congruent belief.

Future research

We have argued that reasoning biases displayed by people with delusions or people who are delusion-prone may combine with other psychological theories of delusions to account for the formation and maintenance of delusional beliefs. In attempting to integrate the various reasoning biases, as well as the other factors (cognition, perception, affect and self-concept), it is evident that they complement each other a great deal when combined. The high-quality empirical and theoretical work on delusions over the past three decades or so has also made it possible to construct this model. However, a number of questions remain and these present opportunities for future research.

Do reasoning deficits in childhood or adolescence represent risk factors for the development of delusions later? Given that schizotypy typically develops in adolescence (Walker & Bollini, 2002), perhaps reasoning biases in early adolescence could signal a vulnerability for delusions. We have recently found that the JTC bias moderates the link between anxiety and subclinical delusions in a cross-sectional study of adolescents (Galbraith, Manktelow, Chen-Wilson, Harris & Nevill, in press), but longitudinal studies are needed to demonstrate a causal link.

Does affect lead to biased reasoning, or does an existing bias converge with negative affect? If heightened negative affect leads one to overuse a danger-confirming reasoning style, even in situations where it is not warranted, then perhaps affect causes the JTC bias and BADE. That is, affect drives the overuse of these styles of reasoning even on abstract materials in the laboratory. This would be an alternative theory to the idea that a pre-existing hasty/confirmatory reasoning style (in addition to negative affect) makes certain people more vulnerable to delusional beliefs.

Does the liberal acceptance bias lead to indecisiveness when more than two hypotheses are considered? There is some inconsistency in the literature here, and further research might examine whether the disappearance of the JTC effect observed by Moritz et al. (2007) in their multiple jar version of the beads task is really (as argued by White and Mansell, 2009) due to their use of a DTC-style format, rather than the DTD format.

Under what circumstances do people ignore disconfirmatory evidence, as found on the BADE tasks (e.g. Woodward et al., 2006) and under what circumstances do they over-react to it, as in the DTC version of the beads task (Moritz & Woodward, 2005)? One tentative suggestion may be that a BADE is more likely when the strength of the initial belief is high, and conversely that over-adjustment occurs when the initial belief is less powerful. At this point though, the reason why strength of belief should discriminate between the beads task and the tasks used by Woodward and colleagues is unclear.

The proposed model posits a complementarity of a range of delusional reasoning biases reported in the literature. If the model is to be supported empirically, further studies must demonstrate that those who exhibit combinations of these biases are more likely to have delusions or to score highly on delusions measures.

Conclusions

These future research questions by no means represent an exhaustive list. This chapter has argued that reasoning biases can help to form a significant part of the delusion formation/maintenance puzzle. This puzzle, however, cannot be completed without considering the role of delusional reasoning in relation to other psychological factors. We contend that progress in research on delusional reasoning depends upon maintaining such a holistic approach.

References

American Psychiatric Association. (2013). *Diagnostic and Statistical Manual of Mental Disorders* (5th ed.). Washington, DC: American Psychiatric Association.

Balzan, R. P., Delfabbro, P. H., Galletly, C., & Woodward, T. S. (2012). Reasoning heuristics across the psychosis continuum: The contribution of hypersalient evidence–hypothesis matches. *Cognitive Neuropsychiatry, 17*, 431–450.

Balzan, R. P., Delfabbro, P. H., Galletly, C., & Woodward, T. S. (2013a). Confirmation biases across the psychosis continuum: The contribution of hypersalient evidence–hypothesis matches. *British Journal of Clinical Psychology, 52*, 53–69.

Balzan, R. P., Delfabbro, P. H., Galletly, C., & Woodward, T. S. (2013b). Illusory correlations and control across the psychosis continuum: The contribution of hypersalient evidence–hypothesis matches. *Journal of Nervous and Mental Disease, 201*, 319–327.

Barrowclough, C., Tarrier, N., Humphreys, L., Ward, J., Gregg, L., & Andrews, B. (2003). Self-esteem in schizophrenia: Relationships between self-evaluation, family attitudes, and symptomatology. *Journal of Abnormal Psychology, 112*, 92–99.

Bensi, L., Giusberti, F., Nori, R., & Gambetti, E. (2010). Individual differences and reasoning: A study on personality traits. *British Journal of Psychology, 101*(3), 545–562.

Bentall, R. P., & Swarbrick, R. (2003). The best laid schemas of paranoid patients: Autonomy, sociotropy and need for closure. *Psychology and Psychotherapy: Theory, Research and Practice, 76*(2), 163–171.

Blackshaw, A. J., Kinderman, P., Hare, D. J., & Hatton, C. (2001). Theory of mind, causal attribution and paranoia in Asperger syndrome. *Autism, 5*, 147–163.

Bora, E., Yücel, M., & Pantelis, C. (2009). Theory of mind impairment: A distinct trait-marker for schizophrenia spectrum disorders and bipolar disorder? *Acta Psychiatrica Scandinavia, 120*, 253–264.

Broome, M. R., Johns, L. C., Valli, I., Woolley, J. B., Tabraham, P., Brett, C., . . . & McGuire, P. K. (2007). Delusion formation and reasoning biases in those at clinical high risk for psychosis. *The British Journal of Psychiatry, 191*(51), s38–s42.

Buchy, L., Woodward, T. S., & Liotti, M. (2007). A cognitive bias against disconfirmatory evidence (BADE) is associated with schizotypy. *Schizophrenia Research, 90*(1), 334–337.

Christopher, G., & MacDonald, J. (2005). The impact of clinical depression on working memory. *Cognitive Neuropsychiatry, 10*(5), 379–399.

Claridge, G. S., & Beech, T. (1995). Fully and quasi-dimensional constructions of schizotypy. In A. Rain, T. Lencz & S.A. Mednick (Eds.), *Schizotypal Personality*. New York: Cambridge University Press.

Clark, D. A., & Beck, A. T. (2010). Cognitive theory and therapy of anxiety and depression: Convergence with neurobiological findings. *Trends in Cognitive Sciences, 14*(9), 418–424.

Cohen, C. I., Magai, C., Yaffee, R., & Walcott-Brown, L. (2004). Racial differences in paranoid ideation and psychoses in an older urban population. *American Journal of Psychiatry, 161*, 864–871.

Colbert, S. M., & Peters, E. R. (2002). Need for closure and jumping-to-conclusions in delusion-prone individuals. *The Journal of Nervous and Mental Disease, 190*(1), 27–31.

Colbert, S. M., Peters, E. R., & Garety, P. A. (2006). Need for closure and anxiety in delusions: A longitudinal investigation in early psychosis. *Behaviour Research and Therapy, 44*(10), 1385–1396.

Coltheart, M., Langdon, R., & McKay, R. (2011). Delusional belief. *Annual Review of Psychology, 62*, 271–298.

Coltheart, M., Menzies, P., & Sutton, J. (2010). Abductive inference and delusional belief. *Cognitive Neuropsychiatry, 15*(1/2/3), 261–287.

Cooper, A. F., Kay, D. W. K., Curry, A. R., Garside, R. F., & Roth, M. (1974). Hearing loss in paranoid and affective disorders of the elderly. *Lancet, 2,* 851–854.

Corcoran, R., Cahill, C., & Frith, C. D. (1997). The appreciation of visual jokes in people with schizophrenia. *Schizophrenia Research, 24,* 319–327.

Davies, M., & Coltheart, M. (2000). Introduction: Pathologies of belief. In M. Coltheart & M. Davies (Eds.), *Pathologies of Belief.* Malden, MA: Blackwell.

de Jong, P. J., Mayer, B. & van den Hout, M. A. (1997). Conditional reasoning and phobic fear: Evidence for a fear-confirming reasoning pattern. *Behaviour Research and Therapy, 35,* 507–516.

Dudley, R., Daley, K., Nicholson, M., Shaftoe, D., Spencer, H., Cavanagh, K., & Freeston, M. (2013). 'Jumping to conclusions' in first-episode psychosis: A longitudinal study. *British Journal of Clinical Psychology, 52*(4), 380–393.

Dudley, R. E. J., John, C. H., Young, A., & Over, D. E. (1997a). Normal and abnormal reasoning in people with delusions. *British Journal of Clinical Psychology, 36,* 243–258.

Dudley, R. E. J., John, C. H., Young, A., & Over, D. E. (1997b). The effect of self-referent material on the reasoning of people with delusions. *British Journal of Clinical Psychology, 36,* 575–584.

Dudley, R. E. J., & Over, D. E. (2003). People with delusions jump to conclusions. *Clinical Psychology and Psychotherapy, 10,* 263–274.

Dudley, R. E. J., Young, A., John, C. H., & Over, D. E. (1998). Conditional reasoning in people with delusions: Performance on the Wason selection task. *Cognitive Neuropsychiatry, 3,* 241–258.

Dunayevich, E., & Keck Jr, P. E. (2000). Prevalence and description of psychotic features in bipolar mania. *Current Psychiatry Reports, 2*(4), 286–290.

Ellett, L., Freeman, D., & Garety, P. A. (2008). The psychological effect of an urban environment on individuals with persecutory delusions: The Camberwell walk study. *Schizophrenia Research, 99,* 77–84.

Evans, J. St. B. T., & Over, D. E. (1996). Rationality in the selection task: Epistemic utility versus uncertainty reduction. *Psychological Review, 103,* 356–363.

Evans, J. St. B. T., & Stanovich, K. E. (2013). Dual-process theories of higher cognition advancing the debate. *Perspectives on Psychological Science, 8*(3), 223–241.

Fine, C., Gardner, M., Craigie, J., & Gold, I. (2007). Hopping, skipping or jumping to conclusions? Clarifying the role of the JTC bias in delusions. *Cognitive Neuropsychiatry, 12*(1), 46–77.

Fowler, D., Freeman, D., Smith, B., Kuipers, E., Bebbington, P., Bashforth, H., . . . & Garety, P. (2006). The Brief Core Schema Scales (BCSS): Psychometric properties and associations with paranoia and grandiosity in non-clinical and psychosis samples. *Psychological Medicine, 36*(6), 749–760.

Freeman, D. (2007). Suspicious minds: The psychology of persecutory delusions. *Clinical Psychology Review, 27,* 425–457.

Freeman, D., Dunn, G., Garety, P. A., Bebbington, P., Slater, M., Kuipers, E., . . . & Ray, K. (2005). The psychology of persecutory ideation I: A questionnaire survey. *The Journal of Nervous and Mental Disease, 193*(5), 302–308.

Freeman, D., Evans, N., & Lister, R. (2012). Gut feelings, deliberative thought, and paranoid ideation: A study of experiential and rational reasoning. *Psychiatry Research, 197*(1), 119–122.

Freeman, D., Garety, P. A., Fowler, D., Kuipers, E., Bebbington, P. E., & Dunn, G. (2004). Why do people with delusions fail to choose more realistic explanations for their experiences? An empirical investigation. *Journal of Consulting and Clinical Psychology, 72*(4), 671.

Freeman, D., Garety, P., Kuipers, E., Colbert, S., Jolley, S., Fowler, D., . . . & Bebbington, P. E. (2006). Delusions and decision-making style: Use of the Need for Closure Scale. *Behaviour Research and Therapy*, *44*(8), 1147–1158.

Freeman, D., Garety, P. A., Kuipers, E., Fowler, D., & Bebbington, P. E. (2002). A cognitive model of persecutory delusions. *British Journal of Clinical Psychology*, *41*, 331–347.

Freeman, D., Pugh, K., & Garety, P. (2008). Jumping to conclusions and paranoid ideation in the general population. *Schizophrenia Research*, *102*(1), 254–260.

Freeman, D., Pugh, K., Vorontsova, N., Antley, A., & Slater, M. (2010). Testing the continuum of delusional beliefs: An experimental study using virtual reality. *Journal of Abnormal Psychology*, *119*, 83–92.

Freeman, D., Startup, H., Dunn, G., Černis, E., Wingham, G., Pugh, K., . . . & Kingdon, D. (2013). The interaction of affective with psychotic processes: A test of the effects of worrying on working memory, jumping to conclusions, and anomalies of experience in patients with persecutory delusions. *Journal of Psychiatric Research*, *47*(12), 1837–1842.

Frith, C. (1992). *The Cognitive Neuropsychology of Schizophrenia*. Hove, UK: Erlbaum.

Galbraith, N. D., Manktelow, K. I., Chen-Wilson, C. H., Harris, R. A., & Nevill, A. (in press). Different combinations of perceptual, emotional and cognitive factors predict three different types of delusional ideation during adolescence. *Journal of Nervous and Mental Disease*.

Galbraith, N. D., Manktelow, K. I., & Morris, N. G. (2008). Sub-clinical delusional ideation and a self-reference bias in everyday reasoning. *British Journal of Psychology*, *99*, 29–44.

Galbraith, N. D., Manktelow, K. I., & Morris, N. G. (2010). Subclinical delusional ideation and appreciation of sample size and heterogeneity in statistical judgment. *British Journal of Psychology*, *101*(4), 621–635.

Galbraith, N. D., Morgan, C. J., Jones, C. L., Ormerod, D. R., Galbraith, V. E., & Manktelow, K. I. (2014). The mediating effect of affect: Different pathways from self and other schemas to persecutory ideation. *Canadian Journal of Behavioural Science*, doi: 10.1037/a0036263.

Garety, P. A., & Freeman, D. (1999). Cognitive approaches to delusions: A critical review of theories and evidence. *British Journal of Clinical Psychology*, *38*(2), 113–154.

Garety, P. A., Gittins, M., Jolley, S., Bebbington, P., Dunn, G., Kuipers, E., . . . & Freeman, D. (2013). Differences in cognitive and emotional processes between persecutory and grandiose delusions. *Schizophrenia Bulletin*, *39*(3), 629–639.

Garety, P. A., Hemsley, D. R., & Wessely, S. (1991). Reasoning in deluded schizophrenic and paranoid patients: Biases in performance on a probabilistic inference task. *Journal of Nervous and Mental Disorder*, *179*, 194–201.

Geyer, M. A., Krebs-Thomson, K., Braff, D. L., & Swerdlow, N. R. (2001). Pharmacological studies of prepulse inhibition models of sensorimotor gating deficits in schizophrenia: A decade in review. *Psychopharmacology*, *156*(2–3), 117–154.

Goel, V., & Bartolo, A. (2004). Logical reasoning deficits in schizophrenia. *Schizophrenia Research*, *66*, 87–88.

Gooding, D. C., & Pflum, M. J. (2011). Theory of mind and psychometric schizotypy. *Psychiatry Research*, *188*(2), 217–223.

Greig, T. C., Bryson, G. J., & Bell, M. D. (2004). Theory of mind performance in schizophrenia. *Journal of Nervous and Mental Disease*, *192*, 12–18.

Hemsley, D. R. (1988). Information processing and schizophrenia. In E. Straube & K. Hahlweg (Eds.), *Schizophrenia: Concepts, Vulnerability and Intervention*. Heidelberg: Springer.

Huq, S. F., Garety, P. A., & Hemsley, D. R. (1988). Probabilistic judgements in deluded and non-deluded subjects. *Quarterly Journal of Experimental Psychology: Human Learning and Memory*, *40A*, 801–812.

John, C. H., & Dodgson, G. (1994). Inductive reasoning in delusional thinking. *Journal of Mental Health*, *3*, 31–49.

Johnson, J., Horwath, E., & Weissman, M. M. (1991). The validity of major depression with psychotic features based on a community study. *Archives of General Psychiatry, 48*(12), 1075.

Kahneman, D. (2003). A perspective on judgment and choice: Mapping bounded rationality. *American Psychologist, 58*(9), 697.

Keefe, K. M., & Warman, D. M. (2011). Reasoning, delusion proneness and stress: An experimental investigation. *Clinical Psychology & Psychotherapy, 18*(2), 138–147.

Kelemen, O., Erdélyi, R., Pataki, I., Benedek, G., Janka, Z., & Kéri, S. (2005). Theory of mind and motion perception in schizophrenia. *Neuropsychology, 19*, 494–500.

Kemp, R., Chua, S., McKenna, P., & David, A. (1997). Reasoning and delusions. *British Journal of Psychiatry, 170*, 398–405.

Kinderman, P., & Bentall, R. P. (1996). The development of a novel measure of causal attributions: The Internal Personal and Situational Attributions Questionnaire. *Personality and Individual Differences, 20*, 261–264.

Kinderman, P., & Bentall, R. P. (1997). Causal attributions in paranoia and depression: Internal, personal and situational attributions for negative events. *Journal of Abnormal Psychology, 106*, 341–345.

Knowles, R., McCarthy-Jones, S., & Rowse, G. (2011). Grandiose delusions: A review and theoretical integration of cognitive and affective perspectives. *Clinical Psychology Review, 31*, 684–696.

Kruglanski, A. W., & Webster, D. M. (1996). Motivated closing of the mind: 'Seizing' and 'freezing'. *Psychological Review, 103*(2), 263.

Langdon, R., Michie, P. T., Ward, P. B., McConaghy, N., Catts, S. V., & Coltheart, M. (1997). Defective self and/or other mentalising in schizophrenia. *Cognitive Neuropsychiatry, 2*, 167–193.

Langdon, R., Still, M., Connors, M. H., Ward, P. B., & Catts, S. V. (2014). Jumping to delusions in early psychosis. *Cognitive Neuropsychiatry, 19*(3), 1–16.

Lee, G., Barrowclough, C., & Lobban, F. (2011). The influence of positive affect on jumping to conclusions in delusional thinking. *Personality and Individual Differences, 50*(5), 717–722.

Lincoln, T. M., Lange, J., Burau, J., Exner, C., & Moritz, S. (2010). The effect of state anxiety on paranoid ideation and jumping to conclusions. An experimental investigation. *Schizophrenia Bulletin, 36*(6), 1140–1148.

Lincoln, T. M., Mehl, S., Exner, C., Lindenmeyer, J., & Rief, W. (2010). Attributional style and persecutory delusions. Evidence for an event independent and state specific external-personal attribution bias for social situations. *Cognitive Therapy and Research, 34*(3), 297–302.

Lincoln, T. M., Ziegler, M., Mehl, S., & Rief, W. (2010). The jumping to conclusions bias in delusions: Specificity and changeability. *Journal of Abnormal Psychology, 119*(1), 40.

Linney, Y. M., Peters, E. R., & Ayton, P. (1998). Reasoning biases in delusion-prone individuals. *British Journal of Clinical Psychology, 37*, 285–302.

Maher, B. A. (1974). Delusional thinking and perceptual disorder. *Journal of Individual Psychology, 30*, 98–113.

Maher, B. A. (1992). Delusions: Contemporary etiological hypotheses. *Psychiatric Annals, 22*, 260–268.

Maher, B. A. (1999). Anomalous experience in everyday life: Its significance for psychopathology. *The Monist, 82*(4), 547–570.

Maher, B. A. (2005). Delusional thinking and cognitive disorder. *Integrative Physiological and Behavioral Science, 40* (3), 136–146.

Mansell, W., & Lam, D. (2006). 'I won't do what you tell me!': Elevated mood and the assessment of advice-taking in euthymic bipolar I disorder. *Behaviour Research and Therapy, 44*(12), 1787–1801.

Mansell, W., Morrison, A. P., Reid, G., Lowens, I., & Tai, S. (2007). The interpretation of and responses to changes in internal states: An integrative cognitive model of mood swings and bipolar disorder. *Behavioural and Cognitive Psychotherapy*, *35*, 515–539.

Martin, J. A., & Penn, D. L. (2001). Brief report: Social cognition and subclinical paranoid ideation. *British Journal of Clinical Psychology*, *40*, 261–265.

McKay, R., Langdon, R., & Coltheart, M. (2005). Paranoia, persecutory delusions and attributional biases. *Psychiatry Research*, *136*, 233–245.

McKay, R., Langdon, R., & Coltheart, M. (2006). The Persecutory Ideation Questionnaire. *The Journal of Nervous and Mental Disease*, *194*(8), 628–631.

McKay, R., Langdon, R., & Coltheart, M. (2007). Models of misbelief: Integrating motivational and deficit theories of delusions. *Consciousness and Cognition*, *16*(4), 932–941.

Menon, M., Pomarol-Clotet, E., McKenna, P. J., & McCarthy, R. A. (2006). Probabilistic reasoning in schizophrenia: A comparison of the performance of deluded and nondeluded schizophrenic patients and exploration of possible cognitive underpinnings. *Cognitive Neuropsychiatry*, *11*(6), 521–536.

Mirian, D., Heinrichs, R. W., & Vaz, S. M. (2011). Exploring logical reasoning abilities in schizophrenia patients. *Schizophrenia Research*, *127*(1), 178–180.

Moritz, S., Veckenstedt, R., Randjbar, S., Hottenrott, B., Woodward, T. S., Eckstaedt, F. V., . . . & Lincoln, T. M. (2009). Decision making under uncertainty and mood induction: Further evidence for liberal acceptance in schizophrenia. *Psychological Medicine*, *39*(11), 1821–1829.

Moritz, S., Veckenstedt, R., Randjbar, S., Vitzthum, F., & Woodward, T. S. (2011). Antipsychotic treatment beyond antipsychotics: Metacognitive intervention for schizophrenia patients improves delusional symptoms. *Psychological Medicine*, *41*(9), 1823–1832.

Moritz, S., & Woodward, T. S. (2004). Plausibility judgment in schizophrenic patients: Evidence for a liberal acceptance bias. *German Journal of Psychiatry*, *7*, 66–74.

Moritz, S., & Woodward, T. S. (2005). Jumping to conclusions in delusional and non delusional schizophrenic patients. *British Journal of Clinical Psychology*, *44*, 193–207.

Moritz, S., & Woodward, T. S. (2006). A generalized bias against disconfirmatory evidence in schizophrenia. *Psychiatry Research*, *142*(2), 157–165.

Moritz, S., Woodward, T. S., Jelinek, L., & Klinge, R. (2008). Memory and metamemory in schizophrenia: A liberal acceptance account of psychosis. *Psychological Medicine*, *38*(6), 825–832.

Moritz, S., Woodward, T. S., & Lambert, M. (2007). Under what circumstances do patients with schizophrenia jump to conclusions? A liberal acceptance account. *British Journal of Clinical Psychology*, *46*, 127–137.

Mujica-Parodi, L. R., Greenberg, T., Bilder, R. M., & Malaspina, D. (2001). Emotional impact on logic deficits may underlie psychotic delusions in schizophrenia. *Proceedings of the 23rd Annual Conference of the Cognitive Science Society*. Mahway, NJ: Lawrence Erlbaum Associates.

Östling, S., & Skoog, I. (2002). Psychotic symptoms and paranoid ideation in a nondemented population-based sample of the very old. *Archives of General Psychiatry*, *59*(1), 53–59.

Pacini, R., & Epstein, S. (1999). The relation of rational and experiential information processing styles to personality, basic beliefs, and the ratio-bias phenomenon. *Journal of Personality and Social Psychology*, *76*(6), 972.

Peralta, V., & Cuesta, M. J. (1999). Dimensional structure of psychotic symptoms: An item-level analysis of SAPS and SANS symptoms in psychotic disorders. *Schizophrenia Research*, *38*, 13–26.

Peters, E. R., Thornton, P., Siksou, L., Linney, Y., & MacCabe, J. H. (2008). Specificity of the jump-to-conclusions bias in deluded patients. *British Journal of Clinical Psychology*, 47(2), 239–244.

Phillips, L. D., & Edwards, W. (1966). Conservatism in a simple probabilistic inference task. *Journal of Experimental Psychology*, 72, 346–354.

Pickup, G. J., & Frith, C. D. (2001). Theory of mind impairments in schizophrenia: Symptomatology, severity and specificity. *Psychological Medicine*, 31(02), 207–220.

Ross, K., Freeman, D., Dunn, G., & Garety, P. (2011). A randomized experimental investigation of reasoning training for people with delusions. *Schizophrenia Bulletin*, 37(2), 324–333.

Smith, B., Fowler, D., Freeman, D., Bebbington, P., Bashforth, H., Garety, P., . . . & Dunn, G. (2006). Emotion and psychosis: Direct links between schematic beliefs, emotion and delusions and hallucinations. *Schizophrenia Research*, 86, 181–188.

So, S. H. W., Freeman, D., & Garety, P. (2008). Impact of state anxiety on the jumping to conclusions delusion bias. *Australian and New Zealand Journal of Psychiatry*, 42(10), 879–886.

Speechley, W. J., Murray, C. B., McKay, R. M., Munz, M. T., & Ngan, E. T. C. (2010). A failure of conflict to modulate dual-stream processing may underlie the formation and maintenance of delusions. *European Psychiatry*, 25(2), 80–86.

Speechley, W. J., Whitman, J. C., & Woodward, T. S. (2010). The contribution of hypersalience to the 'jumping to conclusions' bias associated with delusions in schizophrenia. *Journal of Psychiatry & Neuroscience: JPN*, 35(1), 7.

Speechley, W. J., Woodward, T. S., & Ngan, E. T. (2013). Failure of conflict to modulate central executive network activity associated with delusions in schizophrenia. *Frontiers in Psychiatry*, 4, 113.

Tandon, R., & Maj, M., (2008). Nosological status and definition of schizophrenia: Some considerations for DSM-V. *Asian Journal of Psychiatry*, 1, 22–27.

Taylor, J. L., & Kinderman, P. (2002). An analogue study of attributional complexity, theory of mind deficits and paranoia. *British Journal of Psychology*, 93(1), 137–140.

Teufel, C., Kingdon, A., Ingram, J. N., Wolpert, D. M., & Fletcher, P. C. (2010). Deficits in sensory prediction are related to delusional ideation in healthy individuals. *Neuropsychologia*, 48(14), 4169–4172.

van Os, J., Linscott, R. J., Myin-Germeys, I., Delespaul, P., & Krabbendam, L. (2009). A systematic review and meta-analysis of the psychosis continuum: Evidence for a psychosis proneness-persistence-impairment model of psychotic disorder. *Psychological Medicine*, 39, 179–195.

von Domarus, E. (1944). The specific laws of logic in schizophrenia. In J. Kasanin (Ed.), *Language and Thought in Schizophrenia*. Berkeley, CA: University of California Press.

Walker, E., & Bollini, A. M. (2002). Pubertal neurodevelopment and the emergence of psychotic syndromes. *Schizophrenia Research*, 54, 17–23.

Waller, H., Freeman, D., Jolley, S., Dunn, G., & Garety, P. (2011). Targeting reasoning biases in delusions: A pilot study of the Maudsley Review Training Programme for individuals with persistent, high conviction delusions. *Journal of Behavior Therapy and Experimental Psychiatry*, 42(3), 414–421.

Warman, D. M., Lysaker, P. H., Martin, J. M., Davis, L., & Haudenschield, S. L. (2007). Jumping to conclusions and the continuum of delusional beliefs. *Behaviour Research and Therapy*, 45(6), 1255–1269.

Warman, D. M., & Martin, J. M. (2006). Jumping to conclusions and delusion proneness: The impact of emotionally salient stimuli. *The Journal of Nervous and Mental Disease*, 194(10), 760–765.

Webster, D. M., & Kruglanski, A. W. (1994). Individual differences in need for cognitive closure. *Journal of Personality and Social Psychology, 67*, 1049–1062.

White, L. O., & Mansell, W. (2009). Failing to ponder? Delusion-prone individuals rush to conclusions. *Clinical Psychology & Psychotherapy, 16*(2), 111–124.

Williams, E. B. (1964). Deductive reasoning in schizophrenia. *Journal of Abnormal and Social Psychology, 69*, 47–61.

Woodward, T. S., Buchy, L., Moritz, S., & Liotti, M. (2007). A bias against disconfirmatory evidence is associated with delusion proneness in a nonclinical sample. *Schizophrenia Bulletin, 33*, 1023–1028.

Woodward, T. S., Moritz, S., Cuttler, C., & Whitman, J. C. (2006). The contribution of a cognitive bias against disconfirmatory evidence (BADE) to delusions in schizophrenia. *Journal of Clinical and Experimental Neuropsychology, 28*(4), 605–617.

Woodward, T. S., Munz, M., LeClerc, C., & Lecomte, T. (2009). Change in delusions is associated with change in 'jumping to conclusions'. *Psychiatry Research, 170*(2), 124–127.

Young, H. F., & Bentall, R. P. (1995). Hypothesis testing in patients with persecutory delusions: Comparison with depressed and normal subjects. *British Journal of Clinical Psychology, 34*, 353–369.

Young, H. F., & Bentall, R. P. (1997a). Probabilistic reasoning in deluded, depressed and normal subjects: Effects of task difficulty and meaningful versus non-meaningful material. *Psychological Medicine, 27*, 455–465.

Young, H. F., & Bentall, R. P. (1997b). Social reasoning in individuals with persecutory delusions: The effects of additional information on attributions for the observed behaviours of others. *British Journal of Clinical Psychology, 36*, 569–573.

Zawadzki, J. A., Woodward, T. S., Sokolowski, H. M., Boon, H. S., Wong, A. H. C., & Menon, M. (2012). Cognitive factors associated with subclinical delusional ideation in the general population. *Psychiatry Research, 197*(3), 345–349.

Ziegler, M., Rief, W., Werner, S. M., Mehl, S., & Lincoln, T. M. (2008). Hasty decision-making in a variety of tasks: Does it contribute to the development of delusions? *Psychology and Psychotherapy: Theory, Research and Practice, 81*(3), 237–245.

Ziermans, T., Schothorst, P., Magnée, M., van Engeland, H., & Kemner, C. (2011). Reduced prepulse inhibition in adolescents at risk for psychosis: A 2-year follow-up study. *Journal of Psychiatry & Neuroscience: JPN, 36*(2), 127.

Zimbardo, P. G., Andersen, S. M., & Kabat, L. G. (1981). Induced hearing deficit generates experimental paranoia. *Science, 212*, 1529–1531.

2

PREDICTION-ERROR AND TWO-FACTOR THEORIES OF DELUSION FORMATION

Competitors or allies?

Kengo Miyazono, Lisa Bortolotti and Matthew R. Broome

Introduction

The two-factor theory (Davies, Coltheart, Langdon & Breen 2001; Coltheart 2007; Coltheart, Menzies & Sutton 2010) is an influential account of delusion formation. According to the theory, there are two distinct factors that are causally responsible for delusion formation. The first factor is supposed to explain the content of the delusion, while the second factor is supposed to explain why the delusion is adopted and/or maintained. Recently, another remarkable account of delusion formation has been proposed, in which the notion of "prediction error" plays the central role (Fletcher & Frith 2009; Corlett, Krystal, Taylor & Fletcher 2009; Corlett, Taylor, Wang, Fletcher & Krystal 2010). According to this account, the prediction-error theory, delusions are formed in response to aberrant prediction-error signals, those signals that indicate a mismatch between expectation and actual experience.[1]

Is the prediction-error theory a rival to the two-factor theory? Prediction-error theorists tend to be critical about the two-factor theory and present their views as an alternative to it. Fletcher and Frith wrote, on the two-factor theory: "symptoms reflecting false perception and false beliefs are so intertwined in schizophrenia that a theory relying on coincidental damage seems very unlikely" (Fletcher & Frith 2009, 51). Again, Corlett and colleagues argue that positing two factors is redundant because

> a single deficit in Bayesian inference is able to explain more of what we know about the interactions between perception and belief-based expectation, the neurobiology of the delusions that occur in schizophrenia and the maintenance of delusions in the face of contradictory evidence.
>
> *(Corlett et al. 2010, 357)*

In this chapter, we examine the relationship between the two-factor theory and the prediction-error theory in some detail. Our view is that the prediction-error theory does not have to be understood as a rival to the two-factor theory. We do not deny that there are some important differences between them. However, those differences are not as significant as they have been presented in the literature. Moreover, the core ideas of the prediction-error theory may be incorporated into the two-factor framework. For instance, the aberrant prediction-error signal that is posited by prediction-error theorists can be (or underlie) the first factor contributing to the formation of some delusions, and help explain the content of those delusions. Alternatively, the aberrant prediction-error signal can be (or underlie) the second factor, and help explain why the delusion is adopted and/or maintained.

The second and third sections will offer an overview of the two-factor theory and the prediction-error theory, respectively. The fourth section will host a discussion of the relationship between the two theories. First, we examine the major differences between them. Then, we explore the ways in which some central ideas of the prediction-error theory can be incorporated into the two-factor framework.

The two-factor theory

Why two factors?

The two-factor theory is primarily a theory of monothematic delusions (delusions concerning single themes). The most extensively discussed example of monothematic delusion in the literature is that of the Capgras delusion.

Ellis and Young (1990) argue that the Capgras delusion is formed in response to the abnormal experience of seeing familiar faces. The experience is abnormal in that it lacks the affective component that is usually a part of the experience. The Capgras delusion is formed as an attempt to explain this abnormal perceptual-affective experience.

> [Capgras patients] receive a veridical image of a person they are looking at, which stimulates all the appropriate overt semantic data held about that person, but they lack another, possibly confirming, set of information which [. . .] may carry some sort of affective tone. When patients find themselves in such a conflict, [. . .] they may adopt some sort of rationalisation strategy in which the individual before them is deemed to be an imposter, a dummy, a robot, or whatever extant technology may suggest.
>
> *(Ellis & Young 1990, 244)*

This hypothesis is supported by the finding that people with the Capgras delusion do not show the asymmetrical autonomic responses between familiar faces and unfamiliar faces (Ellis, Young, Quayle & De Pauw 1997).

Is the abnormal perceptual-affective experience of familiar faces sufficient for the development of the Capgras delusion? If it were so, then anyone with this abnormal experience would, other things being equal, develop the delusion. The view that the abnormal experience is sufficient for the formation of the delusion is usually attributed to Maher (1974), who thinks that delusions are a perfectly normal response to abnormal experience. According to him, "a delusion is a hypothesis designed to explain unusual perceptual phenomena and developed through the operation of normal cognitive processes" (Maher 1974, 103).

Two-factor theorists, however, do not think that the abnormal experience is sufficient for the development of Capgras delusion. In addition to the abnormal experience[2], there has to be another causal factor that is responsible for the development of the Capgras delusion. The main argument for the additional factor (Davies *et al.* 2001; Coltheart 2007; Coltheart, Langdon & McKay 2011) goes as follows. Just like people with Capgras delusion, people with damages to the ventromedial prefrontal cortex (VMPFC) fail to show the asymmetrical autonomic responses between familiar faces and unfamiliar faces (Tranel, Damasio & Damasio 1995). This suggests that people with the Capgras delusion and people with VMPFC damage are in similar experiential conditions. However, people with VMPFC damages do not develop the Capgras delusion. This shows that the abnormal experience can be dissociated from Capgras delusion. One can have the abnormal experience without forming the delusion. There are two possible ways to account for the dissociation between experience and delusion. Either the abnormal experience may not be causally responsible for the development of the Capgras delusion after all. Or, in addition to the abnormal experience, there must be an additional factor contributing to the development of the Capgras delusion. The first option is unlikely because the content of the Capgras delusion has an obvious connection to the abnormal experience. Therefore, the only available option is the second one. Let us call this "dissociability argument for the second factor".

The dissociability argument is applicable not only to the Capgras delusion, but also to many other monothematic delusions, because for each monothematic delusion there are some people who might have experiences quite similar to those of people with the relevant delusional subjects, but nonetheless do not develop the relevant delusions. For example, people with schizophrenia who experience global affective flattening might be experientially quite similar to people with the Cotard delusion (who believe that they are dead or disembodied), but do not develop the Cotard delusion. Some people with depersonalisation disorder might be experientially quite similar to the people with delusions of alien control (who believe that the parts of their bodies are controlled by someone else), but do not develop the delusion of alien control. People with severe prosopagnosia (face blindness) might be experientially quite similar to the people with delusions of mirrored-self misidentification (who believe that the reflected images on the mirror are someone else), but do not develop the delusion of mirrored-self misidentification. And the list could go on.

One fundamental commitment of the two-factor theory, therefore, is the idea that *there are two distinct factors that are causally responsible for the development (including adoption and maintenance) of delusions.* Here, to say that two factors are distinct is to say that they can be dissociated from each other. For instance, the second factor of the Capgras delusion, whatever it is, is dissociable from the first factor, the abnormal experience. They are actually dissociated, for instance, in people with VMPFC damage.

Another important commitment of the two-factor theory is the idea that two factors play different explanatory roles. In particular, *the first factor explains the content of the delusion, whilst the second factor explains the fact that the delusional hypothesis is adopted and maintained* (Coltheart 2007). For instance, the abnormal perceptual-affective experience of familiar faces, which is often regarded as the first factor in the Capgras delusion, is certainly explanatory with regard to the content of the Capgras delusion. It explains why, for instance, a person with the Capgras delusion believes that his wife has been replaced by an imposter. It does not equally explain other beliefs the person might have, for instance, that he is followed by CIA agents or that the world is coming to an end. On the other hand, the abnormality in the belief evaluation system located in the right hemisphere, which is the second factor according to Coltheart (2007), explains why delusional hypotheses are adopted and/or maintained. For instance, it explains why, unlike people with VMPFC damage[3], people with Capgras adopt and/or maintain the imposter hypothesis.

Problems with the two-factor theory

There are two main difficulties for the two-factor theory. One is related to the scope of the theory, while the other is related to the nature of the second factor.

Problem of scope: The first problem is that the scope of the theory seems to be rather limited. The two-factor theory is, as we have already noted, primarily concerned with the formation of monothematic delusions. It is not clear how the theory could be applied to other kinds of delusions. In particular, its applicability to polythematic delusions (delusions involving many different themes) is unclear. Coltheart admits that the two-factor theory "has focused principally on monothematic delusion, largely neglecting polythematic delusions, including some that are especially frequently seen in clinical patients" (Coltheart 2013, 105).

The applicability of the theory to motivationally formed delusions is also unclear. McKay, Langdon and Coltheart (2009) refer to a case of a man with Reverse Othello syndrome who, after a serious car accident that caused severe head injury and quadriplegia, believed that he and his former partner had recently married, despite the fact that the former partner severed all contact with him after the accident (Butler 2000). A plausible story about this case is that the man's delusional belief about his recent marriage was formed (partly) because he did not want to accept the stark reality of his situation. Does the two-factor theory have anything to say about this case? McKay and colleagues write, "[t]he problem for the two-factor account as it currently stands is that there are myriad cases of delusions that similarly resist ready identification of potential first deficits, but for which plausible motivational stories can be told" (McKay *et al.* 2009, 313).

Two-factor theorists have some ideas on how to solve these problems. Coltheart and colleagues (2011) suggest three potential scenarios in which two-factor accounts are applicable to polythematic delusions. First, polythematic delusions might be caused by multiple first factors. Second, polythematic delusions might be developed when the second factor is very serious. Third, polythematic delusions might be developed when the first factor is relatively ambiguous and open to different explanations. According to McKay and colleagues (2009), the two-factor account can be applied to motivationally formed delusions if the first factor includes motivational states such as a desire or a suggestion due to a psychological defence mechanism. For instance, the case of Reverse Othello syndrome above might be understood as a case where the first factor is the desire not to accept the loss of one's former romantic partner.

Problem of the second factor. The most serious problem of the two-factor theory is that the nature of the second factor is underspecified. All two-factor theorists agree about the existence of the second factor. But there is no agreement about its nature. Coltheart's proposal, that the second factor is an abnormality in the belief evaluation system located in the right hemisphere, does not specify exactly what kind of abnormality it is. Could it be, for instance, a reasoning bias?

There have been several suggestions as to the nature of the abnormality. The second factor might be the presence of a jumping-to-conclusion bias (the bias of coming to a conclusion with less evidence in comparison to non-clinical samples; see Huq, Garety & Hemsley 1988), an externalising attribution bias (the bias of attributing negative events to external objects or people instead of oneself; see Young 2000), a bias towards observational adequacy (the bias of putting too much weight on observational data, discounting existing beliefs; see Stone and Young 1997) or a failure to inhibit pre-potent doxastic responses to perceptual experience (the failure to adopt a critical stance towards perceptual content and accept it as veridical; see Davies *et al.* 2001). Although some of the above suggestions hold some promise, it is not clear whether one bias would be sufficient in isolation from the other ones to underlie the second factor.

Recently, the nature of the second factor has been investigated by appealing to quantitative models of the inferential step in the delusion formation process (Coltheart *et al.* 2010; McKay 2012; Davies & Egan 2013). Coltheart and colleagues, for instance, argue that the inferential step in the Capgras delusion formation process is perfectly Bayesian-rational. Let H_s be the hypothesis that the woman in front of me is a stranger, H_w be the hypothesis that the woman is my wife, and O be the abnormal perceptual-affective experience. So it follows from Bayes' theorem that:

$$\frac{P(H_s|O)}{P(H_w|O)} = \frac{P(H_s) \times P(O|H_s)}{P(H_w) \times P(O|H_w)}$$

Coltheart *et al.* (2010) argue that:

$$P(H_s) < P(H_w)$$

$$P(O|H_s) \gg P(O|H_w)$$

$$P(H_s|O) > P(H_w|O)$$

In other words, H*w* has a higher prior probability than H*s* (i.e. H*w* is more plausible than H*s* before O becomes available). But it is outweighed by the likelihood ratio that overwhelmingly favours H*s* (i.e. H*s* explains O overwhelmingly better than H*w*). As a result, H*s* gets a higher posterior probability than H*w* (i.e. H*s* is more plausible than H*w* given O). And, assuming that this is the way people with the Capgras delusions actually reason, Coltheart and colleagues (2010) argue that the Capgras delusion is adopted in a Bayesian-rational probabilistic inference. Since this inferential step is Bayesian-rational, they argue, there is no second factor here. The second factor rather operates at the post-adoption stage where counterevidence to H*s* becomes available. For instance, after a person with Capgras adopts H*s*, he will realise that trusted friends or seemingly reliable psychiatrists are saying that the woman in his house is his wife, not an imposter. He will also find that the "imposter" does not just look exactly like his real wife, but also behaves exactly like his real wife, knows everything his real wife knows, and so on. All of this evidence supports H*w* instead of H*s*. The person with Capgras fails to incorporate the new body of evidence into his belief system because he neglects new evidence due to a bias. And this bias of neglecting new evidence is the second factor.

This is certainly an interesting proposal. But does it really solve the problem of the second factor once and for all? Possibly not. If people with the Capgras delusions have the bias of neglecting new evidence, then why do they not neglect the abnormal experience, which is new evidence acquired at the beginning of the process? According to the proposal, people with Capgras adopt H*s* because H*s* is more plausible given the abnormal experience. Here, they do not neglect the abnormal experience at all. Why is it that they do not neglect the abnormal experience despite having a bias that leads them to neglect new evidence? To be consistent, presumably Coltheart and colleagues (2010) need to say that the bias of neglecting new evidence is acquired after H*s* is adopted (so that the abnormal experience is not neglected) and before counterevidence to H*s* becomes available (so that the counterevidence is neglected). But, as McKay (2012) points out, this chronological story is quite unrealistic and implausible.[4]

Summing up, the two-factor theory consists of two main claims: (1) there are two distinct factors that are causally responsible for the development of the delusion; (2) the first factor explains the content of delusion, while the second factor explains why the delusional hypotheses are adopted and/or maintained. The two-factor theory is supported by the dissociability argument in support of the second factor; the existence of the second factor is defended on the basis of the dissociability between the first factor (e.g. an abnormal perceptual–affective experience) and the presence of delusional beliefs (e.g. the Capgras delusion). A problem for the two-factor theory is that the scope of the theory seems to be limited. It is not clear how the theory is applicable to polythematic delusions and motivationally formed delusions. Another problem is that there is no agreement about the nature of the second factor. Even the recent quantitative developments of the two-factor account might not be fully satisfactory.

Prediction-error theory

Salient experience and prediction errors

Kapur (2003) argues that the abnormality in dopamine transmission in schizophrenia leads to an inappropriate attribution of "salience". The attribution of salience is "the process whereby events and thoughts come to grab attention, drive action, and influence goal-directed behaviour because of their association with reward or punishment" (Kapur 2003, 14). When salience is attributed inappropriately to events that are not very interesting as a matter of fact, they grab special attention. Such events, all of a sudden, seem to be important and are invested with special meaning. This hypothesis explains the fact that many people with delusions in the context of schizophrenia report that some events have "special meaning" for them, that they have an "altered experience" of the world, that their awareness is "sharpened", and so on. The delusion, according to Kapur, is produced as the explanation of the inappropriately salient events.

> Delusions are "top-down" cognitive explanations that the individual imposes on these experiences of aberrant salience in an effort to make sense of them. [. . .] Once the patient arrives at such an explanation, it provides an "insight relief" or a "psychotic insight" and serves as a guiding cognitive scheme for further thoughts and actions.
>
> *(Kapur 2003, 15)*

The prediction-error theory of delusion provides a more detailed story about how salience is inappropriately attributed in people with schizophrenia and delusions (Corlett *et al.* 2010; Fletcher & Frith 2009). According to the theory, *inappropriate attribution of salience is the product of aberrant prediction-error signals.*

In general, a prediction error tells us that what we experience does not match our predictions. It indicates that the internal model of the world from which the prediction is derived is incorrect and needs to be updated. By updating the model in such a way as to minimise prediction errors, we improve our understanding of the world. In this framework, prediction-error signals play a fundamental role in allowing us to update our model of the world, and to update our beliefs. Prediction-error theorists posit abnormal prediction-error signalling in people with delusions. In particular, it is hypothesised that, in people with delusions, *prediction-error signals are excessive in the sense that they are produced when there is no real mismatch between prediction and actual inputs.* The excessive prediction-error signals falsely indicate that the internal model of the world needs to be updated even though, as a matter of fact, it does not have to be.

Prediction-error signals also play a crucial role in allocating attention. Attention is allocated to events that defy expectations. This makes sense intuitively since the predictable events do not bring any new information and, thus, do not deserve attention. Due to excessive prediction-error signals, people with delusions allocate attention to events that do not actually deserve it. This is the process where uninteresting events become inappropriately salient, and delusions are produced as explanatory responses to the inappropriately salient events due to aberrant prediction-error signals. Corlett and colleagues (2009) nicely summarise the main claim of the prediction-error theory.

> Prediction error theories of delusion formation suggest that under the influence of inappropriate prediction error signal, possibly as a consequence of dopamine dysregulation, events that are insignificant and merely coincident seem to demand attention, feel important and relate to each other in meaningful ways. Delusions ultimately arise as a means of explaining these odd experiences.
>
> *(Corlett* et al. *2009, 1)*

The remarkable study by Corlett and colleagues (2007) strongly supports this aberrant prediction-error signal hypothesis. In the study, two groups of participants, people with delusions and people without, are tested with a task involving learning the association between certain foods and allergic reactions. The activity of the right prefrontal cortex (which was identified as a reliable marker of prediction-error processing in previous studies) was monitored with fMRI. The authors found that, in the delusional group but not in the control group, the magnitude of the activity of the right prefrontal cortex was not significantly different between the cases where the expectations about allergic reaction were confirmed and the cases where they were violated. They also found that the severity of this abnormal prediction-error signalling was correlated with the severity of their delusion.

Problems with the prediction-error theory

There are two main challenges for the prediction-error theory. First, aberrant prediction-error signals might be dissociable from delusions. Second, the theory (or, at least, its main claim) does not say anything about how delusions are maintained after they are adopted.

Dissociability problem: Prediction-error theorists typically assume that aberrant prediction-error signals are sufficient for the development of delusion. This assumption, however, is problematic. Here is the account of the Capgras delusion offered by Corlett and colleagues (2010). Corlett and colleagues accept Ellis and Young's hypothesis that people with Capgras delusion have an abnormal perceptual-affective experience of familiar faces. They interpret this as a kind of prediction error where the expected affective experience does not match the actual experience. The Capgras delusion is formed as an explanatory response to this affective prediction error. Unlike two-factor theorists, Corlett and colleagues are explicitly committed to the idea that this affective prediction error is sufficient for the development of the Capgras delusion. "[W]e argue that phenomenology of the percepts are such that bizarre beliefs are inevitable; surprising experiences demand surprising explanations" (Corlett *et al.* 2010, 360).

The problem with this commitment is that the affective prediction error is dissociable from the Capgras delusion. For instance, it might be that the affective prediction error is occurring not only in people with Capgras delusion, but also in people with VMPFC damage. But the latter do not develop the Capgras delusion. As we previously discussed, this shows that either the affective prediction error is causally irrelevant to the formation of the Capgras delusion or it is not sufficient for it. The first option cannot be accepted by prediction-error theorists. Thus, it looks as though they need to accept that the affective prediction error is not sufficient.

There are several possible responses from prediction-error theorists. For example, they could argue that the affective prediction error in the people with VMPFC damage is not as serious as the one in people with the Capgras delusion and "the salience of the data in question has simply not passed a certain threshold" (McKay 2012, 348) in the former. Alternatively, they might argue that people with VMPFC damage actually develop something like the Capgras delusion. For example, Corlett and colleagues (2010) argue that some people with damage to the ventromedial and the lateral prefrontal cortex develop delusion-like spontaneous confabulation.

Problem of maintenance: The second problem for the prediction-error theory is that it explains the development of the delusion only up to the point where delusional beliefs are adopted as an account of inappropriately salient events. But, another thing to be explained is the fact that, after the initial adoption, delusions are maintained despite overwhelming counterevidence. The definition of delusion in DSM-5 says that delusion "is firmly sustained despite what almost everyone else believes and despite what constitutes incontrovertible and obvious proof or evidence to the contrary" (American Psychiatric Association 2013, 819). It looks as though the account of this aspect of the delusion is missing from the main tenets of the prediction-error theory. Corlett and colleagues admit that "this model accounts for why delusions emerge but not for why they persist" (Corlett *et al.* 2013, 2).

This explanatory gap is more evident when we compare the prediction-error theory with the two-factor theory. The maintenance of the delusion is the central issue for two-factor theorists. A part of the aim of positing the second factor is to explain the maintenance of delusion. For example, as we have already seen, Coltheart and colleagues (2010) propose that the second factor is the bias of neglecting new evidence. If people with delusions really have this bias, it certainly explains why delusions are firmly maintained despite overwhelming counterevidence. The counterevidence is simply ignored because of the bias.

Presumably, it is not just that an account of delusion maintenance is missing from the prediction-error theory, but also that the theory has a peculiar difficulty in explaining it. It is hypothesised, in the theory, that prediction-error signals are excessive in people with delusions. This presumably does not suddenly come to an end when a delusional hypothesis is adopted. In other words, prediction-error signals will remain excessive even after the adoption of delusional hypotheses. But, this seems to predict that delusions, after adoption, will be unstable instead of firmly maintained. Suppose that a subject adopts a delusional hypothesis as an account of inappropriately salient events due to excessive prediction-error signals. Now, the delusional hypothesis becomes an important part of his internal model of the world. After adopting it, he will be again exposed to recurrent excessive prediction-error signals that indicate, this time, that the delusional internal model of the world is inaccurate and needs to be updated. It is expected, then, that he will update the delusional internal model of the world so that prediction error will be minimised. But, as a matter of fact, people with delusions do not update their delusional hypotheses in this way. They just stick to their commitments even in the face of overwhelming counterevidence. This is quite puzzling.

Corlett and colleagues (2009; 2013) recognise this problem and try to solve it by offering an account of the maintenance of delusion on the basis of the idea of memory reconsolidation.[5] Belief (including delusional belief) is, according to Corlett and colleagues, a kind of memory. Thus, belief is maintained in the same way that memory is maintained. In particular, memory reconsolidation plays a crucial role in the maintenance of delusional beliefs. After the initial adoption of delusion, due to the abnormal activity in the midbrain reminder system:

> aberrant prediction errors might re-evoke the representation of the delusion without definitively disconfirming it. This would drive preferential reconsolidation over and above any new extinction learning. The net effect would be a strengthening of the delusion through reconsolidation rather than a weakening by extinction.
>
> *(Corlett* et al. *2009, 3)*

To summarise, according to the prediction-error theory, a delusion is formed as an explanation of events that are inappropriately salient due to aberrant prediction-error signals. The hypothesis is consistent with the subjective report of delusional subjects, and is supported by empirical studies suggesting abnormal prediction-error signalling in delusional subjects. A problem of the theory is that aberrant prediction-error signals might not be sufficient for the development of the delusion, contrary to the assumption made by many prediction-error theorists. Another problem is that the account of the maintenance of the delusion in the face of overwhelming counterevidence is missing from the main tenets of the prediction-error theory. Thus, it needs to be supplemented by an additional account of maintenance, such as the one appealing to the idea of memory reconsolidation.

Two-factor theory vs. prediction-error theory

In this section, we examine the relationship between the two-factor theory and the prediction-error theory in detail. First, we discuss the main differences between the two theories, and then explore the ways in which the ideas of the prediction-error theory can be incorporated into the two-factor framework.

Differences

There are many differences between the two-factor and the prediction-error theory. But the main differences between them seem to be about (1) target phenomena, (2) the number of factors, and (3) the perceiving–believing relation.

(1) *Target phenomena*: The two-factor theory is primarily about monothematic delusions. In particular, the theory is quite persuasive about monothematic delusions of neuropsychological or organic origins (such as a stroke, traumatic brain injury, etc.). People with monothematic delusions of neuropsychological origins often have abnormalities in the right hemisphere, which supports the existence of the second factor independently from the dissociability argument. On the other hand, the prediction-error theory is primarily about delusions in schizophrenia. Often, the theory is motivated by general neurological hypotheses about schizophrenia, such as the dopamine hypothesis, and presented as a part of the general theory of the positive symptoms of schizophrenia, including delusion and hallucination. Fletcher and Frith note that their proposal is that "a common mechanism, involving minimization of prediction error, may underlie perception and inference, and that a disruption in this mechanism may cause both abnormal perceptions (hallucinations) and abnormal beliefs (delusions)" (Fletcher & Frith 2009, 48). In addition, the empirical support for the prediction-error theory, such as the study involving the allergy detection task by Corlett and colleagues (2007), comes from studies on people with delusions emerging in the context of schizophrenia.

(2) *Number of factors*: It is the essential commitment of the two-factor theory that there are two factors that are causally responsible for the development of delusion. Instead, the prediction-error theory is typically presented as a one-factor account, where the factor is the aberrant prediction-error signal. "Prediction error driven Bayesian models of delusions subsume both factors into a single deficit in Bayesian inference; noise in predictive learning mechanism engender inappropriate percepts which update future priors, leading to the formation and maintenance of delusions" (Corlett *et al.* 2010, 357).

> [T]he positive symptoms of schizophrenia seem to reflect two underlying abnormalities, suggesting that a two-factor explanation is required. However, recent computational models of perception and learning suggest that the same fundamental mechanism (Bayesian inference), by which a model of the world is updated by prediction errors, applies to both perception and belief-formation. [. . .] We suggest that positive symptoms of schizophrenia are caused by an abnormality in the brain's inferencing mechanisms, such that new evidence (including sensations) is not properly integrated, leading to false prediction errors.
>
> *(Fletcher & Frith 2009, 56)*

(3) *Perceiving and believing*: Prediction-error theorists typically assume that there is no categorical distinction between perceiving and believing. Accordingly, they

typically do not draw a sharp distinction between abnormal perception (hallucination) and abnormal belief (delusion). The reason why there is no categorical distinction between perceiving and believing is that, according to their view, both are operating on the same principle, namely, minimising prediction error.

> The boundaries between perception and belief at the physiological level are not so distinct. An important principle that has emerged is that both perception of the world and learning about the world (and therefore beliefs) are dependent on predictions and the extent to which they are fulfilled. This suggests that a single deficit could explain abnormal perceptions and beliefs.
>
> *(Fletcher & Frith 2009, 51)*

> Within this theoretical framework belief itself must, like perception, be a matter of prediction error minimisation. The difference between belief and perception lies in the time scale of the represented processes and their degree of invariance or perceptive independence. There is no further special difference between them and the issue of rationality applies equally to perception and belief.
>
> *(Hohwy & Rajan 2012, 10)*

Two-factor theorists, on the other hand, are typically committed to the categorical distinction between perceptual/experiential processes and believing processes. This is to be expected, because it is the core claim of the two-factor theory that the experiential factor (the first factor) is not sufficient for the development of delusional beliefs.

> As a two-factor theorist, my view is that the distinction between perception and belief is not easily dispensed with – particularly at the personal level of description. As Martin Davies (personal communication) notes, "One indication of this is that obliterating the distinction between perception and belief seems to have the consequence that illusory perceptual states that are informationally encapsulated from most of a person's belief are liable to be counted as delusions."
>
> *(McKay 2012, footnote 26)*

These are the main differences between the two-factor and the prediction-error theory that anyone interested in the relationship between them should be aware of. However, these differences are, in our view, not as significant as one might expect.

The difference in terms of target phenomena is not very significant, given that monothematic delusions and schizophrenic delusions often overlap with each other. For example, the Capgras delusion is a typical example of monothematic delusion, but can be observed in people with schizophrenia. In addition, as Coltheart (2010) points out, if the distinction between monothematic and polythematic delusions is mapped onto the distinction between neuropsychological and non-neuropsychological delusions, then it is not clear-cut. We cannot be sure that there are any non-neuropsychological delusions. Furthermore, it might turn out that the two delusion-formation theories, even though they start from monothematic delusions and schizophrenic delusions respectively, are applicable to other kinds of delusions in the end. For example, as we have already noted, there are some possible scenarios in which the two-factor theory is applicable to polythematic and motivationally formed delusions (without obvious neuropsychological origins). Again, if the prediction-error theory is a persuasive account of, say, the Capgras delusion in schizophrenia, it is perfectly possible that the same account is applicable to the Capgras delusion occurring in other contexts. As Coltheart and colleagues noted, the Capgras delusion is likely to be "cognitively homogeneous" even though it is "etiologically heterogeneous" (Coltheart *et al.* 2007, 645). If the account of the Capgras delusion given by prediction-error theorists is plausible in the context of schizophrenia, then it is also a possible candidate for a general account of the Capgras delusion that is applicable outside the context of schizophrenia.

The difference with regard to the number of factors might not be very significant either. It is not obvious that the prediction-error theory is necessarily a one-factor theory. It is certainly true that the prediction-error theory is, as a matter of fact, often presented as a one-factor account. But are there any reasons to think that the prediction-error theory needs to be a one-factor theory? According to Corlett and colleagues (2010), the affective prediction error is sufficient for the formation of the Capgras delusion, and theirs is certainly a one-factor account. But not all prediction-error theorists have to follow Corlett and colleagues on this issue. Prediction-error theorists could think that the Capgras delusion is an abnormal response to an affective prediction error and that there has to be an additional factor that explains the abnormality of the response. The commitment to an additional factor might give a better account of the dissociability between the Capgras delusion and the affective prediction error. According to the version of the prediction-error theory we are considering, people with VMPFC damage would not develop the Capgras delusion even though they were experiencing affective prediction error because the affective prediction error would not be sufficient for the development of the Capgras delusion. There would have to be an additional factor.

To reiterate, the prediction-error theory is often presented as a one-factor account. But it is not obvious that, strictly speaking, it qualifies as a one-factor account. For example, as we have already noted, an account of the maintenance of delusion is not explicit in the main body of the prediction-error theory. This means that prediction-error theorists need to tell some further story about maintenance. It might turn out that the further story posits an additional abnormal factor. In this case, prediction-error theorists would posit two factors after all: an aberrant prediction-error theory to account for the adoption of the delusion, and an additional factor to account for its maintenance. For instance, think about the account by Corlett and colleagues of the maintenance of the delusion, according to which delusions are maintained through the process of memory reconsolidation. If it turns out that the memory reconsolidation process is abnormal in people with delusions, and this abnormality is dissociable from aberrant prediction-error signals, then the proposal does not qualify as a one-factor account. It posits two distinct factors: aberrant prediction-error signals and an abnormality in the memory reconsolidation process. Such a proposal would also be consistent with the claim by two-factor theorists that the two factors play different explanatory roles. The aberrant prediction error would explain why a hypothesis with delusional content is adopted, and the abnormality in the memory reconsolidation process would explain why the delusional hypothesis is maintained. In this case, the proposal would be just another version of the two-factor theory.

Sometimes, prediction-error theorists show a subtle attitude towards the number of factors. Hohwy and Rajan, for instance, argue that the prediction-error theory is different from the Maher-style one-factor account because it "goes beyond the one- vs two-factor view" (Hohwy & Rajan 2012, 9). Unlike Maher, they posit more than one factor, but, unlike two-factor theorists, they do not believe that there is a categorical distinction between the two factors. The two factors might be *numerically* distinct (in the sense that they are dissociable from each other), but they are not *categorically* distinct (in the sense that they do not belong to different neurological or psychological categories).

The third difference between the two theories concerns the perceiving–believing relation. Is perceiving categorically distinct from believing? This seems an important issue, but we should not overestimate this difference between the two theories. First, the notion of belief in the vocabulary of prediction-error theorists is sometimes peculiar and, accordingly, we need to be careful in interpreting their claim that there is no categorical distinction between perceiving and what they call "believing". Corlett and colleagues characterise belief as "probability distributions that are represented by the brain" (Corlett *et al.* 2010, 347). This notion of belief might not overlap perfectly with the ordinary, folk psychological notion of belief. After all, believing is what we, not our brain, do, in the ordinary usage of the term. We, not our brains, believe something. It seems to be possible that my brain assigns a high probability to a certain hypothesis, but the hypothesis is either not introspectively accessible to me or, if it is accessible, it does not guide my actions or thoughts in the way normal beliefs do. Presumably, I do not believe the hypothesis in this case, at least not in the ordinary usage of the term, even though my brain assigns a high probability to it.

Second, it is not obvious that the two-factor theory is necessarily committed to the claim that perceptual processes and believing processes are categorically different. As we have already noted, the central commitments of the two-factor theory are: (1) there are two distinct factors that are causally responsible for the development of delusion, and (2) those two factors play different explanatory roles. The question that arises is whether these two claims imply a categorical difference between perceptual processes and believing processes.

One might reason in the following way. Those claims imply that there is a categorical difference between the first and the second factor and, since the first–second factor distinction amounts to the perceiving–believing distinction, the commitment to the first distinction implies a commitment to the second distinction. The problem in this line of reasoning is that neither (1) nor (2) entails that there is a categorical difference between the first and the second factor. (1) is committed to the distinctness between the first and the second factors. But, as we have already noted, this notion of "distinctness" only implies that the first and the second factors are dissociable; it does not entail that there is a categorical difference between them. It is perfectly possible that two factors are dissociable, and yet they belong to the same neurological or psychological category. Again, (2) is committed to the explanatory difference between the first and the second factor. But, it is not obvious that this entails a categorical difference between them. It is possible that the two factors play different explanatory roles, and they belong to the same neurological or psychological category.

When emphasising the continuity between perceiving and believing, prediction-error theorists often appeal to Helmholtz's (1878/1971) famous idea that perceiving involves unconscious inferential processes based upon prior knowledge and sensory inputs. Belief formation is often regarded as an inferential process but, according to the Helmholzian picture, perception is inferentially formed too. Thus, there is no categorical distinction between believing and perceiving in this regard. They both involve inferences. This Helmholzian picture would not be incompatible with the two-factor theory. Indeed, Coltheart and colleagues (2010) are very sympathetic to the Helmholzian picture. Their proposal is that the Capgras delusion is formed through an unconscious Bayesian inferential process based upon prior beliefs as well as abnormal data involving reduced autonomic response to familiar faces. They admit that this proposal is similar to the Helmholzian picture.

Again, Coltheart (2010) makes it explicit that the core claims about perception and learning by Corlett and other prediction-error theorists are perfectly compatible with the two-factor theory.

> The first is that much of what we perceive is based in our expectation. That conception is also central to the two-factor theory of delusion because the first factor in most delusions is a violation of expectation (e.g., in Capgras delusion the violation of the expectation of a strong autonomic response upon seeing the face of one's spouse). The second is that perception expectations are learned; that is also consistent with the two-factor theory, because we learn how a mirror works, we learn that objects and people of value to us will generate strong autonomic responses, etc. The third is that mismatches between what we expect and what we experience drive the updating of our expectancies: that too is what the two-factor theory proposes, merely replacing the term "updating of our expectancies" with the term "revision of our belief system".
>
> *(Coltheart 2010, 25)*

Incorporating elements of the prediction-error theory into the two-factor theory

We have just reviewed the major differences between the two-factor and the prediction-error theory. The differences, we argued, are not as significant as one might expect. In this subsection, we explore ways in which some ideas from the prediction-error theory can be incorporated in the framework of the two-factor theory. We also consider the potential advantages of this conciliatory strategy.

There are, broadly speaking, two possible cases. In the first case, *the aberrant prediction-error signal is, or underlies, the first factor*. This means that the content of the relevant delusions is explained in terms of aberrant prediction-error signals. In the second case, *the aberrant prediction-error signal is, or underlies, the second factor*. This means that the adoption and/or maintenance of delusional hypotheses are explained in terms of aberrant prediction-error signals.

Let us first look at the latter case. The potential advantage of this idea is that it might give us some further insight into the nature of the second factor, which is still underspecified. The conciliatory strategy might help us to solve the main problem of the two-factor theory, namely, the problem of the second factor. Coltheart (2010) argues that the allergy detection task study by Corlett and colleagues is consistent with and supportive of the claim by him and colleagues that the second factor concerns the hypothesis evaluation system and is located in the right hemisphere. The study, according to Coltheart, is informative about the exact location of the second factor (right lateral prefrontal cortex) as well as the nature of it.

> In the patients, surprising and unsurprising events *both* evoked responses of RLPFC [right lateral prefrontal cortex], and to an equal degree. Hence *unsurprising* events evoked such activity in the patients when no such activity was evoked in the controls. The implication for two-factor theory, if one assumes that RLPFC is a signature of hypothesis *evaluation*, is that what is abnormal about the patients is that they are evaluating hypotheses even on those trials where the hypothesis was confirmed and so did not need evaluation.
>
> (*Coltheart 2010, 24, italics original*)

The general idea seems to be as follows: assuming that belief updating is operating on the principle of prediction-error minimisation, excessive prediction-error signals in people with delusions would lead to revising beliefs that do not have to be revised. In short, people with delusions would be too revisionist when they update their beliefs. This bias might constitute the second factor. This idea is not entirely novel. Stone and Young (1997) already proposed that the second factor in delusion formation is a bias towards observational adequacy, which is due to putting too much weight on observational data and discounting existing beliefs. Obviously, this bias makes people too revisionist in belief updating.

McKay (2012) develops Stone and Young's idea in detail and connects the proposal with the prediction-error theory. Unlike Coltheart and colleagues (2010), McKay does not think that the inferential step in the delusion adoption stage is Bayesian-rational. The step deviates from Bayesian rationality and the deviation is characterised by the bias of discounting the prior probability ratio. Here is McKay's story about how people with the Capgras delusion reason.

$$P(Hs) \ll P(Hw)$$

$$P(O|Hs) \gg P(O|Hw)$$

$$P(Hs|O) > P(Hw|O)$$

Hw has a much higher prior probability than Hs. But, the likelihood ratio overwhelmingly favours Hs. Due to a bias, the prior probability ratio in favour of Hw is discounted, and the likelihood ratio in favour of Hs is overemphasised. As a result, Hs gets a higher posterior probability than Hw. This bias of discounting the prior probability ratio is the second factor. The difference between people with the Capgras delusion and people with VMPFC damage is explained by the assumption that this bias is peculiar to the former and absent in the latter. Unlike the proposal by Coltheart and colleagues (2010), there is no need to posit the bias of neglecting new evidence as the second factor, which might be problematic, as we have already noted. McKay suggests that excessive prediction-error signals might underlie the bias of discounting the prior probability ratio.

> Prediction error signals are triggered by discrepancies between the data expected and the data encountered. Such signals render salient the unexpected data and initiate a revision to accommodate these data. If there is an excess of prediction error signal, an appropriately heightened salience is attached to the data, and belief revision is excessively accommodatory – biased towards explanatory adequacy.[6]
>
> *(McKay 2012, 348)*

The first case, the case where an aberrant prediction-error signal is the first factor, has not been explored seriously yet. But it seems to be an attractive option. According to the prediction-error theory, delusions are explanations of events that are inappropriately salient due to aberrant prediction-error signals. And most two-factor theorists (explanationist two-factor theorists) think that delusions are explanations of the first factor.[7] For instance, Coltheart and colleagues (2010) regard the probabilistic inference in the delusion adoption stage as an inference to the best *explanation* (of the first factor). Then, it is tempting to identify "events that are inappropriately salient due to aberrant prediction-error signals" with "the first factor".

This proposal has some potential benefits. First, it would solve the problem of dissociation (for the prediction-error theory). Since, in this proposal, aberrant prediction-error signal is merely the first factor, it is not expected to be sufficient for the development of delusion. People with VMPFC damage have the first factor, but they presumably do not have the second factor. Second, the problem of maintenance (for the prediction-error theory) might be solved if the second factor helps explain the maintenance of delusion. It is no longer an issue if an aberrant prediction-error signal does not satisfactorily explain maintenance. The second factor explains it. Third, the problem of scope (for the two-factor theory) might be solved if aberrant prediction-error signals explain the first factor in the formation of delusions whose first factors are unknown. For example, it is not clear how the two-factor theory is applied to the delusion of reference because there the first factor is unknown. But, according to this proposal, the first factor in the formation of delusions of reference might just be the inappropriate salience attached to some uninteresting events.

To say that the aberrant prediction-error signal is the first factor in the formation of some delusions is to say that it helps explain the content of those delusions. But how exactly can aberrant prediction-error signals be explanatory with regard to the content of delusions? The key would be the role of prediction error in attention allocation. Aberrant prediction-error signals render some events inappropriately attention-grabbing. Delusions are formed as the explanations of those events. Here, aberrant prediction-error signals influence the allocation of attention, which is certainly explanatory with regard to the content of delusions that are formed as the explanations of the attention-grabbing events. Corlett and colleagues (2009) discuss a subject who formed the delusional belief that "The Organisation" painted the doors of the houses on a street as a message for him. This was based on his observation that many doors on the right-hand side of the street were red, while many doors on the left side were green (Chadwick 2001). In this case, aberrant prediction-error signals render this uninteresting pattern of red doors and green doors inappropriately attention-grabbing, and this attention-grabbingness is explanatory with regard to the content of his delusion. It explains, for instance, why he thinks that the pattern of the colour of the doors, as opposed to cars or trees on the street, conveys the message for him.

There are two possibilities to explore. One possibility is that the aberrant prediction-error signal underlies the first factor in the formation of some, but not all, delusions. For instance, one might think that inappropriate prediction-error signalling is the first factor in the formation of delusions of reference or persecutory delusions, but it has nothing to do with the first factor in the formation of monothematic delusions.

The other possibility is that the first factor in the formation of all delusions, including monothematic ones, has something to do with prediction error. Two-factor theorists often assume that the second factor is shared by all (monothematic) delusions, but the first factor is different in different delusions. But, in this proposal, the first factor would also be shared by all delusions in the sense that it would have something to do with prediction error. This idea is attractive because, as Coltheart points out in the earlier quote, "the first factor in most delusions is a violation of expectation". As Corlett and colleagues (2010) suggest, the abnormal perceptual-affective experience, which is a good candidate for the first factor in the formation of the Capgras delusion, constitutes an affective prediction error. The same thing was true of the Cotard delusion, whose first factor is often regarded as an abnormal affective experience about things in general. Corlett and colleagues argue that this abnormal experience also constitutes an affective prediction error. Again, delusions of control, thought control and thought insertion are very likely to be linked to prediction error. These delusions are likely to be generated by the failure to identify self-generated physical behaviour or mental events as self-generated (Blakemore, Oakley & Frith 2003; Frith 2005). This failure can be easily linked to a prediction error because the most obvious feature that differentiates self-generated physical behaviour and mental events from externally generated ones is their predictability. Due to the erroneous prediction error attributed to self-generated physical behaviour and mental events, such events are mistakenly regarded as defying predictions and, hence, as externally generated.

Conclusion

In this chapter, we reviewed the basic commitments of the two-factor theory as well as the prediction-error theory and discussed the relationship between the two. We acknowledged that there are some important differences between the two. They have been developed as accounts for different kinds of delusions. The prediction-error theory is often presented as a one-factor account, whereas the two-factor theory is committed to two distinct factors. Prediction-error theorists tend to blur the distinction between perceiving and believing, whereas two-factor theorists tend to draw a sharp line there. However, when we examined these differences further, we realised that they were not as significant as one might expect. Moreover, we argued that it is possible to incorporate the basic ideas of the prediction-error theory into the two-factor framework.

This conciliatory strategy might offer some interesting solutions to the existing challenges that the two theories face when considered in isolation. The aberrant prediction-error signal might explain the content of the delusion via its impact on attention allocation, in which case it could underlie the first factor in delusion formation. Alternatively, aberrant prediction-error signals might explain the adoption and/or maintenance of delusional hypotheses by making belief updating excessively revisionist, in which case it could underlie the second factor in delusion formation. If both theories of delusion formation, the two-factor theory and the prediction-error theory, continue to be largely supported by the empirical evidence and provide plausible enough explanations for the phenomenon of delusion formation, then the conciliatory strategy strikes us as appealing. A good story about delusion formation will probably need to incorporate ideas from both.

Notes

1 There are many different versions of two-factor and prediction-error theory. In this chapter, we will focus on the most influential version of the two-factor theory (by Coltheart and others) and the most influential version of the prediction-error theory (by Corlett and others).
2 Some two-factor theorists avoid the term "abnormal experience" because they think that the first factor is an unconscious event involving abnormal autonomic activity (Coltheart *et al.* 2010). For the sake of simplicity, however, we will stick to this terminology in the rest of the paper.

3 Some two-factor theorists maintain that people with VMPFC damage do not *adopt* the imposter hypothesis (e.g. McKay 2012), whilst others argue that they adopt it but they do not *maintain* it (e.g. Coltheart *et al.* 2010).

4 For more discussions on the proposal, see McKay (2012) and Davies and Egan (2013).

5 See also Murray (2011).

6 For McKay, "bias toward explanatory adequacy" is another name for the bias of neglecting the prior probability ratio.

7 However, endorsement-type two-factor theory (e.g. Davies *et al.* 2001) maintains that delusions are not the explanation, but rather the endorsement of the content of abnormal experience.

References

American Psychiatric Association. (2013). *Diagnostic and Statistical Manual of Mental Disorders* (5th ed.). Arlington: American Psychiatric Association.

Blakemore, S., Oakley, D., & Frith, C. (2003). Delusions of alien control in the normal brain. *Neuropsychologia, 41,* 1058–1067.

Butler, P. (2000). Reverse Othello syndrome subsequent to traumatic brain injury. *Psychiatry, 63*(1), 85–92.

Chadwick, P. (2001). Psychotic consciousness. *Internal Journal for Social Psychiatry, 47,* 52–62.

Coltheart, M. (2007). The 33rd Sir Frederick Barlett Lecture: Cognitive neuropsychiatry and delusional belief. *The Quarterly Journal of Experimental Psychology, 60*(8), 1041–1062.

Coltheart, M. (2010). The neuropsychology of delusions. *Annals of The New York Academy of Sciences, 1191,* 16–26.

Coltheart, M. (2013). On the distinction between monothematic and polythematic delusions. *Mind & Language, 28*(1), 103–112.

Coltheart, M., Langdon, R., & McKay, R. (2007). Schizophrenia and monothematic delusions. *Schizophrenia Bulletin, 33,* 642–647.

Coltheart, M., Langdon, R., & McKay, R. (2011). Delusional belief. *Annual Review of Psychology, 62,* 271–298.

Coltheart, M., Menzies, P., & Sutton, J. (2010). Abductive inference and delusional belief. *Cognitive Neuropsychiatry, 15*(1/2/3), 261–287.

Corlett, P., Cambridge, V., Gardner, J., Piggot, J., Turner, D., Everott, J., . . . & Fletcher, P. C. (2013). Ketamine effects on memory reconsolidation favor a learning model of delusions. *PLOS ONE, 8*(6), 1–17.

Corlett, P., Krystal, J., Taylor, J., & Fletcher, P. (2009). Why do delusions persist? *Frontiers in Human Neuroscience, 3*(12), 1–9.

Corlett, P. R., Murray, G. K., Honey, G. D., Aitken, M. R., Shanks, D. R., Robbins, T., . . . & Fletcher, P. C. (2007). Disrupted prediction-error signal in psychosis: Evidence for an associative account of delusions. *Brain, 130,* 2387–2400.

Corlett, P., Taylor, J., Wang, X.-J., Fletcher, P., & Krystal, J. (2010). Toward a neurobiology of delusions. *Progress in Neurobiology, 92,* 345–369.

Davies, M., Coltheart, M., Langdon, R., & Breen, N. (2001). Monothematic delusions: Toward a two-factor account. *Philosophy, Psychiatry, & Psychology, 8*(2/3), 133–158.

Davies, M., & Egan, A. (2013). Delusion: Cognitive approaches – Bayesian inference and compartmentalisation. In K. Fulford, M. Davies, R. Gipps, G. Graham, J. Sadler, G. Strangellini & T. Thornton (Eds.), *The Oxford Handbook of Philosophy and Psychiatry* (pp. 689–730). Oxford: Oxford University Press.

Ellis, H., & Young, A. (1990). Accounting for delusional misidentifications. *British Journal of Psychiatry, 157,* 239–248.

Ellis, H., Young, A., Quayle, A., & De Pauw, K. (1997). Reduced autonomic responses to faces in Capgras delusion. *Proceedings of the Royal Society Biological Sciences, 264*, 1085–1092.

Fletcher, P., & Frith, C. (2009). Perceiving is believing: A Bayesian approach to explaining the positive symptoms of schizophrenia. *Nature Reviews Neuroscience, 10*, 48–58.

Frith, C. (2005). The neural basis of hallucinations and delusions. *Comptes Rendus Biologies, 328*, 169–175.

Helmholtz, H. (1878/1971). The facts of perception. In R. Kahl (Ed.), *Selected Writings of Herman von Helmholtz* (R. Kahl, Trans., pp. 366–408). Middletown: Wesleyan University Press.

Hohwy, J., & Rajan, V. (2012). Delusions as forensically disturbing perceptual inferences. *Neuroethics, 5*(1), 5–11.

Huq, S., Garety, P., & Hemsley, D. (1988). Probabilistic judgments in deluded and non-deluded subjects. *Quarterly Journal of Experimental Psychology A, 40*, 801–812.

Kapur, S. (2003). Psychosis as a state of aberrant salience: A framework linking biology, phenomenology, and pharmacology in schizophrenia. *The American Journal of Psychiatry, 160*(1), 13–23.

Maher, B. (1974). Delusional thinking and perceptual disorder. *Journal of Individual Psychology, 30*(1), 98–113.

McKay, R. (2012). Delusional inference. *Mind & Language, 27*(3), 330–355.

McKay, R., Langdon, R., & Coltheart, M. (2009). "Sleights of mind": Delusions and self-deception. In T. Bayne & J. Fernández (Eds), *Delusion and Self-Deception: Affective and Motivational Influences on Belief Formation* (pp. 165–186). New York: Psychology Press.

Murray, G. (2011). The emerging biology of delusions. *Psychological Medicine, 41*(1), 7–13.

Stone, T., & Young, A. (1997). Delusions and brain injury: The philosophy and psychology of belief. *Mind & Language, 12*(3/4), 327–364.

Tranel, D., Damasio, H., & Damasio, A. (1995). Double dissociation between overt and covert face recognition. *Journal of Cognitive Neuroscience, 7*, 425–432.

Young, A. (2000). Wondrous strange: The neuropsychology of abnormal beliefs. In M. Coltheart & M. Davies (Eds.), *Pathologies of Belief* (pp. 47–73). Oxford: Blackwell.

3

REASONING AND DELUSIONS

Do people with delusions really jump to conclusions?

*Robert Dudley, Kate Cavanagh, Kate Daley
and Stephen Smith*

Delusional beliefs can cause distress or disability and commonly occur in the context of psychotic illness such as schizophrenia. Persecutory delusions are the most common type of delusion, found in around 80% of people suffering with schizophrenia (Freeman, 2007) and grandiose delusions are reported by between 20–50% of individuals with schizophrenia (Knowles, McCarthy-Jones & Rowse, 2011). Given this prevalence, such beliefs, along with auditory hallucinations, were considered the very hallmark of madness (Berrios, Luque & Villagrán, 2003, p.122).

Delusions were defined as fixed, false personal beliefs that are resistant to counter evidence (American Psychiatric Association, 1994). In effect, people with delusions were seen to have formed such beliefs as a result of faulty reasoning. This conceptualisation of delusions posed a real challenge to clinicians interested in extending psychological treatments like cognitive behavioural therapy (CBT) to working with people with psychosis. Whilst CBT had been proven helpful for people with mood and anxiety disorders, if people with psychosis and delusions were unable to reason, then there would be little value in utilising a CBT approach. CBT is based on the cognitive model of emotional disorders that emphasises that the way a person views a situation will affect their emotions and behaviours. Unhelpful, or unrealistic, appraisals and beliefs are revised and changed by the therapist and patient working together to consider new or neglected evidence that may not fit with the original belief. In short, CBT asks people to evaluate their ideas and consider whether there may be another way of seeing the situation (Turkington & Dudley, 2004; Turkington, Dudley, Warman & Beck, 2004).

This view of delusions has been revised over time, in part because it is not unusual to find delusion-like beliefs in the non-clinical population, who are not obviously suffering from faulty reasoning. For example, Freeman et al. (2005) report that 10–15% of the general population regularly experience paranoid thoughts involving suspicion and mistrust of others. Second, the idea that delusions are fixed and resistant to counter evidence has not necessarily stood up to scrutiny. Some people with clinical levels of delusional ideation report changes over time in their beliefs, and some may be open to the possibility that they are mistaken (Freeman, 2007). Related to this, cognitive behavioural therapy for psychosis (CBTp) has been shown to have a modest effect for positive symptoms like delusions (Turner, van der Gaag, Karyotaki & Cuijpers, 2014). There is still considerable room for improvement in terms of the efficacy of CBTp but the demonstration that a talking treatment can improve symptoms like delusions has helped question the fixity of delusional beliefs. In the recent revision of DSM, it has introduced a more subtle and nuanced description of delusions:

> Delusions are fixed beliefs that are not amenable to change in light of con-
> flicting evidence. [. . .] The distinction between a delusion and a strongly
> held idea is sometimes difficult to make and depends in part on the degree of
> conviction with which the belief is held despite clear or reasonable contra-
> dictory evidence regarding its veracity.
>
> *(American Psychiatric Association, 2013, p.87)*

This revision does not emphasise that the reasoning of people with delusions is fundamentally aberrant. There may not be overarching and pervasive problems in reasoning but there may be specific differences in reasoning that help form and maintain a delusional belief. With the aim of better understanding abnormal beliefs, a number of reasoning processes have been investigated, including Wason's 2-4-6 and card selection tasks (Dudley, Young, John & Over, 1998; Linney, Peters & Ayton, 1998), the 20-questions game (John & Dodgson, 1994) and syllogistic reasoning tasks (Kemp, Chua, McKenna & David, 1997). However, a wealth of studies spanning some 25 years have consistently reported that people with delusions make decisions on the basis of less evidence than people without delusions. In effect they jump to conclusions (JTC). This finding has been demonstrated on a measure of probabilistic reasoning called the beads task (Phillips & Edwards, 1966). In this task, two jars containing coloured beads in equal but opposite ratios are shown to the participant. The jars may contain 85 blue beads and 15 pink and vice versa (Figure 3.1). The person is told that one of the jars has been chosen and beads from the selected jar will be presented one at a time. The person's task is to decide when they are certain they know whether it is the mainly blue bead jar or the mainly pink bead jar that the beads are being drawn from. On this task, as a group, people with delusions see fewer beads (i.e. less draws to decision, or DTD) before making a decision than clinical and non-clinical controls (Fine, Gardner, Craigie & Gold, 2007).

There are a number of variants of the task that have manipulated the ratios of the beads in the jars, thereby making the task easier or harder. Typically, people with delusions decide more rapidly on the easy (usually at 85:15 ratio) and harder tasks (usually at 60:40) than controls. However, they take account of the task demands and increase the amount of evidence they view on the harder task, but still remain

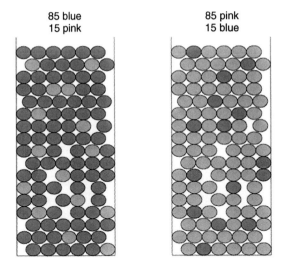

85 blue
15 pink

85 pink
15 blue

FIGURE 3.1 The beads task

hasty relative to the other groups (Dudley, John, Young & Over, 1997a). Importantly, it has been shown that this is a specific data-gathering bias and is not the result of people being impulsive and not actually reasoning (Dudley, John, Young & Over, 1997b). The number of errors is relatively small even when people decide rapidly, which would imply some comprehension of the task demands (though see Balzan, Delfabbro, Galletly & Woodward, 2012).

These tasks have used material unrelated to the content of the delusional belief. This is valuable as if people were to reason about their delusional beliefs, it could lead to tautological explanations (why can't they reason, because they are delusional, and vice versa). However, clearly delusions tend to have a limited number of themes, and in the case of grandiose and persecutory delusional beliefs, the theme is around whether a person is liked or valued, and essentially is about their worth (Freeman, 2007). Hence, one criticism of the beads task is that it lacks ecological validity (Lincoln, Salzmann, Ziegler & Westermann, 2011). People make decisions in a social environment, and the consequences of their decisions are likely to differ from the consequences of deciding between two jars of beads. Consequently, some researchers have changed the content of the beads task to be more self-referent or to reflect more emotionally salient themes. For example, a variant of the task is to imagine that a survey has been undertaken about a "person very much like you" and the participant is presented with positively or negatively valenced words from the survey. The task is to decide if the survey is mainly positive or negative. Using such methods, there has been some indication that it may increase the data-gathering bias and/or lead to more errors in decision making (Young & Bentall, 1997; Lincoln et al., 2011).

This data-gathering bias has been incorporated into a number of multifactorial models of delusion formation and maintenance (e.g. Freeman, Garety, Kuipers,

Fowler & Bebbington, 2002), in which emotional processes, anomalous experiences and cognitive biases all play a role in the pathogenesis of delusions. Having a reduced data-gathering bias is hypothesised to limit the amount of information an individual gathers to support an explanation, resulting in an early (and potentially inaccurate) decision, and contributes to the formation of a delusional belief. This belief is then maintained, in part by the "JTC" bias, preventing the individual gathering enough information for it to be disproved (Freeman, 2007).

As noted, a number of reasoning tasks have been investigated but studies of probabilistic reasoning using the beads task have flourished over the past few years, and this chapter will overview and consider studies investigating reasoning and JTC and consider a number of questions related to these findings. These include i) how prevalent is this style in people with delusions, and is it common across all phases or stages of psychosis, ii) is it affected by changes in content of the task that reflect more self-referent or salient task materials, iii) is it specific to delusions, iv) does it change over time, and/or is it amenable to intervention, and v) what leads people to JTC? The questions are addressed in the form of a narrative review in order to inform the reader of the key studies and findings.

Prevalence of reduced data gathering

The relationship between delusional ideation and the reduced data gathering is supported by a significant body of literature that includes correlational studies of symptoms such as paranoia and DTD and group studies comparing people with delusions against those without such beliefs (e.g. Fine *et al.*, 2007). As noted, people with delusions see less evidence than control participants before making a decision (Garety & Freeman, 2013). However, group means mask the fact that some people with delusions are not deciding on the basis of less evidence than other people. Hence, a second outcome variable is extreme responding (or JTC), which has been defined as making a decision on the basis of two or fewer beads (Garety *et al.*, 2005).

In terms of prevalence, it seems that the presence of a reduced data-gathering style is pretty common in people with psychosis. In the original study that launched this area of research by Huq, Garety and Hemsley (1988), 11 out of 27 (41%) of the participants with schizophrenia/delusions decided after seeing only one bead on the easier 85:15 ratio task. Similarly, Mortimer *et al.* (1996) reported that 18 out of 43 (or 42%) of people with schizophrenia decided after one bead.

Garety *et al.* (2005) introduced a now widely used definition of JTC as deciding on the basis of two or fewer beads. Using this criterion with a group of 100 people with delusional beliefs (recruited as part of a large treatment study; see Garety *et al.*, 2008) 53% of the sample showed jumping to conclusions on the 85:15 task, and 41% on the harder 60:40 version. Freeman *et al.* (2006) report data from some of the same sample (the sample size was 149) and found 76 out of 149 (51%) reported JTC on the easy task and 57 out of 148 (39%) on the harder task. Similarly, Moritz and Woodward (2005) reported that 65% of people with delusions JTC, whereas it was 21% for clinical and 6% for non-clinical controls. Seemingly, around 40–70% of people with delusions demonstrate JTC (Freeman, 2007).

A meta-analysis (Fine *et al.*, 2007) on DTD indicated a large effect size for the comparison between people with delusions and non-clinical controls on DTD. The differences were smaller between people with delusions and psychiatric controls.

Nevertheless, the consistency of this finding is a point of discussion. On close inspection of the results of DTD, it is evident that there is quite considerable variation in mean DTD between some studies. To illustrate this point, Table 3.1 reports some studies that have used what would seem to be the same 85:15 DTD methodology, yet report quite wide variation in mean DTD.

In essence, what is important to note is that, whilst relative to a control group in any one study people with delusions/psychosis may decide on the basis of less evidence, across studies, performance by the control groups could be the same as the patient group. What accounts for this variability is unclear. One possible contender is that the order in which the beads are presented may differ between studies. So, for example, on an 85:15 ratio, one trial may have an order of Pink (P) or Blue (B) beads that may encourage an earlier decision, whilst another trial may encourage a later decision. For example, PPPPPBPPBP or PPPBPPPPPP are both entirely possible bead sequences at an 85:15 ratio, and yet they could encourage different decision points. Another important consideration is whether people have a practice trial to ensure that there are no miscomprehension issues, and it may be helpful to have more than one trial of each task as it tends to reduce the variance between participants, which can be large.

Whilst JTC is well established in those with psychosis, it has also been found in populations without delusions. For example, Freeman, Pugh and Garety (2008) reported that 20% of a sample of 200 members of the general population showed a JTC bias and, importantly, the level of conviction in paranoid ideation was

TABLE 3.1 Variation in responses across studies.

Authors/Date	Participants	Mean (and SD) on 85:15	Non-clinical participants	Mean (and SD) on 85:15
Huq *et al.* (1988)	15 people with delusions	1.22 (1.57)	10 non-clinical controls	3.58 (3.51)
Garety *et al.* (1991)	14 people with delusions	2.38 (1.94)	13 non-clinical controls	5.38 (3.15)
Dudley *et al.* (1997a)	15 people with delusions	2.45 (0.70)	15 non-clinical controls	4.10 (1.40)
Colbert *et al.* (2010)	17 current delusions	8.35 (7.82)	35 non-clinical controls	7.03 (5.51)
	17 remission delusions	9.59 (7.83)		
Peters & Garety (2006)	22 people with delusions	6.4 (5.1)	36 non-clinical controls	10.3 (7.1)

associated with the bias. Using the more stringent criteria of two beads or fewer on the harder 60:40 task, only 2 out of 117 non-clinical participants JTC (Menon *et al.*, 2013). Moreover, in people high in delusion proneness (Colbert & Peters, 2002; Warman, Lysaker, Martin, Davis & Haudenschield, 2007), at high risk of developing psychosis (Broome *et al.*, 2007), and who are first-degree relatives of those with schizophrenia (Van Dael *et al.*, 2006), the JTC style is common. This suggests that this data-gathering bias could predate psychosis onset, and may therefore be a trait or vulnerability factor (Van Dael *et al.*, 2006) for the emergence of psychosis and delusional beliefs. In a large study of people in their first episode of psychosis by the criterion of requesting two or fewer beads on the 85:15 task, 36 out of 77 (47%) participants exhibited JTC (Dudley *et al.*, 2011).

So JTC and reduced data gathering appear to be a feature of people with psychosis and it appears to be present across the phases of psychosis, but it is apparent that this reduced data-gathering style alone does not explain why people hold delusional beliefs. Around half of people with delusions do not JTC. Hence, it would seem that people may develop delusions without demonstrating a reduced data-gathering style. Second, a number of people in the non-clinical population report a JTC style and, whilst associated with paranoid ideation, it does not seem that they are necessarily delusional. Given this caveat, it is important to consider our next question of whether changes in content affect the data-gathering style.

The effect of self-referent or emotionally laden materials

It is an important question as to whether performance is different when reasoning with emotionally salient material. Dudley and colleagues (Dudley *et al.*, 1997a) reported reduced data gathering (but not significantly so) with emotionally salient material for people with delusions, clinical and non-clinical controls, indicating a possible general effect of reasoning about emotionally laden materials. Warman and Martin (2006) found that negative emotionally salient material led to hastier decision making in delusion-prone individuals in a normal population, whereas neutral task material did not, implying that the bias may be more evident with emotional materials. However, in their meta-analysis, Fine *et al.* (2007) compared the results from three studies (Dudley *et al.*, 1997a; Young & Bentall, 1997, Exp. 2; and Menon, Pomarol-Clotet, McKenna & McCarthy, 2006, Exp. 1) that investigated the role of emotional saliency on variants of the beads task and found that effect sizes for the comparison between with delusions and clinical and non-clinical controls were not statistically greater for emotionally salient stimuli when compared with neutral stimuli. It was concluded that the results revealed no support for the idea that JTC is exacerbated by emotional material in people with delusions. Since this time, a number of large, well-conducted studies have used both neutral and salient tasks with clinical and non-clinical participants. It would seem that on balance there is some evidence that self-referent or salient material may decrease DTD in all groups but it seems less likely that there is a specific effect for people with delusions. It is important to note that the materials that have been used are assumed to be salient or self-referent to people. It may not be the case that a particular person has concerns about being liked by others (which is one of the commonly used tasks). Equally, one challenge of these more self-referent tasks is that, unlike the beads, the words or materials used are no longer homogenous or of equal value. Words such as "cruel", "loved", "friendly" or "lazy" may be rated as equivalent in emotional salience but may resonate with an individual. Hence the informational value of any one word may not be consistent in the way that a bead is uniform.

Specificity to delusional beliefs

It is clear that people with psychosis, often with delusions, demonstrate a JTC style. It is thought likely that this is associated with the presence of delusional beliefs, and possibly specifically with paranoia and persecutory beliefs. Of course most of the studies mentioned so far have compared people with delusions in the context of psychosis against non-psychotic controls. So, it is possible that it is not specific to delusions but may be associated with other symptoms of psychosis, like hallucinations. To address this issue of specificity, some studies have recruited people without delusions but still diagnosed with schizophrenia as a control group (Menon et al., 2006; Moritz & Woodward, 2005) and found no substantial difference between those with and those without delusions.

Lincoln and colleagues (Lincoln, Ziegler, Mehl & Rief, 2010) compared 71 patients with a diagnosis of schizophrenia with 68 participants from a non-clinical control group. The schizophrenia group was further divided into 44 people with acute delusions and 27 with a history of delusions who were in remission. They found that people with delusions took fewer draws to decision than the non-clinical control group and that participants with current delusions took fewer draws than those in remission. Corcorran and colleagues (Corcoran et al., 2008) recruited people who were currently paranoid (diagnosed with schizophrenia), people with remitted paranoia (diagnosed with schizophrenia), people with paranoia in the context of depression, people with non-psychotic depression, and a non-clinical control group. They found that people with current paranoid ideation (irrespective of diagnosis) had fewer DTD than the other non-paranoid groups, which indicates that it was the presence of paranoid ideation rather than diagnosis that was key. Garety and colleagues (Garety et al., 2005) reported a specific association between delusional conviction and DTD, which together with the other studies (e.g. Startup, Freeman & Garety, 2008) would seemingly indicate an association between persecutory beliefs/paranoia/delusions and a data-gathering bias.

Garety and colleagues (Garety, Gittins et al., 2013) recently reported another well-powered, methodologically strong study that compared persecutory and grandiose delusional beliefs. Using a sample for a large treatment study (PRP trial), they identified persecutory delusions in 192 people, grandiose delusions in 97, and 58 had both delusional beliefs. In this large sample, 51% demonstrated JTC on the easier task, and 39% on the harder task. Interestingly, people with neither persecutory nor grandiose delusions also displayed JTC (46%) on the easier task.

However, the percentage of people with grandiose delusions who JTC was much higher (80%) than the persecutory delusions group (48%) on the easy and hard tasks (46% vs 38%). This would seem to indicate an association of JTC and delusions, but more with grandiose rather than persecutory beliefs.

A number of other studies call into question a specific association with paranoia, and with delusions more broadly. For example, Mortimer *et al.* (1996) found negative symptoms significantly correlated with DTD (−0.41), whereas for delusions it was more modest (−0.17). Bentall and colleagues (Bentall *et al.*, 2009), using structural equation modelling in a large sample of people with delusional beliefs, indicated that JTC was better explained by general cognitive performance (and specifically measures of executive reasoning) than with any association with paranoid ideation. As noted above, Lincoln, Ziegler *et al.* (2010) found DTD was associated with the presence of delusion, but this association was non-significant when IQ score and negative symptoms were controlled for. Furthermore, So and colleagues (So *et al.*, 2012) found that delusional belief conviction was independent of JTC and DTD, which is at odds with the work of Garety *et al.* (2005). Finally, Wittorf *et al.* (2012) recruited people with schizophrenia, depression or anorexia nervosa and non-clinical controls. People with schizophrenia exhibited more JTC (58%) than people with depression (30%), anorexia nervosa (36%) and non-clinical controls (42%). In the people with schizophrenia, reduced data gathering was not associated with delusions, but rather it was most related to negative symptoms. So it would seem that the bias may not be specific to delusions, and may be a general association with psychosis or with other features of psychosis, such as negative symptoms.

There is a parallel story in relation to non-clinical participants which indicates that data gathering is not specific to paranoia, or delusions. For example, Warman *et al.* (2007) found no relationship between JTC and delusional ideation in the general population (see also Warman, 2008; Freeman *et al.*, 2005, 2008; Ziegler, Rief, Werner, Mehl & Lincoln, 2008). Any association may be with positive symptoms in general, or paranormal or religious beliefs (Lim, Gleeson & Jackson, 2012; see Chapter 6 in this volume; Menon *et al.*, 2013).

Further reasons to be cautious about the specific association comes from work that has considered whether people with other diagnoses also demonstrate reduced data gathering. People with other diagnoses, usually consisting of people with anxiety disorders or mood disorders, have commonly been used as psychiatric control groups. However, given that unrealistic beliefs may also be core features of both anxiety and mood disorders, some studies have specifically recruited client groups with the express intention of considering if data gathering is also different in such groups.

Performance on the beads task by people with OCD is an interesting area. Volans (1976) found that people with OCD asked for more beads before a decision than controls (once neuroticism was controlled for). So people with OCD were overly cautious and delayed their decision making. Fear and Healy (1997) reported a non-significant trend that an OCD group required more beads before a decision than controls. They also had a group of people with delusions who requested less evidence than the control group. Pelissier and O'Connor (2002) reported people with OCD requested more beads before a decision than people with generalised anxiety disorder and a non-clinical control group. This would imply people with OCD perform in the opposite manner to people with delusions, and that OCD is associated with a cautious approach to decision making (Dudley & Over, 2003). However, as Jacobsen and colleagues (Jacobsen, Freeman & Salkovskis, 2012) noted, some OCD beliefs can be held with very high conviction and appear to be almost delusion like. Therefore, they queried if the belief processes in high-conviction OCD would be the same as people with delusions or different and hence compared people with high conviction in their OCD ideation, low conviction in OCD ideation, people with delusions, and non-clinical controls. The people with delusions requested less evidence than the OCD groups (but not significantly different from the non-clinical controls) and the other groups did not differ from each other. This implies the processes in high conviction may not be trans-diagnostic. The study was limited by small sample sizes, however.

People with body dysmorphic disorder (BDD) can report delusion-like ideas (Phillips, 2004). Consequently, Reese, McNally and Wilhelm (2011) compared people with BDD, people with obsessive compulsive disorder and non-clinical controls on the beads task. The BDD group exhibited higher levels of delusional-like beliefs than the patients with OCD but there was no evidence of a JTC bias in comparison to the OCD or the healthy controls. A secondary consideration of participants with poor-insight BDD indicated that they requested significantly less information before making a decision than did patients with higher levels of insight about their BDD.

The Autism-Psychosis Model (Crespi & Badcock, 2008) proposes that people with autistic spectrum disorder (ASD) show the opposite JTC pattern to that seen in psychosis, and hence would be expected to demonstrate greater DTD on a beads task. Recent research has demonstrated that people from the general population who self-report high "Empathising" scores alongside low "Systemising" scores, which is the opposite cognitive pattern to that seen in ASD (Baron-Cohen, 2009), also report higher levels of psychosis experiences and view less evidence on the beads task (Brosnan, Ashwin, Walker & Donaghue, 2010; Brosnan, Ashwin & Gamble, 2013). In a recent study, people with ASD and non-clinical controls undertook a trial on a harder 60:40 task. The ASD group requested more beads (M = 9.95, SD = 3.33) than the controls (M = 6.83, SD = 1.67). This would seem consistent with the theory. Note, however, the low number of beads viewed by the controls on the hard task. In previous studies, this performance would be somewhere between that of people with psychosis and the control groups (see Dudley et al., 1997b, for example, where on the 60:40 task the delusion group mean was 5.2, SD = 2.4, psychiatric controls M = 8.3, SD = 2.8 and non-clinical controls M = 8.55, SD = 2.8). Whilst it is hard to compare across studies, given the potential differences in methodologies, it does raise a query as to whether the control group were unusually quick to decide.

Jänsch and Hare (2014) reported that a group of people with Asperger syndrome made decisions on the basis of less evidence on the easy 85:15 beads task, with 50% demonstrating JTC, whereas none of the control group showed such a bias. Reduced data gathering was not associated with paranoid ideation. The authors report medians rather than means, but for the easier task the ASD group requested 2.5 beads; for the controls it was 6. On the harder (60:40) version, the medians were 5 and then 10 for the controls. In short, the differences in these findings between the two studies are difficult to reconcile.

As will be discussed later, working memory and executive processes have been considered as potential explanations for why people demonstrate reduced data gathering. Another potential explanation is that people are not really reasoning at all but are merely being impulsive. To help shed light on these possible explanations, Lunt and colleagues (Lunt *et al.*, 2012) recruited people with attention deficit hyperactivity disorder (ADHD, who were thought likely to be impulsive) and people who had surgery within their prefrontal cortex (and hence would have greater difficulties with executive processes) and compared these groups to a non-clinical control group. The prefrontal group requested fewer beads before a decision on the easier task (M = 3.47, SD = 2.29) than the other two groups (ADHD M = 5.05, SD = 2.42; non-clinical controls M = 5.58, SD = 2.12), who did not differ. Of the prefrontal group, 26% met the criterion for JTC, whereas it was 9% and 4% in the other groups, respectively. So, impulsivity in the context of ADHD was not obviously a factor in reduced data gathering, but impaired executive functioning may be important.

Another group of participants who have undertaken the easy beads task are people with functional neurological disorder (Pareés *et al.*, 2012). This study reported that 40% of the sample (n = 18) displayed JTC, whereas none of the non-clinical control group did on an easy version of the task (mean DTD = 2.5, SD = 1.2 and 5.56, SD =2.0, respectively). Paranoia was not associated with DTD so it is not evident that the performance was owing to a comorbid delusional disorder.

Garety and Freeman (2013) in a recent review consider that, in general, the larger studies showed evidence of a specific association of JTC with current delusional status and that the larger non-clinical studies also provided support for a specific association of JTC with delusional thinking or delusion proneness in the general population or in at-risk groups (see Langdon, Still, Connors, Ward & Catts, 2014). However, overall, there is reason to be cautious about accepting the claim that people with delusions jump to conclusions.

Longitudinal and intervention studies

Reduced data gathering is demonstrated by the non-clinical population, in people at risk of transition to psychosis as well as first-degree relatives. People with more acute symptoms seem to have higher rates of JTC but it is still fairly common in people with remitted symptoms. This then raises the question of whether JTC is a trait or more of a state-like variable. Consequently, in a systematic review, So and colleagues (So, Garety, Peters & Kapur, 2010) considered whether there was evidence that data gathering changed over time, and whether medication affects this style. They discuss a limited number of studies, including the work of Peters and Garety (2006), who investigated JTC stability in those with delusions and clinical controls. Number of beads requested (on the 85:15 task) by those with delusions (n = 17) remained stable over time, despite a reduction in delusional symptomatology over an average of 17 weeks. It was noteworthy though that the controls reduced their DTD, perhaps owing to practice effects. This provides some evidence that JTC is stable over time, at least in a group who had been unwell for some time (on average it was five years or more).

In contrast, Woodward, Munz, LeClerc and Lecomte (2009) found a reduction in DTD in an early psychosis sample (n = 19) over a 12-week period in which a structured intervention was offered which led to a reduction in delusional beliefs. They used a 60:40 beads task. Findings were against predictions. It was concluded that these findings may be due to practice effects rather than a lack of inherent JTC stability.

In terms of the effect of medication, Menon and colleagues examined the effects of antipsychotics on the JTC bias in a group of people who had not previously been given medication (Menon, Mizrahi & Kapur, 2008). There was an increase in DTD and a decrease in symptomatology over a two-week period, following the introduction of antipsychotic medication and the proportion of JTC reduced on the hard task from 6/19 to 4/19 and from 8/19 to 5/19 on the salient task after two weeks of medication. Performance on the salient task was a considered to be a moderator of symptom improvement. Those that did not show JTC (on the salient task) at baseline had a greater reduction in symptoms. So, Peters, Swendsen, Garety and Kapur (2014) also tracked changes in symptoms following the initiation of medication in people primarily in their first episode of psychosis and noted that those who did not demonstrate the JTC style seemed to demonstrate a greater reduction in conviction and distress associated with their delusions.

Subsequently, a large study considered change in JTC over a one-year period in a cohort of people (once again those in the PRP trial; Garety et al., 2008). Unfortunately, the treatment (CBTp) was not effective so this study provided an opportunity to consider if JTC changes over a period of a year. It was found that JTC remained stable (with about 52% reporting a JTC style at baseline and 55% at follow up) over the course of a year and showed no response to medication or a psychological intervention. Andreou and colleagues (2013) considered predictors of remission in people with schizophrenia and tracked whether performance on the beads task was associated with remission. Somewhat unusually they found high rates of JTC in their non-clinical control group (11/25) that was not different to the clinical group (43/79). Data gathering did not predict remission status, whereas some factors, such as positive symptoms and performance on a measure of attention, did.

Ormrod and colleagues (2012) investigated JTC stability in a sample of people with first-episode psychosis over an eight-month time period and found the number of people who JTC on the neutral beads tasks changed over time (17/29 at baseline, 9/29 at follow up). Given time between testing, change may be less likely to be the result of practice effects. Similarly, Dudley and colleagues (2013) recruited 31 service users in their first episode of psychosis, and followed them up over a two-year time scale. Over time, the number that JTC on the easy task reduced from 19/31 (or 61%) to 8/31 (26%). Of the 19 who JTC at baseline, only 7 continued to do so at follow up. The group who demonstrated JTC at both time points appeared to have a worsening of symptoms (particularly delusions) over time, whereas those who never JTC, or changed from JTC to not, tended to show improvement. This may reflect a crystallisation or hardening of symptoms in those people who continue to JTC. This would suggest persistence of JTC may be a marker of poor response and may well warrant additional resources and help to be targeted at such people. However, this is a small study and needs replication and extension with larger samples.

Given the findings of Garety *et al.* (2008) it would seem that CBT does not appear to affect reasoning style (see also Brakoulias *et al.*, 2008, but also Sanford, Veckenstedt, Moritz, Balzan & Woodward, 2014). In a way, this is not surprising as most CBTp approaches would not necessarily assess for and target hasty data gathering. Hence, a potential bias is not specifically addressed either as part of a CBT package or perhaps prior to undertaking CBT in a pre-CBT intervention.

To address this, a number of researchers have developed interventions that address reasoning and the JTC style, the argument being that if we can tailor treatment to account for JTC, it could improve therapy efficacy. Warman, Martin and Lysaker (2013) found that even drawing people's attention to the bias could seemingly increase DTD in people with psychosis, and others have developed more extensive, though still relatively brief, interventions targeting JTC (Ross, Freeman, Dunn & Garety, 2011; Waller, Freeman, Jolley, Dunn & Garety, 2011). For example, Moritz and Woodward (2007) are developing a meta-cognitive training (MCT) programme for people with schizophrenia. This aims to raise awareness of the bias, encouraging further reasoning and challenging of beliefs. MCT is more effective at reducing JTC and positive symptoms than standard treatment (Aghotor, Pfueller, Moritz, Weisbrod & Roesch-Ely, 2010; Moritz, Veckenstedt, Randjbar, Vitzthum & Woodward, 2011) and a matched control condition (Moritz *et al.*, 2013; these findings are discussed elsewhere in detail in this volume). So, there is an indication that reduced data-gathering style can be changed.

Why do people JTC?

Whilst there have been a proliferation of studies demonstrating this data-gathering bias, there is less understanding of what accounts for JTC. Broadly speaking, there are four main theories. First, it is hypothesised that people who JTC may have problems integrating information. Second, motivational accounts posit that in some way people find managing uncertainty unpleasant and are motivated to end that state. Third, it is hypothesised that people who JTC may have cognitive deficits or impairments, particularly with working memory, that lead to early decision making. Finally, a role for heightened anxiety has been suggested as a possible exacerbating factor in decision making.

Hypersalience

It has long been proposed (Hemsley, 1993) that people with delusions and psychosis experience current stimuli with abnormally high salience (Kapur, 2003). Owing to this hypersalience, immediate experience is given more emphasis than prior experience, leading a person to place inappropriate weight on the current bead in decision-making tasks (Menon et al., 2006). These accounts seem particularly well suited to explaining why someone would revise their beliefs or change them rapidly (Langdon et al., 2014).

It has also been shown that people with delusions (and delusion-prone people) demonstrate a bias against disconfirming evidence (BADE). This is almost the opposite to the hypersalience hypothesis as people are thought to disregard new information that is inconsistent (e.g. Moritz & Woodward, 2005; Moritz et al., 2010; Woodward, Moritz, Cuttler & Whitman, 2006; see Chapter 8 in this volume).

Motivational factors

Cognitive biases such as an inability to tolerate uncertainty (Broome et al., 2007) or the need for closure (Freeman et al., 2006) have also been proposed as reasons people JTC. When an individual is confronted with an ambiguous or unclear situation, they may rush to find an explanation (to obtain closure, shortening the time in an uncertain state), making a decision on the basis of minimal evidence. Hence, jumping to conclusions is a motivated top-down strategy to reduce or end the presence of distressing uncertainty. Rather than dealing with doubt, a decision is rapidly made (Dudley & Over, 2003).

Need for closure

"Need for closure" (NFC) is defined as "individuals' desire for a firm answer to a question and an aversion toward ambiguity" (Kruglanski & Webster, 1996). NFC is high in people with delusions, and those with a predisposition to delusional ideation (Bentall & Swarbrick, 2003; Colbert & Peters, 2002; Freeman et al., 2005). Clearly the natural question to ask is whether NFC accounts for JTC (McKay, Langdon & Coltheart, 2007). Unfortunately, when tested, the relationship between NFC and reduced data gathering is not evident (McKay, Langdon & Coltheart, 2006; McKay et al., 2007). For example, Freeman et al. (2006) recruited 187 patients with psychosis, and need for closure was unrelated to jumping to conclusions.

Intolerance of uncertainty

Individuals high in intolerance of uncertainty (IOU) find uncertainty stressful and upsetting, and have difficulty functioning in uncertain situations (Freeston, Rhéaume, Letarte, Dugas & Ladouceur, 1994). A person who is high in IOU may JTC as the rapid acceptance of explanations, even if they are implausible and based on scant evidence, would end the state of uncertainty. Broome *et al.* (2007) found higher levels of intolerance of uncertainty to be associated with less data gathering in the beads task in a combined high risk of psychosis (n = 35) and non-clinical control (n = 23) group. However, a number of other studies with people with first-episode psychosis (Dudley *et al.*, 2011) or more enduring difficulties (Freeman *et al.*, 2014) found no relationship between DTD and IOU or with JTC status. Overall, there is little reason to accept a motivational account of JTC.

Cognitive deficits

Neurocognitive deficits have, for example, been proposed to lead to JTC, and we have already seen that impaired cognitive processes such as working memory (Broome *et al.*, 2007; Menon *et al.*, 2006) or lowered IQ (Garety *et al.*, 1991; Moritz *et al.*, 2010) feature within the literature on JTC. It has been suggested that an inability to retain information could lead to a rapid decision (Colbert & Peters, 2002), or that there may be difficulty understanding the task (Balzan *et al.*, 2012; Fine *et al.*, 2007).

IQ

A number of studies have measured IQ and memory performance, and controlled for this in analyses of JTC, with the majority finding the two not to be related (Colbert & Peters, 2002; Fraser, Morrison & Wells, 2006; Freeman *et al.*, 2008; Garety *et al.*, 2005; Langdon, Ward & Coltheart, 2010). Many of these studies used premorbid rather than current IQ performance, and as noted, however, a larger and more recent study found intelligence contributed to JTC in a clinical sample (Lincoln, Ziegler *et al.*, 2010), albeit only in the more difficult task (e.g. the 60:40 bead ratio).

Working memory

Working memory has long been proposed as a possible explanation for performance on the beads task (Dudley *et al.*, 1997a; Mortimer *et al.*, 1996; Menon *et al.*, 2006). In part, this is owing to the long associations between cognitive impairments in working memory and severe mental illness like schizophrenia (Horan *et al.*, 2008). More specifically, though, with the beads tasks the person has to hold in mind bead sequences, and consider the current ratio of beads against the proportions in the jars. Hence, there is potential demand on working memory. Consequently, early versions of the beads tasks added memory aides to try to reduce demands on working memory and ensure it was reasoning rather than memory differences that accounted for the JTC (Dudley *et al.*, 1997b). A number of papers have investigated memory, one finding a positive association between JTC and impaired memory in those with an at-risk mental state (Broome *et al.*, 2007). However, some using clinical samples have found little or no relationship (Lunt *et al.*, 2012; Moritz & Woodward, 2005), such as in a group of people with first-episode psychosis (n = 29) (Ormrod *et al.*, 2012). Recent studies appear to point clearly to memory and cognitive processes as being central to understanding reasoning. As noted, Bentall *et al.* (2009) found that JTC was more associated with cognitive functioning (including working memory) than it was with paranoia. Also, Garety, Joyce *et al.* (2013) recruited 126 people with schizophrenia spectrum disorders and current delusions and compared working memory performance in those with and without JTC bias. Around 40% demonstrated JTC on the easy (85:15) task and 27% on the harder (60:40) task. Whilst those who were defined by the easier task as JTC or not did not differ on premorbid IQ or other measures (although it was at trend level for a number), those that JTC on the harder task performed worse on tests of working memory (including digit span total and forwards, and letter number sequencing). Hence, there was a difference in working memory, albeit with small to medium effect sizes. This work, however, has been subject to independent replication with another sample of participants (n = 123) with persecutory beliefs (Freeman *et al.*, 2014). Whilst JTC and non-JTC participants did not differ in symptoms, those that did JTC had poorer performance on measures of working memory and IQ. Those who JTC did have higher levels of negative symptoms and lower IQ. This study also tested the contribution of IOU and found no support for the motivational account.

This evidence of impairments in working memory has support from neuroimaging studies which indicate probabilistic reasoning, which indicates that performance on the beads tasks rely on executive functions (Esslinger *et al.*, 2013; Krug *et al.*, 2014).

Further exploration of the mechanism that leads people to reduced data gathering have included studies that have tried to manipulate neurochemicals associated with symptoms of schizophrenia. Some aspects of schizophrenia have been induced in non-clinical participants following ketamine administration, hence Evans and colleagues (Evans *et al.*, 2012) expected that people given ketamine in comparison to placebo controls would adopt a JTC style. They also recruited people with schizophrenia who demonstrated the expected reduced DTD but those on ketamine did not. Similarly, Andreou and colleagues (Andreou, Moritz, Veith, Veckenstedt & Naber, in press) examined the effects of a dopaminergic agonist (l-dopa) and a dopaminergic antagonist (haloperidol) on the JTC bias in non-clinical participants. There were no significant effects of substance on draws to decision. So, to date, we have been limited in our ability to experimentally induce or alter reduced data gathering by neurochemical means.

Anxiety/arousal

Freeman *et al.*'s (2002) model emphasises a central role for anxiety as it helps create thoughts with a paranoid content and that anxiety-related processes contribute to the maintenance and distress associated with the experience. Consequently, a number of studies have investigated the relationship between anxiety and data gathering by either considering the relationship between anxiety and delusions (Dudley *et al.*, 2011; Garety *et al.*, 2005) or by experimentally manipulating arousal levels and examining their effect on the decision-making process. Of nine papers that have investigated anxiety and reasoning, three found anxiety to be related to DTD: two employed correlational designs (Bensi & Giusberti, 2007; Bensi, Giusberti, Nori & Gambetti, 2010) and one an experimental manipulation (Lincoln, Lange, Burau, Exner & Moritz, 2010). The remaining six studies found no such relationship (Dudley *et al.*, 2011; Fraser *et al.*, 2006; Freeman *et al.*, 2008; Garety *et al.*, 2005; So, Freeman & Garety, 2008; White & Mansell, 2009). So the relationship between anxiety and data gathering, at least at a correlational level, is not strong.

Evidence for the effect of experimentally manipulating anxiety and its impact on JTC is limited to a few studies that have so far produced inconsistent findings. For example, Ellett, Freeman and Garety (2008) found that increased anxiety levels (manipulated by walking in a busy urban environment) led to reduced data gathering on the beads task in a clinical population. Conversely, So *et al.* (2008) tried to experimentally increase anxiety in people with delusions and a non-clinical control. Only the controls responded to the anxiety manipulation (which was understandably a mild induction asking people to recall an everyday situation in which they had felt anxious). There was no significant effect of increased anxiety levels on the standard beads task for the non-clinical samples. This study was also interesting as it used a group of first-episode population, and the rates of JTC were very high, with 90% of clinical participants meeting the criteria on the easy task, and 76% on the harder version; for the controls, it was 66.7% and 33.3%, respectively. A recent worry induction did not lead to change in JTC in a clinical population of people with delusional beliefs (Freeman *et al.*, 2013).

Working with a non-clinical population, Lincoln and colleagues (Lincoln, Lange *et al.*, 2010) successfully increased levels of anxiety and state paranoia, and noted a higher rate of JTC (51%) in comparison to a control condition (24%) on a beads-like task (that is, conceptually similar fish in lakes task) at the 80:20 ratio. Unfortunately, there was no statistical difference in DTD (M = 3.6, SD = 2.6, and M = 4.6, SD = 3.0) between the two conditions. Moreover, as this assessment of reasoning was only undertaken after the anxiety manipulation, it is not possible to discount that there may have been baseline differences between the groups in rate of JTC.

Interestingly, in non-clinical participants an experimental induction of positive affect led to more evidence being seen before making a decision than those in a neutral condition (Lee, Barrowclough & Lobban, 2011), perhaps indicating some sort of bidirectional relationship (although low mood seems to be unrelated to DTD; Garety *et al.*, 2005).

Of course the main issue with such work is to consider the specific relationship between anxiety and data gathering. If JTC were a trait characteristic, perhaps then higher levels of trait anxiety may be expected. However, it may be that reduced data gathering is more of a state (given the changes over time in some individuals, and the experimental manipulations of anxiety affecting DTD). In which case, measures of state anxiety may be associated with decision making. However, once again we need to consider the nature of the measurement of the arousal/anxiety. Kate Daley (2011) conducted a small pilot study in which she asked people with psychosis to rate their level of anxiety about making a decision when undertaking the beads tasks. Participants rated anxiety on a Visual Analogue Scale (0–10) whilst undertaking an emotionally salient task (Dudley *et al.*, 1997b), completing the VAS at baseline and between presentations of each bead (up to a minimum of four, even if they decided after two or fewer). Participants were divided into those who did and did not JTC on the 85:15 task, and on the salient task which led to the creation of three groups: those who did not JTC on either the 85:15 or salient task (n = 27); those who JTC on the 85:15 task only (n = 8); and those who JTC on the 85:15 and salient anxiety tasks (n = 5). As can be seen, the rate of JTC was quite low (see Dudley *et al.*, 2011 for cohort details). Given the numbers involved and unequal spread, visual analysis is preferred to any form of inferential analysis. The results are shown in Figure 3.2.

Those who JTC on the salient anxiety task (n = 5) demonstrate higher levels of anxiety than other groups when asked how anxious they felt about making a decision. They increase anxiety level prior to making a decision, and notably decrease after the decision has occurred. The other groups appear to have relatively stable profiles, although most will not have yet made their decision. This suggests that those experiencing higher levels of anxiety demonstrate the JTC style and experience a considerable reduction in anxiety once a decision is made. This is a small

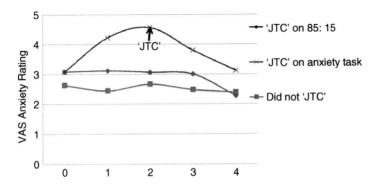

FIGURE 3.2 VAS ratings for the three groups for the first four beads drawn on the salient task

Source: Illustration used with permission from Daley, 2011

pilot needing replication, but obviously if state anxiety were linked to "JTC", this could be a target within a treatment package.

Clearly anxiety and arousal are unlikely to cause reduced data gathering. However, increased arousal may affect and reduce data gathering in those prone to JTC.

Future directions and the next 25 years

From this review, it is evident that there is an association between data gathering and psychosis and, despite the inconsistencies in the literature, it is most likely with the presence of delusional beliefs. However, reduced data gathering cannot account for the formation of the delusional belief, given the prevalence in the non–clinical population and the absence in many people with delusions. So we are still dealing with one potential contributory factor that, in combination with other biological and genetic vulnerabilities, early adversity, current life stressors and unhelpful coping, may help explain the onset and maintenance of distressing and disabling beliefs.

There seems to be no end of interest in the role of reasoning and particularly beads task performance of people with delusions. There are a number of issues emerging from the narrative review that may be helpful to consider in future research studies. First, it may be helpful if the research community could agree on standardised measures, materials and procedures. Obviously, standardised administration perhaps involving practice trials or multiple measures of data gathering would help reduce any problems with comprehension or experimenter effects. Similarly, it would help to report the specific order of materials presented (i.e. BPBBBPPP etc.). This would allow easier comparison across studies.

Second, consideration perhaps needs to be given to the extension of this research to other non-psychotic participants. The differences or not with people with ASD, with BDD and other conditions begs the question of whether the data-gathering style is driven by other processes, be it neurocognitive factors like memory, or processes that reflect how people hold their beliefs (i.e. with high levels of conviction or with insight). Without such consideration, it may well be that we see differences in rates of JTC in other client groups, but are not more knowledgeable as to why this would be.

Third, given emerging evidence for the role of working memory and anxiety processes, further work perhaps considering whether clear, specific manipulations of working memory capacity or anxiety levels can further test our understanding of factors that lead people to JTC would be helpful. Presumably some concurrent working memory demand would be expected to reduce capacity and perhaps hasten decision making.

From this overview of the research, it is evident that each question could and possibly should be subject to formal systematic review and/or meta-analysis for a more robust consideration of each question. This chapter intended to overview the research and guide the reader to the key questions and literature, rather than answer any one question in the depth required in a more formal review. However, it would seem timely to update the review of Fine *et al.* (2007) and consider some of these questions in more detail.

Clinical implications

They are very preliminary data but if reduced data gathering is associated with response to medication (So *et al.*, 2010) and delusion persistence (Menon *et al.*, 2008; Dudley *et al.*, 2013), this does then raise the question of whether we can use this to help identify people who are not benefitting sufficiently from existing treatments. It potentially raises the possibility of some form of personalised medicine for psychosis, where the persistence over time of an observable behaviour (data-gathering style) may be an indicator that additional, targeted treatments are necessary. This is potentially exciting as our current treatments for people with psychosis, whilst of some help to some people some of the time, are not highly specific or tailored to the individual's presentation.

Acknowledgements

RD has worked with the following people who have particularly helped shape the ideas in this chapter: Aoibhinn Tormey, Stephen Smith, Kate Daley, John Ormrod, Andy Young, David Over and Carolyn John. Of course the responsibility for the content rests with RD. Work on reasoning and delusions has been supported by an award from the Lena Teague Bequest fund.

References

Aghotor, J., Pfueller, U., Moritz, S., Weisbrod, M., & Roesch-Ely, D. (2010). Metacognitive training for patients with schizophrenia (MCT): feasibility and preliminary evidence for its efficacy. *Journal of Behavior Therapy and Experimental Psychiatry, 41*(3), 207–211.

American Psychiatric Association. (1994). *Diagnostic and Statistical Manual of Mental Disorders DSM-IV*. Washington, DC: American Psychiatric Association.

American Psychiatric Association. (2013). *Diagnostic and Statistical Manual of Mental Disorders* (5th ed.). Washington, DC: American Psychiatric Association.

Andreou, C., Moritz, S., Veith, K., Veckenstedt, R., & Naber, D. (in press). Dopaminergic modulation of probabilistic reasoning and overconfidence in errors: A double-blind study. *Schizophrenia Bulletin*.

Andreou, C., Roesch-Ely, D., Veckenstedt, R., Bohn, F., Aghotor, J., Köther, U., . . . & Moritz, S. (2013). Predictors of early stable symptomatic remission after an exacerbation of schizophrenia: The significance of symptoms, neuropsychological performance and cognitive biases. *Psychiatry Research, 210*(3), 729–734.

Balzan, R. P., Delfabbro, P. H., Galletly, C. A., & Woodward, T. S. (2012). Overadjustment or miscomprehension? A re-examination of the jumping to conclusions bias. *Australian and New Zealand Journal of Psychiatry, 46*(6), 532–540.

Baron-Cohen, S. (2009). Autism: The empathizing-systemizing (E-S) theory. *Annals of the New York Academy of Sciences, 1156*(1), 68–80.

Bensi, L., & Giusberti, F. (2007). Trait anxiety and reasoning under uncertainty. *Personality and Individual Differences, 43*(4), 827–838.

Bensi, L., Giusberti, F., Nori, R., & Gambetti, E. (2010). Individual differences and reasoning: A study on personality traits. *British Journal of Psychology, 101*(3), 545–562.

Bentall, R. P., Rowse, G., Shryane, N., Kinderman, P., Howard, R., Blackwood, N., . . . & Corcoran, R. (2009). The cognitive and affective structure of paranoid delusions: A transdiagnostic investigation of patients with schizophrenia spectrum disorders and depression. *Archives of General Psychiatry, 66*(3), 236–247.

Bentall, R. P., & Swarbrick, R. (2003). The best laid schemas of paranoid patients: Autonomy, sociotropy and need for closure. *Psychology and Psychotherapy: Theory, Research and Practice, 76*(2), 163–171.

Berrios, G. E., Luque, R., & Villagrán, J. M. (2003). Schizophrenia: A conceptual history. *International Journal of Psychology and Psychological Therapy, 3*(2), 111–140.

Brakoulias, V., Langdon, R., Sloss, G., Coltheart, M., Meares, R., & Harris, A. (2008). Delusions and reasoning: A study involving cognitive behavioural therapy. *Cognitive Neuropsychiatry, 13*(2), 148–165.

Broome, M. R., Johns, L. C., Valli, I., Woolley, J. B., Tabraham, P., Brett, C., . . . & McGuire, P. K. (2007). Delusion formation and reasoning biases in those at clinical high risk for psychosis. *The British Journal of Psychiatry, 191*(51), s38–s42.

Brosnan, M., Ashwin, C., & Gamble, T. (2013). Greater empathizing and reduced systemizing in people who show a jumping to conclusions bias in the general population: Implications for psychosis. *Psychosis, 5*(1), 71–81.

Brosnan, M., Ashwin, C., Walker, I., & Donaghue, J. (2010). Can an "extreme female brain" be characterised in terms of psychosis? *Personality and Individual Differences, 49*(7), 738–742.

Colbert, S. M., & Peters, E. R. (2002). Need for closure and jumping-to-conclusions in delusion-prone individuals. *The Journal of Nervous and Mental Disease, 190*(1), 27–31.

Colbert, S. M., Peters, E., & Garety, P. (2010). Jumping to conclusions and perceptions in early psychosis: Relationship with delusional beliefs. *Cognitive Neuropsychiatry, 15*(4), 422–440.

Corcoran, R., Rowse, G., Moore, R., Blackwood, N., Kinderman, P., Howard, R., . . . & Bentall, R. P. (2008). A transdiagnostic investigation of "theory of mind" and "jumping to conclusions" in patients with persecutory delusions. *Psychological Medicine, 38*(11), 1577.

Crespi, B., & Badcock, C. (2008). Psychosis and autism as diametrical disorders of the social brain. *Behavioral and Brain Sciences, 31*(03), 241–261.

Dudley, R., Daley, K., Nicholson, M., Shaftoe, D., Spencer, H., Cavanagh, K., & Freeston, M. (2013). "Jumping to conclusions" in first-episode psychosis: A longitudinal study. *British Journal of Clinical Psychology, 52*(4), 380–393.

Dudley, R. E. J., John, C. H., Young, A., & Over, D. E. (1997a). The effect of self-referent material on the reasoning of people with delusions. *British Journal of Clinical Psychology, 36*, 575–584.

Dudley, R. E. J., John, C. H., Young, A., & Over, D. E. (1997b). Normal and abnormal reasoning in people with delusions. *British Journal of Clinical Psychology, 36*, 243–258.

Dudley, R. E. J., & Over, D. E. (2003). People with delusions jump to conclusions. *Clinical Psychology and Psychotherapy, 10*, 263–274.

Dudley, R., Shaftoe, D., Cavanagh, K., Spencer, H., Ormrod, J., Turkington, D., & Freeston, M. (2011). "Jumping to conclusions" in first-episode psychosis. *Early Intervention in Psychiatry, 5*(1), 50–56.

Dudley, R. E. J., Young, A., John, C. H., & Over, D. E. (1998). Conditional reasoning in people with delusions: Performance on the Wason selection task. *Cognitive Neuropsychiatry, 3*, 241–258.

Ellett, L., Freeman, D., & Garety, P. A. (2008). The psychological effect of an urban environment on individuals with persecutory delusions: The Camberwell walk study. *Schizophrenia Research, 99*, 77–84.

Esslinger, C., Braun, U., Schirmbeck, F., Santos, A., Meyer-Lindenberg, A., Zink, M., & Kirsch, P. (2013). Activation of midbrain and ventral striatal regions implicates salience processing during a modified beads task. *PloS One, 8*(3), e58536.

Evans, S., Almahdi, B., Sultan, P., Sohanpal, I., Brandner, B., Collier, T., . . . & Averbeck, B. B. (2012). Performance on a probabilistic inference task in healthy subjects receiving ketamine compared with patients with schizophrenia. *Journal of Psychopharmacology, 26*(9), 1211–1217.

Fear, C. F., & Healy, D. (1997). Probabilistic reasoning in obsessive-compulsive and delusional disorders. *Psychological Medicine, 27*, 199–208.

Fine, C., Gardner, M., Craigie, J., & Gold, I. (2007). Hopping, skipping or jumping to conclusions? Clarifying the role of the JTC bias in delusions. *Cognitive Neuropsychiatry, 12*, (1) 46–77.

Fraser, J., Morrison, A., & Wells, A. (2006). Cognitive processes, reasoning biases and persecutory delusions: A comparative study. *Behavioural and Cognitive Psychotherapy, 34*(04), 421–435.

Freeman, D. (2007). Suspicious minds: the psychology of persecutory delusions. *Clinical Psychology Review, 27*, 425–457.

Freeman, D., Dunn, G., Garety, P. A., Bebbington, P., Slater, M., Kuipers, E., . . . & Ray, K. (2005). The psychology of persecutory ideation I: A questionnaire survey. *The Journal of Nervous and Mental Disease, 193*(5), 302–308.

Freeman, D., Garety, P., Kuipers, E., Colbert, S., Jolley, S., Fowler, D., . . . & Bebbington, P. (2006). Delusions and decision-making style: Use of the need for closure scale. *Behaviour Research and Therapy, 44*(8), 1147–1158.

Freeman, D., Garety, P. A., Kuipers, E., Fowler, D., & Bebbington, P. E. (2002). A cognitive model of persecutory delusions. *British Journal of Clinical Psychology, 41*, 331–347.

Freeman, D., Pugh, K., & Garety, P. (2008). Jumping to conclusions and paranoid ideation in the general population. *Schizophrenia Research, 102*(1), 254–260.

Freeman, D., Startup, H., Dunn, G., Černis, E., Wingham, G., Pugh, K., . . . & Kingdon, D. (2013). The interaction of affective with psychotic processes: A test of the effects of worrying on working memory, jumping to conclusions, and anomalies of experience in patients with persecutory delusions. *Journal of Psychiatric Research, 47*(12), 1837–1842.

Freeman, D., Startup, H., Dunn, G., Černis, E., Wingham, G., Pugh, K., . . . & Kingdon, D. (2014). Understanding jumping to conclusions in patients with persecutory delusions: Working memory and intolerance of uncertainty. *Psychological Medicine, First View* Article, 1–8.

Freeston, M. H., Rhéaume, J., Letarte, H., Dugas, M. J., & Ladouceur, R. (1994). Why do people worry? *Personality and Individual Differences, 17*(6), 791–802.

Garety, P. A., Fowler, D. G., Freeman, D., Bebbington, P., Dunn, G., & Kuipers, E. (2008). Cognitive-behavioural therapy and family intervention for relapse prevention and symptom reduction in psychosis: Randomised controlled trial. *The British Journal of Psychiatry, 192*(6), 412–423.

Garety, P. A., & Freeman, D. (2013). The past and future of delusions research: From the inexplicable to the treatable. *The British Journal of Psychiatry, 203*(5), 327–333.

Garety, P. A., Freeman, D., Jolley, S., Dunn, G., Bebbington, P. E., Fowler, D. G., . . . & Dudley, R. (2005). Reasoning, emotions, and delusional conviction in psychosis. *Journal of Abnormal Psychology, 114*(3), 373.

Garety, P. A., Gittins, M., Jolley, S., Bebbington, P., Dunn, G., Kuipers, E., . . . & Freeman, D. (2013). Differences in cognitive and emotional processes between persecutory and grandiose delusions. *Schizophrenia Bulletin, 39*(3), 629–639.

Garety, P. A., Hemsley, D. R., & Wessely, S. (1991). Reasoning in deluded schizophrenic and paranoid patients: Biases in performance on a probabilistic inference task. *Journal of Nervous and Mental Disorder, 179*, 194–201.

Garety, P., Joyce, E., Jolley, S., Emsley, R., Waller, H., Kuipers, E., . . . & Freeman, D. (2013). Neuropsychological functioning and jumping to conclusions in delusions. *Schizophrenia Research, 150*(2), 570–574.

Hemsley, D. R. (1993). A simple (or simplistic?) cognitive model for schizophrenia. *Behaviour Research and Therapy, 31*(7), 633–645.

Horan, W. P., Braff, D. L., Nuechterlein, K. H., Sugar, C. A., Cadenhead, K. S., Calkins, M. E., . . . & Green, M. F. (2008). Verbal working memory impairments in individuals with schizophrenia and their first-degree relatives: Findings from the Consortium on the Genetics of Schizophrenia. *Schizophrenia Research, 103*(1), 218–228.

Huq, S., Garety, P., & Hemsley, D. (1988). Probabilistic judgments in deluded and non-deluded subjects. *Quarterly Journal of Experimental Psychology A, 40*, 801–812.

Jacobsen, P., Freeman, D., & Salkovskis, P. (2012). Reasoning bias and belief conviction in obsessive-compulsive disorder and delusions: Jumping to conclusions across disorders? *British Journal of Clinical Psychology, 51*(1), 84–99.

Jänsch, C., & Hare, D. J. (2014). An investigation of the "jumping to conclusions" data-gathering bias and paranoid thoughts in Asperger Syndrome. *Journal of Autism and Developmental Disorders, 44*(1), 111–119.

John, C. H., & Dodgson, G. (1994). Inductive reasoning in delusional thinking. *Journal of Mental Health, 3*, 31–49.

Kapur, S. (2003). Psychosis as a state of aberrant salience: A framework linking biology, phenomenology, and pharmacology in schizophrenia. *American Journal of Psychiatry, 160*(1), 13–23.

Kemp, R., Chua, S., McKenna, P., & David, A. (1997). Reasoning and delusions. *British Journal of Psychiatry, 170*, 398–405.

Knowles, R., McCarthy-Jones, S., & Rowse, G. (2011). Grandiose delusions: A review and theoretical integration of cognitive and affective perspectives. *Clinical Psychology Review, 31*, 684–696.

Krug, A., Cabanis, M., Pyka, M., Pauly, K., Kellermann, T., Walter, H., . . . & Kircher, T. (2014). Attenuated prefrontal activation during decision-making under uncertainty in schizophrenia: A multi-center fMRI study. *Schizophrenia Research, 152*(1), 176–183.

Kruglanski, A. W., & Webster, D. M. (1996). Motivated closing of the mind: "Seizing" and "freezing". *Psychological Review, 103*(2), 263.

Langdon, R., Still, M., Connors, M. H., Ward, P. B., & Catts, S. V. (2014). Jumping to delusions in early psychosis. *Cognitive Neuropsychiatry, 19*(3), 241–256.

Langdon, R., Ward, P. B., & Coltheart, M. (2010). Reasoning anomalies associated with delusions in schizophrenia. *Schizophrenia Bulletin, 36*(2), 321–330.

Lee, G., Barrowclough, C., & Lobban, F. (2011). The influence of positive affect on jumping to conclusions in delusional thinking. *Personality and Individual Differences, 50*(5), 717–722.

Lim, M. H., Gleeson, J. F., & Jackson, H. J. (2012). The jumping-to-conclusions bias in new religious movements. *The Journal of Nervous and Mental Disease, 200*(10), 868–875.

Lincoln, T. M., Lange, J., Burau, J., Exner, C., & Moritz, S. (2010). The effect of state anxiety on paranoid ideation and jumping to conclusions. An experimental investigation. *Schizophrenia Bulletin, 36*(6), 1140–1148.

Lincoln, T. M., Salzmann, S., Ziegler, M., & Westermann, S. (2011). When does jumping-to-conclusions reach its peak? The interaction of vulnerability and situation-characteristics in social reasoning. *Journal of Behavior Therapy and Experimental Psychiatry, 42*(2), 185–191.

Lincoln, T. M., Ziegler, M., Mehl, S., & Rief, W. (2010). The jumping to conclusions bias in delusions: Specificity and changeability. *Journal of Abnormal Psychology, 119*(1), 40.

Linney, Y. M., Peters, E. R., & Ayton, P. (1998). Reasoning biases in delusion-prone individuals. *British Journal of Clinical Psychology, 37*, 285–302.

Lunt, L., Bramham, J., Morris, R. G., Bullock, P. R., Selway, R. P., Xenitidis, K., & David, A. S. (2012). Prefrontal cortex dysfunction and "jumping to conclusions": Bias or deficit? *Journal of Neuropsychology, 6*(1), 65–78.

McKay, R., Langdon, R., & Coltheart, M. (2006). Need for closure, jumping to conclusions, and decisiveness in delusion-prone individuals. *The Journal of Nervous and Mental Disease, 194*(6), 422–426.

McKay, R., Langdon, R., & Coltheart, M. (2007). Models of misbelief: Integrating motivational and deficit theories of delusions. *Consciousness and Cognition, 16*(4), 932–941.

Menon, M., Mizrahi, R., & Kapur, S. (2008). "Jumping to conclusions" and delusions in psychosis: Relationship and response to treatment. *Schizophrenia Research, 98*(1), 225–231.

Menon, M., Pomarol-Clotet, E., McKenna, P. J., & McCarthy, R. A. (2006). Probabilistic reasoning in schizophrenia: A comparison of the performance of deluded and nondeluded schizophrenic patients and exploration of possible cognitive underpinnings. *Cognitive Neuropsychiatry, 11*(6), 521–536.

Menon, M., Quilty, L. C., Zawadzki, J. A., Woodward, T. S., Sokolowski, H. M., Boon, H. S., & Wong, A. H. C. (2013). The role of cognitive biases and personality variables in subclinical delusional ideation. *Cognitive Neuropsychiatry, 18*(3), 208–218.

Moritz, S., Veckenstedt, R., Bohn, F., Hottenrott, B., Scheu, F., Randjbar, S., . . . & Roesch-Ely, D. (2013). Complementary group metacognitive training (MCT) reduces delusional ideation in schizophrenia. *Schizophrenia Research, 151*(1), 61–69.

Moritz, S., Veckenstedt, R., Hottenrott, B., Woodward, T. S., Randjbar, S., & Lincoln, T. M. (2010). Different sides of the same coin? Intercorrelations of cognitive biases in schizophrenia. *Cognitive Neuropsychiatry, 15*(4), 406–421.

Moritz, S., Veckenstedt, R., Randjbar, S., Vitzthum, F., & Woodward, T. S. (2011). Antipsychotic treatment beyond antipsychotics: Metacognitive intervention for schizophrenia patients improves delusional symptoms. *Psychological Medicine, 41*(9), 1823–1832.

Moritz, S., & Woodward, T. S. (2005). Jumping to conclusions in delusional and non delusional schizophrenic patients. *British Journal of Clinical Psychology, 44*, 193–207.

Moritz, S., & Woodward, T. S. (2007). Metacognitive training in schizophrenia: From basic research to knowledge translation and intervention. *Current Opinion in Psychiatry, 20*(6), 619–625.

Mortimer, A. M., Bentham, P., McKay, A. P., Quemada, I., Clare, L., Eastwood, N., & McKenna, P. J. (1996). Delusions in schizophrenia: A phenomenological and psychological exploration. *Cognitive Neuropsychiatry, 1*, 289–303.

Ormrod, J., Shaftoe, D., Cavanagh, K., Freeston, M., Turkington, D., Price, J., & Dudley, R. (2012). A pilot study exploring the contribution of working memory to "jumping to conclusions" in people with first episode psychosis. *Cognitive Neuropsychiatry, 17*(2), 97–114.

Pareés, I., Kassavetis, P., Saifee, T. A., Sadnicka, A., Bhatia, K. P., Fotopoulou, A., & Edwards, M. J. (2012). "Jumping to conclusions" bias in functional movement disorders. *Journal of Neurology, Neurosurgery & Psychiatry, 83*(4), 460–463.

Phillips, L. D., & Edwards, W. (1966). Conservatism in a simple probabilistic inference task. *Journal of Experimental Psychology, 72*, 346–354.

Pelissier, M. C., & O'Connor, K. P. (2002). Deductive and inductive reasoning in obsessive compulsive disorder. *British Journal of Clinical Psychology, 41*(Pt 1), 15–27.

Peters, E., & Garety, P. (2006). Cognitive functioning in delusions: A longitudinal analysis. *Behaviour Research and Therapy, 44*(4), 481–514.

Phillips, K. A. (2004). Psychosis in body dysmorphic disorder. *Journal of Psychiatric Research, 38*(1), 63–72.

Reese, H. E., McNally, R. J., & Wilhelm, S. (2011). Probabilistic reasoning in patients with body dysmorphic disorder. *Journal of Behavior Therapy and Experimental Psychiatry, 42*(3), 270–276.

Ross, K., Freeman, D., Dunn, G., & Garety, P. (2011). A randomized experimental investigation of reasoning training for people with delusions. *Schizophrenia Bulletin, 37*(2), 324–333.

Sanford, N., Veckenstedt, R., Moritz, S., Balzan, R. P., & Woodward, T. S. (2014). Impaired integration of disambiguating evidence in delusional schizophrenia patients. *Psychological Medicine, FirstView* Article, 1–10.

So, S. H., Freeman, D., Dunn, G., Kapur, S., Kuipers, E., Bebbington, P., . . . & Garety, P. A. (2012). Jumping to conclusions, a lack of belief flexibility and delusional conviction in psychosis: A longitudinal investigation of the structure, frequency, and relatedness of reasoning biases. *Journal of Abnormal Psychology, 121*(1), 129–139.

So, S. H. W., Freeman, D., & Garety, P. (2008). Impact of state anxiety on the jumping to conclusions delusion bias. *Australian and New Zealand Journal of Psychiatry, 42*(10), 879–886.

So, S. H. W., Garety, P. A., Peters, E. R., & Kapur, S. (2010). Do antipsychotics improve reasoning biases? A review. *Psychosomatic Medicine, 72*(7), 681–693.

So, S. H. W., Peters, E. R., Swendsen, J., Garety, P. A., & Kapur, S. (2014). Changes in delusions in the early phase of antipsychotic treatment – an experience sampling study. *Psychiatry Research, 215*(3), 568–573.

Startup, H., Freeman, D., & Garety, P. A. (2008). Jumping to conclusions and persecutory delusions. *European Psychiatry, 23*(6), 457–459.

Turkington, D., & Dudley, R. (2004). Cognitive behavioral therapy in the treatment of schizophrenia. *Expert Review of Neurotherapeutics, 4*(5), 861–868.

Turkington, D., Dudley, R., Warman, D. M., & Beck, A. T. (2004). Cognitive-behavioral therapy for schizophrenia: A review. *Journal of Psychiatric Practice, 10*(1), 5–16.

Turner, D. T., van der Gaag, M., Karyotaki, E., & Cuijpers, P. (2014). Psychological interventions for psychosis: A meta-analysis of comparative outcome studies. *American Journal of Psychiatry, 171*(5), 523–538.

Van Dael, F., Versmissen, D., Janssen, I., Myin-Germeys, I., van Os, J., & Krabbendam, L. (2006). Data gathering: Biased in psychosis? *Schizophrenia Bulletin, 32*(2), 341–351.

Volans, P. J. (1976). Styles of decision making and probability appraisal in selected obsessional and phobic patients. *British Journal of Social and Clinical Psychology, 15*, 305–317.

Waller, H., Freeman, D., Jolley, S., Dunn, G., & Garety, P. (2011). Targeting reasoning biases in delusions: A pilot study of the Maudsley Review Training Programme for individuals with persistent, high conviction delusions. *Journal of Behavior Therapy and Experimental Psychiatry, 42*(3), 414–421.

Warman, D. M. (2008). Reasoning and delusion proneness: Confidence in decisions. *The Journal of Nervous and Mental Disease, 196*(1), 9–15.

Warman, D. M., Lysaker, P. H., Martin, J. M., Davis, L., & Haudenschield, S. L. (2007). Jumping to conclusions and the continuum of delusional beliefs. *Behaviour Research and Therapy, 45*(6), 1255–1269.

Warman, D. M., & Martin, J. M. (2006). Jumping to conclusions and delusion proneness: The impact of emotionally salient stimuli. *The Journal of Nervous and Mental Disease, 194*(10), 760–765.

Warman, D. M., Martin, J. M., & Lysaker, P. (2013). Jumping to conclusions and delusions: The impact of discussion of the bias on the bias. *Schizophrenia Research, 150*(2), 575–579.

White, L. O., & Mansell, W. (2009). Failing to ponder? Delusion-prone individuals rush to conclusions. *Clinical Psychology & Psychotherapy, 16*(2), 111–124.

Wittorf, A., Giel, K. E., Hautzinger, M., Rapp, A., Schönenberg, M., Wolkenstein, L., . . . & Klingberg, S. (2012). Specificity of jumping to conclusions and attributional biases: A comparison between patients with schizophrenia, depression, and anorexia nervosa. *Cognitive Neuropsychiatry, 17*(3), 262–286.

Woodward, T. S., Moritz, S., Cuttler, C., & Whitman, J. C. (2006). The contribution of a cognitive bias against disconfirmatory evidence (BADE) to delusions in schizophrenia. *Journal of Clinical and Experimental Neuropsychology, 28*(4), 605–617.

Woodward, T. S., Munz, M., LeClerc, C., & Lecomte, T. (2009). Change in delusions is associated with change in "jumping to conclusions". *Psychiatry Research, 170*(2), 124–127.

Young, H. F., & Bentall, R. P. (1997). Probabilistic reasoning in deluded, depressed and normal subjects: Effects of task difficulty and meaningful versus non-meaningful material. *Psychological Medicine, 27*, 455–465.

Ziegler, M., Rief, W., Werner, S. M., Mehl, S., & Lincoln, T. M. (2008). Hasty decision-making in a variety of tasks: Does it contribute to the development of delusions? *Psychology and Psychotherapy: Theory, Research and Practice, 81*(3), 237–245.

4

AFFECT, DUAL PROCESSES AND SOME PERTINENT QUESTIONS ABOUT DELUSIONAL REASONING

Stephanie Rhodes and Claire Jones

Psychotic delusions are present in a number of psychological disorders but are most common in patients with schizophrenia (Mujica-Paraodi, Greenberg, Bilder & Malaspina, 2001), with schizophrenia affecting around 1% of the population (Johns & van Os, 2001) and delusions occurring in around three-quarters of these cases (Sartorius *et al.*, 1986).

The concept of delusions has a long history (Berrios, 1991). However, the attempts most recently to define delusions have mainly concentrated on the ideas first introduced by Karl Jaspers (1913). Jaspers defined three main areas concerned with psychiatric patients' beliefs: these included the conviction with which the belief is held, the tendency for the belief/s to be unreceptive to evidence or counterarguments and often the tendency to have bizarre content. However, Jaspers also made the distinction that, for a belief to be delusional rather than a delusion-like idea, it must also be un-understandable. As some have noted (Bentall, Corcoran, Howard, Blackwood & Kinderman, 2001), it is difficult to operationalise the criteria of un-understandability and thus definitions of delusions have mainly concentrated on the first three criteria highlighted by Jaspers (1913). Until most recently, delusions have been defined as:

> A false belief based on incorrect inference about external reality that is firmly sustained despite what almost everyone else believes and despite what constitutes incontrovertible and obvious proof or evidence to the contrary. The belief is not one ordinarily accepted by other members of the person's culture or subculture (e.g. it is not an article of religious faith).
>
> *(DSM-IV, American Psychiatric Association, 2000, p. 765)*

However, this definition has received criticism. For example, non-bizarre delusions could essentially occur in real-life situations, such as believing you are being followed, poisoned or deceived by someone (Bell, Halligan & Ellis, 2003). In other words, the belief does not necessarily have to be false and it is left to clinicians to make a judgement about whether this is, indeed, a false belief.

This has been so-called the 'Martha Mitchell Effect', whereby psychiatrists dismissed the claims of corruption in the Nixon White House as mental illness, even though the claims were later proved to be correct by the Watergate investigation. As Maher (1988) suggests, although patient reports may appear improbable, they can sometimes be erroneously assumed to be delusional, as was the case with Martha Mitchell. This has led researchers to question the 'falsity' criterion (Spitzer, 1990) and it is left unclear what level of evidence would be required for a belief to be 'incontrovertibly false' (Bell et al., 2003).

Furthermore, delusions need not be about 'external reality'. Indeed, delusions of control or passivity delusions usually refer to a person's own mental state, such as experiencing one's thoughts and actions as not being their own. Some researchers have also questioned whether the delusional belief is firmly sustained. A study conducted by Myin-Germeys, Nicolson and Delespaul (2001) found that patients' conviction of the truthfulness of a belief can vary over short periods of time, even over the course of a day; while Garety and colleagues (2005) found that approximately half of patients with delusions will accept the possibility that they may be mistaken about their beliefs. This suggests that delusional beliefs are not always firmly sustained. Despite this evidence, when looking at the long-term, the delusions of psychotic patients can persist for many years (Harrow, MacDonald, Sands & Silverstein, 1995). In light of this, therapeutic interventions are slowly beginning to emerge that specifically target delusional beliefs, with the intent to change belief systems (Kumar et al., 2010; Moritz & Woodward, 2007; Ross, Freeman, Dunn & Garety, 2009).

Given that the delusional belief is not one ordinarily accepted by other members of a person's culture or subculture, the DSM definition assumes that the criterion of abnormality and/or bizarreness of a belief should be obvious (Bell et al., 2003). This implies that the first consideration is that of the clinician – and whether the clinician's initial evaluation regards the patient's belief as plausible. However, the clinician may only have their own beliefs to compare this to and the beliefs of his/her own peer group. In clinical practice, how widely accepted the belief is is typically not based on empirical data (Bell, Halligan & Ellis, 2006). Furthermore, research demonstrates that inter-rater reliability between psychiatrists for bizarre delusions has been less than satisfactory for clinical practice (Mojtabai & Nicholson, 1995).

Second, the clinician must consider whether the belief is typically held by that person's culture or subculture. This information may not be readily available, thus many clinicians may find this difficult to know or even find out. As demonstrated in a poll measuring paranormal beliefs in the UK (Ipsos MORI, 1998), 45% of respondents believed in life after death, while 64% believed in the power of premonition and ESP – to name just a few unusual beliefs. Polls such as these can tell us about cultural differences in unusual beliefs and, consequently, such beliefs may be regarded as unusual but not necessarily delusional in western countries.

With the publication of the fifth Diagnostic and Statistical Manual of Mental Disorders (DSM V, 2013), the definition of delusions has recently undergone some revisions. The new DSM has tried to address some of the above issues associated with defining delusions. According to DSM V, (American Psychiatric Association, 2013):

> Delusions are fixed beliefs that are not amenable to change in light of conflicting evidence. Their content may include a variety of themes (e.g. persecutory, referential, somatic, religious, grandiose). [. . .] The distinction between a delusion and a strongly held idea is sometimes difficult to make and depends in part on the degree of conviction with which the belief is held despite clear or reasonable contradictory evidence regarding its veracity.
>
> *(DSM V; American Psychiatric Association, 2013, p. 87)*

Although the changes do not appear overly significant at first glance, they do have implications for the current understanding of delusions. For example, what is most noticeable is the change of a *false* belief now being a *fixed* belief. In other words, beliefs no longer need to be false to be classed as a delusion in DSM V. In addition, delusions no longer need to be based on 'incorrect inference' about 'external reality' but can be about one's self or one's life experiences, for example. It must also be considered that proof is not always available that the belief is false and, therefore, 'despite what constitutes incontrovertible and obvious proof or evidence to the contrary' has now been changed to 'despite clear or reasonable contradictory evidence regarding its veracity' in the new definition, reflecting more flexibility regarding the truthfulness of a belief than was afforded by the old definition. These appear to be positive changes; however, only time, clinical application and research will tell.

Delusions: dichotomous or continuous?

Despite psychosis generally being defined dichotomously for clinical purposes (van Os, Hanssen, Bijl & Ravelli, 2000), a growing body of evidence suggests that psychosis exists on a continuum (Claridge, 1988; van Os, Linscott, Myin-Germeys, Delespaul & Krabbendam, 2009) and that those in the general population experience delusional ideation more often than previously thought. By this reasoning, there are people in the general population whose experiences, cognitions and behaviours are comparable to patients with schizophrenia but milder and would not generally warrant a clinical diagnosis of psychosis. Some authors have noted that general population samples who engage in delusional ideation may be distinguished from clinical populations on their levels of distress and preoccupation with a belief (Peters, Joseph & Garety, 1999).

The idea of dimensionality between normality and psychosis is by no means a new one (Bleuler, 1911; Rado, 1953; Meehl, 1962). Personality and individual differences were thought to be implicated in psychosis proneness some decades ago. This emphasised, in the schizophrenia literature, the idea of continuity in the disorder and that certain features of schizophrenia could be observed without the associated clinical signs of illness (Claridge, 1994).

It has subsequently been proposed that it would be more beneficial to study individuals in this sub-clinical category of psychosis proneness (e.g. Linney, Peters & Ayton, 1998). As some have noted, this avoids methodological difficulties such as medication effects, motivational issues, variation over time of severity of symptoms and general cognitive decline as a consequence of mental illness (Claridge, 1988). Research on sub-clinical delusions allows researchers to make inferences regarding the clinical population.

In psychology, this has led to the development of a number of questionnaires to measure liability to psychosis. These range from the Magical Ideation Scale (Eckblad & Chapman, 1983) measuring unusual experiences, the Schizotypal Personality Scale (Jackson & Claridge 1991) modelled on DSM-III criteria for schizotypal and borderline personality disorders and the Psychoticism Scale (Eysenck & Eysenck, 1975, 1976) measuring personality traits, through to the more recent Oxford-Liverpool Inventory of Feelings and Experiences (O-LIFE; Mason, Claridge & Jackson, 1995; Mason, Linney & Claridge, 2005) measuring 'Unusual Experiences', 'Cognitive Disorganisation', 'Introvertive Anhedonia' and 'Impulsive Nonconformity'.

From these and other measures that have been developed, it can be argued that there has been a limitation on the number of questionnaires available that exclusively measure delusional thinking, especially in non-clinical populations (Peters et al., 1999). One such scale, the Foulds Delusions-Symptoms-State Inventory (Foulds & Bedford 1975), was designed to measure four main types of delusion (delusions of grandeur, disintegration, persecution and contrition); however, this was designed for clinical use and would be considered inappropriate for use in non-clinical populations since the items reflect florid symptoms and would be unlikely to be consistent with delusional ideation in non-clinical populations (Peters et al., 1999). Thus in the 1990s, the Peters et al. Delusions Inventory (PDI; Peters, Day & Garety, 1996) was constructed to specifically measure delusional ideation in general population samples. This measure emphasises the importance of the distress associated with a belief, how much the person is preoccupied with the belief and the conviction with which the belief is held. In doing this, it also emphasises the importance of continuity in delusional thinking and the potential for this to develop into psychotic disorder and also the multi-dimensionality of delusions (Peters et al., 1999). For example, a person may believe with absolute conviction that things in magazines or on TV are written especially for them but they may not be particularly distressed or preoccupied with this. Conversely, they may be somewhat preoccupied with the idea that people communicate telepathically but not be distressed about it or really believe that it is true. Therefore, delusions can no longer be defined as 'all or nothing' phenomena, but as multi-dimensional beliefs that lie on a continuum with normality.

What is reflected in the literature and in this diverse range of psychosis proneness measures is that there is some confusion in the field regarding the difference between delusional *experiences* and delusional *beliefs* (Peters et al., 1999).

Garety and Hemsley (1994) described delusions as *evaluations* of mental events and that the mental events (or perception) are not what is delusional – it is the evaluation or judgement of these events that represent the delusion. For example, one person may hear a crackling sound when they use the telephone and assume that there is simply a fault with the line. However, another person may hear the crackling sound and believe that their telephone has been sophisticatedly bugged in order for someone else to listen to their conversations. A further endorsement of each person's belief would be 'technicians' outside their house, pointing to the telephone lines and making notes. How each person evaluates these events in each case can be seen to be quite different. However, Garety has argued more recently that there is not a straightforward distinction between perception and cognition *per se*. As Peters and Garety (2006) point out, perception is not necessarily independent of interpretations; therefore, delusions may also influence abnormal perceptual experiences.

Anomalous perceptual experiences and cognitive biases

In contrast to the views of Garety and Hemsley (1994), Maher (1974) argued that delusions arise as explanations of abnormal perceptual experiences through normal reasoning processes. A number of studies provide evidence to support this theory. For example, delusions are not limited to one type of disorder but rather can occur in a number of psychological and medical conditions (Maher & Ross, 1984). In non-clinical populations, hearing loss has been found to be linked to paranoia (Zimbardo, Andersen & Kabat, 1981). Ellis, Young, Quayle and de Pauw (1997) found that, when Capgras patients (having the delusion that a friend, spouse, parent or close family member has been replaced by an identical looking imposter) and controls were shown pictures of familiar and unfamiliar faces, Capgras patients failed to discriminate between the two on a measure of skin-conductance response in comparison to controls. However, Maher's theory does not account for all delusions (Garety & Freeman, 1999). Some delusions occur in the absence of an anomalous perceptual experience (Chapman & Chapman, 1988). Additionally, some people have perceptual anomalies but do not develop delusions (e.g. Tranel, Damasio & Damasio, 1995).

Nonetheless, Maher (1988) argued against a cognitive impairment and maintained that there was a lack of evidence for reasoning biases in deluded individuals. However, over time evidence has emerged that challenges Maher's position and suggests that reasoning biases are indeed implicated in delusion formation and maintenance (e.g. Garety & Freeman, 1999).

Jumping to conclusions or pushed to conclusions?

Reasoning biases are amongst the many cognitive constituents considered to be implicated in delusion formation and/or maintenance. Garety and Hemsley (1994) and Garety and Freeman (1999) speculated that individuals with delusions display 'a tendency or bias to the early acceptance and, to a lesser extent, the early rejection of hypotheses' (Garety & Freeman, 1999, p. 127). In plainer terms, it was proposed that those with delusions jump to conclusions, are prone to making snap judgements and may form decisions quickly on the basis of little evidence (Huq, Garety & Hemsley, 1988).

It is extensively documented that patients experiencing delusional beliefs jump to conclusions when faced with probabilistic reasoning tasks (Averbeck, Evans, Chouhan, Bristow & Shergill, 2011; Garety et al., 2013). Indeed, the supposition that patients with delusions jump to conclusions when forming decisions is so strongly upheld by psychologists that many meta-cognitive training programmes designed to treat patients with delusions specifically aspire to reduce the rate of this jump to conclusions bias (Moritz et al., 2011; Waller, Freeman, Jolley, Dunn & Garety, 2011).

Likewise, the tendency to jump to conclusions when faced with experimental decision-making tasks has also been observed in healthy individuals within the sub-clinical range of delusional ideation (Cafferkey, Murphy & Shevlin, 2013; Orenes, Navarrete, Beltran & Santamaria, 2012; Zawadzski et al., 2012). As a result, it has been implied that the tendency to jump to conclusions appears to be associated with the presence of delusions rather than psychotic symptoms per se (Freeman, Pugh & Garety, 2008).

The picture appears well-supported: patients with delusions jump to conclusions and this inherent reasoning bias serves to contribute to the formation and/or maintenance of delusional ideas (Huq et al., 1988). However, the picture may not be as clear-cut as first impressions may imply. According to Dudley et al. (2011), studies indicate that only around 40–70% of patients exhibit the jump to conclusions reasoning style and, as outlined by Freeman et al. (2008), around 20% without delusions display the data-gathering bias. Additional studies observed the reasoning bias amongst only 4% of patients with schizophrenia (Rossell & O'Regan, 2008), whilst other studies failed to detect the emergence of a jump to conclusions bias amongst participants with current or remitted delusions (Colbert, Peters & Garety, 2010). Indeed, a more recent study concluded that delusion-proneness did not significantly influence the emergence of the jump to conclusions bias even when hasty decision making was demonstrated, rather that miscomprehension of the task was the more likely cause of the bias (Balzan, Delfabbro & Galletly, 2012).

The suggestion that a propensity to jump to conclusions is an inherent and influential bias involved in the formation and/or maintenance of delusional beliefs (Huq et al., 1988) is a persuasive one. Nevertheless, the proposition is not entirely convincing. It is evident, given the extensive support amongst clinical (Dudley, John, Young & Over, 1997a, 1997b; Fear & Healy, 1997; Freeman, 2007) and non-clinical samples (Orenes et al., 2012; Zawadzki et al., 2012) that the jump to conclusions bias does, in many instances, although not all, emerge amongst individuals engaging in delusional thinking. However, in order to obtain a richer perspective we must first question, and not ignore, why some individuals experiencing delusional beliefs jump to conclusions whilst others do not.

Methodological considerations

Typically, studies detecting a jump to conclusions bias amongst delusional schizophrenic patients (Huq *et al.*, 1988) have frequently implemented the renowned 'beads' task. The beads task was initially employed by Phillips and Edwards (1966) to investigate probabilistic inference. The task presented participants with two jars of beads, one of which had a ratio of largely black compared to white beads (85:15) and the second had a ratio of largely white compared to black (15:85). The jars were hidden from view and participants were required to request as many or as few beads as they deemed necessary in order to infer from which of the two jars a sequence of beads was drawn. Those that typically display the jump to conclusions bias reach final decisions abnormally early in the process of data gathering. Typically, schizophrenic or delusional disorder patients display an increased tendency to decide after the first bead drawn in comparison with control participants (Dudley & Over, 2003; Fine, Gardner, Craigie & Gold, 2007; Freeman *et al.*, 2004; Garety & Freeman, 1999).

The obvious irrelevance of the task in relation to how people gather evidence in order to form beliefs is clear; people are not encouraged to gather information for the very purpose of generating an opinion or perspective. The artificial nature of the task demands that participants merely make a decision and opt for a choice, from essentially one of only two options. Whilst attempts have been made to make the original beads task, or variations of the beads task, more realistic by including emotionally salient, self-referent (Dudley *et al.*, 1997b) or lexical task material (Ziegler, Rief, Werner, Mehl & Lincoln, 2008), the methodologies implemented continue to fail to provide the opportunity for individuals to gather information for the very purpose of developing a real belief or perspective. The type of task presented to participants, and the way in which the tasks are presented, has only recently received attention in research. It has been highlighted that increasing the ambiguity of the beads task (Moritz, Woodward & Lambert, 2007) and factors such as task miscomprehension (i.e. misunderstanding task instructions; Balzan *et al.*, 2012) could influence performance on tasks employed to measure the jump to conclusions bias.

However, of particular interest is how decision-making tasks make participants *feel* and how this may consequently impact upon how participants *behave*. Interestingly, it has recently been proposed that delusion-prone individuals may display a tendency to jump to conclusions in scenarios that induce a sense of feeling rushed (White & Mansell, 2009). Similarly, it has been found that delusion-prone individuals report greater confidence in their ideas when they encounter a stressful situation or feel particularly hurried in their decision making (Keefe & Warman, 2011). Likewise, the jump to conclusions phenomenon has been observed amongst high trait anxiety individuals in particular (Bensi & Guisberti, 2007).

The potential influence of stress/anxiety has received considerable investigation in relation to the jump to conclusions bias amongst delusional and delusion-prone individuals (Ellett, Freeman & Garety, 2008; Lincoln, Lange, Burau, Exner & Moritz, 2010). Whilst studies have consistently linked the presence of anxiety and/or stress to an increased tendency to jump to conclusions (Ellett *et al.*, 2008; Lincoln *et al.*, 2010), many have focussed heavily upon stress that may be induced prior to the decision-making task/s. Few studies have investigated and appreciated the stress that may arise as a result of completing the very decision-making task used to measure the jump to conclusions bias itself. It is possible that the jump to conclusions effect observed amongst patients with delusions, and healthy individuals from the sub-clinical range, is merely a response action to the perceived threat and/or stress of the data-gathering task itself. Is it possible that a task designed to measure hastiness in decision making could in fact, paradoxically, promote its emergence?

Imagine, for a moment, that you yourself were participating in such an experiment. You enter a room with a researcher and are informed that there are two jars of coloured beads hidden beneath the table. The two jars contain contrasting ratios of the coloured beads and you need to decide, whilst the researcher presents a sequence of beads to you one at a time, from which of the two jars the beads are drawn, whilst taking into account the prospective ratio of coloured beads in each jar. Before you begin the experiment, you realise you are going to need to remember the colour of each bead that the researcher presents and then hides from view, in order to add up the number of each of the coloured beads you see, in order to work out the most likely ratio – and then there is the possibility that you may still get the answer wrong.

It is easy to appreciate why participants may become flustered or stressed when completing data-gathering tasks such as this. Perhaps, it is a far more rational option to avoid the stress and to take a guess at it after the first bead drawn, and consequently jump to conclusions. Your alternative is to invest effort and time and, whilst you may increase your chances of getting the answer correct, you still run the risk of getting the answer wrong, which, by your own evaluation, may leave you feeling a little silly after such a lengthy investment.

In a recent study conducted by Rhodes, Galbraith and Manktelow (2012), it was concluded that modifications in the type of task presented to participants (abstract vs. realistic) and the way the task is presented (computerised vs. face to face) can influence the quantity of information that a participant will request prior to finalising a decision amongst individuals engaging in delusional thinking. The findings therefore support the notion that data gathering may be influenced by domain-specific factors.

If the stress of a given task can influence our susceptibility to jump to conclusions, you may still ask why some individuals jump to conclusions whilst others do not. It is possible that emotions experienced at the time of testing may influence consequent action and that the emotions experienced may vary between individuals. Exactly *how* emotions may impact upon the subsequent behaviour remains to be seen but can almost positively be linked to how the experienced emotion influences our reasoning.

Liberal acceptance

Steffen Moritz and Todd Woodward (2004) have proposed a liberal acceptance bias as an underlying mechanism of the jump to conclusions bias. According to this account, those with delusions have a lower threshold of acceptance, suggesting that rather than simply being hasty, as would be predicted by the jump to conclusions bias, patients with delusions cross the threshold of what is acceptable evidence for a decision to be made sooner than others. This, in turn, can lead them to accept implausible information more easily. Furthermore, according to this account, ambiguous situations (rather than situations with only one strong alternative, e.g. the 'beads task') can lead to increased ambivalence and could actually delay a decision, rather than lead to a hasty one, since multiple alternatives cross this lowered threshold of acceptance and deciding between them becomes more difficult (Moritz et al., 2007).

In their study (Moritz & Woodward, 2004), patients with schizophrenia were shown pictures from the Thematic Apperception Task (Murray, 1943). The Thematic Apperception Task was specifically chosen due to the pictures being fairly ambiguous and could invoke a number of interpretations. Twenty-nine delusional and non-delusional patients with schizophrenia and 28 healthy participants were asked to rate the plausibility of various (randomly presented) interpretations of the pictures. A strict jump to conclusions account would mean that patients would quickly decide on a single interpretation. However, patients gave relatively high plausibility ratings for numerous interpretations that were rated as poor or unlikely by controls. Yet on plausibility ratings that were rated as good or excellent by controls, patients were comparable to them (Moritz & Woodward, 2004). What is compelling is that the findings indicated that a liberal acceptance bias was more pronounced for scenarios that were absurd or less likely and are usually discounted either through 'common sense' or prior knowledge.

As discussed above, how decision-making tasks make people *feel* may influence the way they subsequently *behave*. However, unlike the jump to conclusions bias, the way people feel and the way these emotions affect the subsequent behaviour of individuals exhibiting a liberal acceptance bias has received much less attention.

In a recent study, LaRocco and Warman (2009) were interested in how people reason about the primary variable of interest – delusional stimuli. The investigation was based on a previous study conducted by McGuire, Junginger, Adams, Burright and Donovick (2001). In the original study (McGuire et al., 2001), there were delusional, previously delusional, psychiatric inpatients and non-psychiatric participants who were asked to assign probability estimates of the likelihood that emotionally neutral and delusional narratives (thought to be emotionally salient) could be true. No differences between the groups emerged for the emotionally neutral narratives. However, it was found that those with delusions assigned higher probability estimates (i.e. thought they were likely to be true or possible) to delusional narratives than the other groups. LaRocco and Warman (2009) replicated McGuire et al.'s (2001) study in a non-clinical population, investigating how high and low delusion-prone participants reason about delusional and neutral material.

They found that those high in delusional ideation were biased, in that they rated unusual scenarios as more likely. To put it another way, unusual scenarios surpassed a lowered threshold of acceptance that is not present in those low in delusional ideation but appears to be present in high delusion-prone individuals as well as patients with delusions. This is consistent with a liberal acceptance account.

It can be seen how delusional narratives, unlike the abstract 'beads task', may invoke various emotions that may lead one to believe that they could be true. To illustrate, an extract from one of the persecutory narratives read: 'He said people were out to kill him. He said he was afraid he might get gunned down', while an extract from one of the grandiose narratives read: 'He said he was Jesus Christ. He said if someone followed him, that person would find his way. [. . .] He said he couldn't work miracles yet, but he would some-day' (LaRocco & Warman, 2009, p. 199). The authors (LaRocco & Warman, 2009) suggest that delusional material in particular affects reasoning in a unique way in those high in delusional ideation and those with delusions. Indeed, research has suggested that those high in delusional ideation are significantly more emotionally creative in comparison to those low in delusional ideation – in addition to displaying a liberal acceptance bias for delusional stimuli (Jones, Galbraith, Manktelow & Fullwood, in prep).

In a further study, it was found that those high in delusional ideation (compared to those low in delusional ideation) exhibit a liberal acceptance bias in relation to delusional stimuli because they find it more exciting (Jones, Galbraith, Fullwood & Manktelow, in prep). This supports the theory that holding unusual beliefs may offer greater excitement than a more rational view of the world (Kumar, Pekala & Cummings, 1993; Zuckerman, 1979). However, when asked how disturbing participants found delusional stimuli and how disturbing it would be to most other people, no differences emerged between those high and low in delusional ideation, implying that both groups found the delusional stimuli equally disturbing.

As mentioned earlier, emotions experienced at the time of testing may influence consequent actions. In line with this notion, some studies have investigated the effects of mood induction. Bouhuys, Bloem and Groothuis (1995) showed healthy participants 12 'ambiguous' faces displaying equal amounts of positive or negative emotions and six 'clear' faces expressing either positive or negative emotions which were further distinguished by the intensity of the emotions they expressed. Participants judged the faces after listening to either depressing or elating music. Eleven participants who were particularly affected by listening to the depressing music were selected for further analysis. They found that these participants reported more sadness and rejection in ambiguous faces and less happiness and more fear in clear faces. Studies such as this demonstrate that manipulating mood can affect the way people reason about various stimuli.

In relation to liberal acceptance, Moritz et al. (2009) have tested this theory of mood induction further by showing participants (27 patients with schizophrenia and 32 healthy controls) classical paintings with four alternative titles (one correct title and three lure titles) and asking them to rate the plausibility of the titles while either anxiety-evoking music, happy music or no music was played. In particular, those with delusions made more decisions overall than healthy participants. Implausible titles were judged as significantly more plausible by patients and anxiety-invoking music resulted in more decisions made by those with delusions compared to non-deluded patients and healthy controls. However, despite these findings, no overall effect was found for the mood induction manipulation.

Indeed, previous research has provided mixed results regarding the effects of emotional material on reasoning, with some studies reporting that emotional materials lead to biased reasoning in delusions and control groups (Dudley *et al.*, 1997b; Fraser, Morrison & Wells, 2006), while other studies have reported no difference in reasoning when using emotional or neutral materials (Garety *et al.*, 2005; Warman, Lysaker, Martin, Davis & Haudenschield, 2007). This begs the question of why emotion sometimes leads to biased reasoning and sometimes not.

Reasoning with your heart or your head?

When faced with numerous dilemmas in life, we often experience an internal struggle between what our 'heart' *feels* is the right course of action to take and what our 'head' *thinks* is right. Dilemmas become such when what the heart feels and what the head thinks conflict with one another. The concept of this invisible battle of wills is certainly not a new one.

The concept of a divided mind has existed for centuries. Plato (1993) was one of the first to claim that the soul was partitioned into three individual units: reason, spirit and appetite. Subsequently, Freud (1933) extended the notion that separated mental phenomena could influence both unconscious and conscious behaviour with his in-depth and detailed descriptions of the id, ego and superego. Since the beginning of the early 1970s, early split-mind speculations have been applied to the discipline of human cognitive psychology. Specifically in relation to the study of deductive reasoning, decision making and social judgement. Here lay the foundations of what is now known as the dual process approach to decision making (Evans & Stanovich, 2013; Kahneman & Frederick, 2002, 2005).

The postulation of the dual process theory is the existence of two mental systems labelled System 1 and System 2 (Evans, 2008; Stanovich, 1999). System 1 is described as a default mechanism that produces quick, automatic and intuitive answers to decision-making dilemmas. In contrast, System 2 is far more analytical in its approach to the decision-making task and has been associated with conscious activation and operation. Whilst the framework has been criticised for being simplistic (Stanovich, 2009), the concept has been applied to explain a variety of reasoning biases and heuristic strategies (Evans, 2008; Tversky & Kahneman, 1974).

Of particular interest is the Cognitive- Experiential Self Theory of Personality (CEST) developed by Seymour Epstein (2003). Whilst there remains considerable debate regarding the relevance of CEST to current dual process theories (Newstead, Handley, Harley, Wright & Farrelly, 2004), acknowledgements of the similarities between rational-experiential processing and System 1 and 2 models have been supported (Norenzayan, Choi & Peng, 2007). Epstein (2003) describes the experiential system as rapid, effortless, automatic and minimally demanding of cognitive resources; the rational system is conscious, analytical, relatively slow and demanding of cognitive resources. It is clear that the description of the rational and experiential systems closely mirrors the concept of System 1 and 2, as earlier suggested by Stanovich (1999). However, in contrast to preceding dual process approaches to decision making, CEST (Epstein, 2003) accounts for the impact of *affect* upon the decision-making process.

Esptein (2003) contends that the experiential system learns from experience rather than logical inference. It is suggested that the system works in two ways: 1) encoding experiences and cross-referencing these to a memory bank of prior experiences that were highly emotionally stimulating; 2) reasoning in the more general, abstract sense. In relation to CEST (Epstein, 2003), the experiential system is considered to not only influence but also be influenced by affect. To elaborate, whilst the experiential system is highly motivated to promote positive outcomes and avoid the negative (as a result of memories of prior emotionally significant events), the cognitions themselves are also vulnerable to the influence of affect.

In many previous theories, the automatic 'unconscious' system of reasoning was almost indirectly linked to our animal or primitive-like instincts; perceived as an unruly system driven by speed and prior experience that required restraint from the superior and all knowledgeable rational pathway of reasoning and decision making. However, a reasoning system that is driven by our emotions is a powerful one. As outlined by Epstein (2003), it is possible to live in the world with an experiential system in the absence of a rational system, as the existence of animals attests, but you could not exist with only rational system at play. The simplest of tasks would demand extensive cognitive power and calculation in order to execute; exposing oneself to potential hazards and dangers in the interim. Most interesting of all is the suggestion that our experiential system can trick our rational system into believing it is responsible for the given decision made (Epstein, 2003). If our emotions are influential to our reasoning processes, is it possible that specific emotions may elicit a particular reasoning style preference?

Reasoning style

Whilst psychological investigation has highlighted that the experiential and rational scales of the Rational Experiential Inventory measure are uncorrelated (Handley, Newstead & Wright, 2000; Pacini & Epstein, 1999), an individual predominance or preference to execute one particular system more than another appears to exist (Epstein, 1985; Strack & Deutsch, 2004). For example, age-related differences have been identified, with older adolescents employing a rational decision-making style most frequently, and an intuitive style less frequently in comparison with younger teenagers (Baiocco, Laghi & D'Alessio, 2009).

Interestingly, it has been suggested that the experience of certain emotions can influence specific reasoning style preferences. A review of the literature suggests that positive emotional traits such as openness to experience, conscientiousness and open-minded thinking are indicative of a rational reasoning style (Handley *et al.*, 2000; Marks, Hine, Blore & Phillips, 2008; Toyosawa & Karasawa, 2004). In a more recent study, a preference for deliberation significantly predicted positive affect (Laborde, Dosseville & Scelles, 2010). This may help to explain why increases in positive affect have been associated with a reduction in the jump to conclusion bias (Lee, Barrowclough & Lobban, 2011). Furthermore, an intuitive or experiential reasoning style has been linked to negative affect (Laborde *et al.*, 2010). Individuals with paranormal/superstitious and/or peculiar beliefs have demonstrated a lesser degree of analytical thinking (Pennycook, Cheyne, Koehler & Fugelsang, 2012; Shenhav, Rand & Greene, 2012), whilst an intuitive reasoning style has been linked with the presence of such beliefs (Aarnio & Lindeman, 2005; Genovese, 2005; Sadler-Smith, 2011). Interestingly, it has been suggested elsewhere that the amalgamation of high experiential reasoning but low rational reasoning was particularly associated with persecutory ideation (Freeman, Evans & Lister, 2012). Furthermore, an experiential reasoning style may be associated with anxiety, which itself may be related to the jump to conclusions bias (Lincoln *et al.* 2010).

However, the findings in studies of delusional reasoning and affect are often mixed. For example, So, Freeman and Garety (2008) found that an anxiety manipulation had no effect upon patients with delusions (or controls). Similarly, whilst there is considerable support that positive affective states are linked with a rational reasoning style and negative affective states are linked with experiential reasoning, the findings are not always replicated. King and Hicks (2009) found that positive affect and intuitive thinking interacted to predict ideas of reference. In contrast though, Boden, Berenbaum and Topper (2012) found that peculiar beliefs were predicted by intuitive thinking and negative affect separately, but these predictors did not interact and no association with positive affect was found at all.

It is clear that the potential relationship between our emotions, our reasoning systems and our consequent beliefs is a complex one – but yet from a lay perspective can seem simple. From personal experience, to which I am sure many of us can attest and/or empathise, when we experience particularly distressing events and feelings in life (for which we cannot always understand as a result of logical analysis), we often cling to beliefs that bring about comfort; irrespective, and often at the expense, of plausibility. It can be argued that to experimentally examine perceived reasoning biases, such as the jump to conclusions bias, whilst lacking an appreciation for our emotional states and traits, is an ill-advised venture.

Closing comments

The presence of the jump to conclusions bias amongst both patients with delusions (Huq *et al.*, 1988) and those from within the sub-clinical range of delusion proneness (Orenes *et al.*, 2012) cannot directly or entirely be attributed to the presence of delusional beliefs per se. It is possible emotional reactions to tasks interfere with reasoning style that the previous methodological techniques employed to investigate the jump to conclusions bias may have contributed to its emergence. It is imperative that a multifaceted perspective and methodology is adopted in the future in order to understand the contributing factors that may influence the susceptibility to jump to conclusions and other reasoning biases amongst individuals that may or may not engage in delusional thinking. This will inevitably enrich our understanding of how delusions form and continue to persist over time.

References

Aarnio, K., & Lindeman, M. (2005). Paranormal beliefs, education, and thinking styles. *Personality and Individual Differences, 39,* 1227–1236.

American Psychiatric Association. (2000). *Diagnostic and Statistical Manual of Mental Disorders* (4th ed., text rev.). Washington, DC: American Psychiatric Association.

American Psychiatric Association. (2013). *Diagnostic and Statistical Manual of Mental Disorders* (5th ed.). Washington, DC: American Psychiatric Association.

Averbeck, B. B., Evans, S., Chouhan, V., Bristow, E., & Shergill, S. S. (2011). Probabilistic learning and inference in schizophrenia. *Schizophrenia Research, 127,* 115–122.

Baiocco, R., Laghi, F., & D'Alessio, M. (2009). Decision-making style amongst adolescents: Relationship with sensation seeking and locus of control. *Journal of Adolescence, 32*(4), 963–976.

Balzan, R. P., Delfabbro, P. H., & Galletly, C. (2012). Delusion-proneness or miscomprehension? A re-examination of the jumping to conclusions bias. *Australian Journal of Psychology, 64,* 100–107.

Bell, V., Halligan, P. W. & Ellis, H. D. (2003). Beliefs about delusions. *The Psychologist, 16*(8), 418–423.

Bell, V., Halligan, P. W. & Ellis, H. D. (2006). Explaining delusions: A cognitive perspective. *Trends in Cognitive Sciences, 10*(5), 219–226.

Bensi, L., & Guisberti, F. (2007). Trait anxiety and reasoning under uncertainty. *Personality and Individual Differences, 43,* 827–838.

Bentall, R. P., Corcoran, R., Howard, R., Blackwood, N. & Kinderman, P. (2001). Persecutory delusions: A review and theoretical integration. *Clinical Psychology Review, 21*(8), 1143–1192.

Berrios, G. (1991). Delusions as 'wrong beliefs': A conceptual history. *British Journal of Psychiatry, 159,* 6–13.

Bleuler, E. (1911). *Dementia Praecox oder Gruppe der Schizophrenien.* Leipzig, Germany: Deuticke.

Boden, M. T., Berenbaum, H., & Topper, M. (2012). Intuition, affect and peculiar beliefs. *Personality and Individual Differences, 52,* 845–848.

Bouhuys, A. L., Bloem, G. M., & Groothuis, T. G. G. (1995). Induction of depressed and elated mood by music influences the perception of facial emotional expressions in healthy subjects. *Journal of Affective Disorders, 33,* 215–226.

Cafferkey, K., Murphy, J., & Shevlin, M. (2013). Jumping to conclusions: The association between delusional ideation and reasoning biases in a healthy student population. *Psychosis,* (ahead-of-print), 1–9.

Chapman, L. J., and Chapman, J. P. (1988). Scales for rating psychotic and psychotic-like experiences as continua. *Schizophrenia Bulletin, 6,* 476–489.

Claridge, G. S. (1988). Schizotypy and schizophrenia. In P. Bebbington & P. McGuffin (Eds.), *Schizophrenia: The Major Issues.* Oxford: Heinemann Professional.

Claridge, G. S. (1994). Single indicator of risk for schizophrenia: Probable fact or likely myth? *Schizophrenia Bulletin, 20*(l), 151–168.

Colbert, S. M., Peters, E., & Garety, P. (2010). Jumping to conclusions and perceptions in early psychosis: Relationship with delusional beliefs. *Cognitive Neuropsychiatry, 15*(4), 422–440.

Dudley, R. E. J., John, C. H., Young, A. W., & Over, D. E. (1997a). Normal and abnormal reasoning in people with delusions. *British Journal of Clinical Psychology, 36*, 243–258.

Dudley, R. E. J., John, C. H., Young, A. W., & Over, D. E. (1997b). The effect of self-referent material on the reasoning of people with delusions. *British Journal of Clinical Psychology, 364*, 575–584.

Dudley, R. E. J., & Over, D. E. (2003). People with delusions jump to conclusions. *Clinical Psychology and Psychotherapy, 10*, 263–274.

Dudley, R., Shaftoe, D., Cavanagh, K., Spencer, H., Ormrod, J., Turkington, D., & Freeston, M. (2011). 'Jumping to conclusions' in first-episode psychosis. *Early Intervention in Psychiatry, 5*, 50–56.

Eckblad, M., & Chapman, L. J. (1983). Magical ideation as an indicator of schizotypy. *Journal of Consulting and Clinical Psychology, 51*, 215–225.

Ellett, L., Freeman, D., & Garety, P. A. (2008). The psychological effect of an urban environment on individuals with persecutory delusions: The Camberwell walk study. *Schizophrenia Research, 99*, 77–84.

Ellis, H. D., Young, A. W., Quayle, A. H., & de Pauw, K. W. (1997). Reduced autonomic responses to faces in Capgras delusion. *Proceedings of the Royal Society B: Biological Sciences, 264*(1384), 1085–1092.

Epstein, S. (1985). The implications of cognitive-experiential self-theory for research in social psychology and personality. *Journal for the Theory of Social Behaviour, 15*, 283–310.

Epstein, S. (2003). Cognitive-experiential self-theory of personality. In T. Millon & M. J. Lerner (Eds.), *Comprehensive Handbook of Psychology, Vol. 5: Personality and Social Psychology*. Hoboken, NJ: Wiley & Sons.

Evans, J. St. B. T. (2008). Dual-processing accounts of reasoning, judgment, and social cognition. *Annual Review of Psychology, 59*, 255–278.

Evans, J. St. B. T., & Stanovich, K. E. (2013). Dual-process theories of higher cognition: advancing the debate. *Perspectives on Psychological Science, 8*(3), 223–241.

Eysenck H. J., & Eysenck S. B. G. (1975) *Manual of the Eysenck Personality Questionnaire.* London: Hodder & Stoughton.

Eysenck, H. J., & Eysenck, S. B. (1976). *Manual of the Eysenck Personality Inventory.* San Diego: Educational and Industrial Testing Service.

Fear, C. F., & Healy, D. (1997). Probabilistic reasoning in obsessive-compulsive and delusional disorders. *Psychological Medicine, 27*, 199–208.

Fine, C., Gardner, M., Craigie, J., & Gold, I. (2007). Hopping, skipping or jumping to conclusions? Clarifying the role of the JTC bias in delusions. *Cognitive Neuropsychiatry, 12*(1), 46–77.

Foulds, G. A., & Bedford, A. (1975). Hierarchy of classes of personal illness. *Psychological Medicine, 5*, 181–192.

Fraser, J., Morrison, A. P. & Wells, A. (2006). Cognitive processes, reasoning biases and persecutory delusions: A comparative study. *Behavioural & Cognitive Psychotherapy, 34*(4), 421–435.

Freeman, D. (2007). Suspicious minds: The psychology of persecutory delusions. *Clinical Psychology Review, 27*, 425–457.

Freeman, D., Evans, N., & Lister, R. (2012). Gut feelings, deliberative thought and paranoid ideation: A study of rational and experiential reasoning. *Psychiatry Research, 197*, 119–122.

Freeman, D., Garety, P. A., Fowler, D., Kuipers, E., Bebbington, P. E., & Dunn, G. (2004). Why do people with delusions fail to choose more realistic explanations for their experiences? An empirical investigation. *Journal of Consulting and Clinical Psychology, 72,* 671–680.

Freeman, D., Pugh, K., & Garety, P. (2008). Jumping to conclusions and paranoid ideation in the general population. *Schizophrenia Research, 102,* 254–260.

Freud, S. (1933). *New Introductory Lectures on Psychoanalysis* (J. Strachey, trans.). New York: W. W. Norton.

Garety, P. A., & Freeman, D. (1999). Cognitive approaches to delusions: A critical review of theories and evidence. *British Journal of Clinical Psychology, 38,* 113–154.

Garety, P. A., Freeman, D., Jolley, S., Dunn, G., Bebbington, P. E., Fowler, D. G., . . . & Dudley, R. (2005). Reasoning, emotions, and delusional conviction in psychosis. *Journal of Abnormal Psychology, 114*(3), 373.

Garety, P. A., & Hemsley, D. R. (1994) *Delusions: Investigations into the Psychology of Delusional Reasoning.* London: Psychology Press.

Garety, P., Joyce, E., Jolley, S., Emsley, R., Waller, H., Kuipers, E., . . . & Freeman, D. (2013). Neuropsychological functioning and jumping to conclusions in delusions. *Schizophrenia Research, 150*(2), 570–574.

Genovese, J. E. C. (2005). Paranormal beliefs, schizotypy, and thinking styles among teachers and future teachers. *Personality and Individual Differences, 39,* 93–102.

Handley, S. J., Newstead, S. E., & Wright, H. (2000). Rational and experiential thinking: A study of the REI. In R. J. Riding & S. G. Rayner (Eds.), *International Perspectives on Individual Differences: Vol. 1.* Stamford, CO: Ablex.

Harrow, M., MacDonald, A. W., Sands, J. R., & Silverstein, M. L. (1995). Vulnerability to delusions over time in schizophrenia and affective disorders. *Schizophrenia Bulletin, 21*(1), 95–109.

Huq, S. F., Garety, P. A., & Hemsley, D. R. (1988). Probabilistic judgements in deluded and non-deluded subjects. *Quarterly Journal of Experimental Psychology: Human Experimental Psychology, 40,* 801–812.

Ipsos MORI. (1998). Paranormal Survey. Retrieved from www.ipsos-mori.com/research-publications/researcharchive/poll.aspx?oItemId=2082

Jackson, M., & Claridge, G. (1991). Reliability and validity of a psychotic traits questionnaire (STQ). *British Journal of Clinical Psychology, 30,* 311–323.

Jaspers, K. (1913/1963). *General Psychopathology* (J. Hoenig & M. W. Hamilton, Eds., trans.). Manchester: Manchester University Press.

Johns, L. C. & van Os, J. (2001). The continuity of psychotic experiences in the general population. *Clinical Psychology Review, 21*(8), 1125–1141.

Jones, C. L., Galbraith, N. D., Fullwood, C., & Manktelow, K. I. (in prep). Beliefs, creativity and reasoning.

Jones, C. L., Galbraith, N. D., Manktelow, K. I., & Fullwood, C. (in prep). Delusional ideation and probability estimations of delusional and neutral stimuli.

Kahneman, D., & Frederick, S. (2002). Representativeness revisited: Attribute substitution in intuitive judgment. In T. Gilovich, D. Griffin, & D. Kahneman (Eds.), *Heuristics & Biases: The Psychology of Intuitive Judgment.* Cambridge, UK: Cambridge University Press.

Kahneman, D., & Frederick, S. (2005). A model of heuristic judgment. In K. J. Holyoak & R. G. Morrison (Eds.), *The Cambridge Handbook of Thinking and Reasoning.* Cambridge, UK: Cambridge University Press.

Keefe, K. M., & Warman, D. (2011). Reasoning, delusion proneness and stress: An experimental investigation. *Clinical Psychology and Psychotherapy, 18*(2), 138–147.

King, L. A., & Hicks, J. A. (2009). Positive affect, intuition and referential thinking. *Personality and Individual Differences, 46,* 719–724.

Kumar, V. K., Pekala, R. J., & Cummings, J. (1993). Sensation seeking, drug use and reported paranormal beliefs and experiences. *Personality and Individual Differences, 14*(5), 685–681.

Kumar, D., Zia Ul Haq, M., Dubey, I., Dotivala, K. N., Siddiqui, S. V., Prakash, R., . . . & Nizamie, H. (2010). Effect of meta-cognitive training in the reduction of positive symptoms in schizophrenia. *European Journal of Psychotherapy and Counselling, 12*(2), 149–158.

Laborde, S., Dosseville., & Scelles, N. (2010). Trait emotional intelligence and preference for intuition and deliberation: Respective influence on academic performance. *Personality and Individual Differences, 49*, 784–788.

LaRocco, V. A., & Warman, D. M. (2009). Probability estimations and delusion-proneness. *Personality and Individual Differences, 47*(3), 197–202.

Lee, G., Barrowclough, C., & Lobban, F. (2011). The influence of positive affect on jumping to conclusions in delusional thinking. *Personality and Individual Differences, 50*, 717–722.

Lincoln, T. M., Lange, J., Burau, J., Exner, C., & Moritz, S. (2010). The effect of state anxiety on paranoid ideation and jumping to conclusions. An experimental investigation. *Schizophrenia Bulletin, 36*(6), 1140–1148.

Linney, Y., Peters, E., & Ayton, P. (1998). Reasoning biases in delusion-prone individuals. *British Journal of Clinical Psychology, 37*(3), 247–370.

Maher, B. A. (1974). Delusional thinking and perceptual disorder. *Journal of Individual Psychology, 30*(1), 98–113.

Maher, B. A. (1988). Anomalous experience and delusional thinking: The logic of explanations. In T. F. Maher & B. A. Maher (Eds.), *Delusional Beliefs*. New York: Wiley.

Maher, B. A., & Ross, J. S. (1984). Delusions. In H. E. Adams & P. B. Sutker (Eds.), *Comprehensive Handbook of Psychopathology*. New York: Plenum.

Marks, A. D. G., Hine, D. W., Blore, R. L., & Phillips, W. J. (2008). Assessing individual differences in adolescents' preferences for rational and experiential cognition. *Personality and Individual Differences, 44*, 42–52.

Mason, O., Claridge, G., & Jackson, M. (1995). New scales for the assessment of schizotypy. *Personality and Individual Differences, 18*(1), 7–13.

Mason, O., Linney, Y., & Claridge, G. (2005). Short scales for measuring schizotypy. *Schizophrenia Research, 78*(2–3), 293–296.

McGuire, L., Junginger, J., Adams, S. G., Burright, R., & Donovick, P. (2001). Delusions and delusional reasoning. *Journal of Abnormal Psychology, 110*, 259–266.

Meehl, P. E. (1962). Schizotaxia, schizotypy, schizophrenia. *American Psychologist, 17*, 827–838.

Mojtabai, R., & Nicholson, R. A. (1995). Interrater reliability of ratings of delusions and bizarre delusions. *The American Journal of Psychiatry, 152*(12), 1804–1806.

Moritz, T., Kerstan, A., Veckenstedt, R., Randjbar, S., Vitzthum, F., Schmidt, C., . . . & Woodward, T.S. (2011). Further evidence for the efficacy of a metacognitive group training in schizophrenia. *Behaviour Research and Therapy, 49*, 151–157.

Moritz, S., Veckenstedt, R., Randjbar, S., Hottenrott, B., Woodward, T. S., Eckstaedt, F. V. . . . & Lincoln, T. M. (2009). Decision making under uncertainty and mood induction: Further evidence for liberal acceptance in schizophrenia. *Psychological Medicine, 39*, 1821–1829.

Moritz, S., & Woodward, T. S. (2004). Plausibility judgment in schizophrenic patients: Evidence for a liberal acceptance bias. *German Journal of Psychiatry, 7*, 66–74.

Moritz, S., & Woodward, T. S. (2007). Metacognitive training in schizophrenia: From basic research to knowledge translation and intervention. *Current Opinion in Psychiatry, 20*, 619–625.

Moritz, S., Woodward, T. S., & Lambert, M. (2007). Under what circumstances do patients with schizophrenia jump to conclusions? A liberal acceptance account. *British Journal of Clinical Psychology, 46*, 127–137.

Mujica-Parodi, L. R., Greenberg, T., Bilder, R. M., & Malaspina, D. (2001). Emotional impact on logic deficits may underlie psychotic delusions in schizophrenia. *Proceedings of the 23rd Annual Conference of the Cognitive Science Society*. Mahway, NJ: Lawrence Erlbaum Associates Inc.

Murray, H. A. (1943). *The Thematic Apperception Test Manual*. Cambridge, MA: Harvard University Press.

Myin-Germeys, I., Nicolson, N. A., & Delespaul, P. A. E. G. (2001). The context of delusional experiences in the daily life of patients with schizophrenia. *Psychological Medicine, 31*(3), 489–498.

Newstead, S. E., Handley, S. J., Harley, C., Wright, H., & Farrelly, D. (2004). Individual differences in deductive reasoning. *Quarterly Journal of Experimental Psychology Section A, 57*(1), 33–60.

Norenzayan, A., Choi, I., & Peng, K. (2007). Cognition and perception. In S. Kitayama & D. Cohen (Eds.), *Handbook of Cultural Psychology*. New York: Guilford Publications.

Orenes, I., Navarrete, G., Beltran, D., & Santamaria, C. (2012). Schizotypal people stick longer to their first choices. *Psychiatry Research, 200*, 620–628.

Pacini, R., & Epstein, S. (1999). The relation of rational and experiential information processing styles to personality, basic beliefs, and the ratio-bias phenomenon. *Journal of Personality and Social Psychology, 76*(6), 972–987.

Pennycook, G., Cheyne, J. A., Koehler, D. J., & Fugelsang, J. A. (2012). Analytic cognitive style predicts religious and paranormal belief. *Cognition, 123*, 335–346.

Peters, E. R., Day, S., & Garety, P. A. (1996). The Peters *et al.* Delusion Inventory (PDI): New norms for the 21-item version. *Schizophrenia Research, 18*(2–3), 118–119.

Peters, E., & Garety, P. (2006). Cognitive functioning in delusions: A longitudinal analysis. *Behaviour Research and Therapy, 44*, 481–514.

Peters, E. R., Joseph, S. A., & Garety, P. A. (1999). Measurement of delusional ideation in the normal population: Introducing the PDI (Peters *et al* Delusions Inventory). *Schizophrenia Bulletin, 25*(3), 553–576.

Phillips, L. D., & Edwards, W. (1966). Conservatism in a simple probability inference task. *Journal of Experimental Psychology, 72*, 346–354.

Plato. (1993). *Republic* (R. Waterfield, trans.). Oxford: Oxford University Press.

Rado, S. (1953). Dynamics and classification of disordered behaviour. *American Journal of Psychiatry, 110*, 406–416.

Rhodes, S. K., Galbraith, N. D., & Manktelow, K. I. (2012). Investigating the domain-specificity of the jump to conclusions bias. *Unpublished manuscript*, University of Wolverhampton, UK.

Ross, K., Freeman, D., Dunn, G., & Garety, P. (2009). A randomized experimental investigation of reasoning training for people with delusions. *Schizophrenia Bulletin, 37*(2), 324–333.

Rossell, S., & O'Regan, A. (2008). Jumping to conclusions in delusions: Fact or fallacy? *Abstracts Schizophrenia Research, 102*(1–3), 127.

Sadler-Smith, E. (2011). The intuitive style: Relationships with local/global and verbal/visual styles, gender and superstitious reasoning. *Learning and Individual Differences, 21*, 263–270.

Sartorius, N., Jablensky, A., Korten, A., Ernberg, G., Anker, M., Cooper, J. E., & Day, R. (1986). Early manifestations and first contact incidence of schizophrenia in different cultures. *Psychological medicine, 16*(4), 909–928.

Shenhav, A, Rand, D. G., & Greene, J. D. (2012) Divine intuition: Cognitive style influences belief in God. *Journal of Experimental Psychology: General, 141*, 423–428.

So, S. H. W., Freeman, D., & Garety, P. A. (2008). Impact of state anxiety on the jumping to conclusions delusion bias. *Australian and New Zealand Journal of Psychiatry, 42*, 879–886.

Spitzer, M. (1990). On defining delusions. *Comprehensive Psychiatry, 31*, 377–397.

Stanovich, K. E. (1999). *Who Is Rational? Studies of Individual Differences in Reasoning*. Mahwah, NJ: Erlbaum.

Stanovich, K. E. (2009). Distinguishing the reflective, algorithmic, and autonomous minds: Is it time for a tri-process theory? In J. St. B. T Evans & K. Frankish (Eds.), *In Two Minds: Dual Processes and Beyond*. Oxford: Oxford University Press.

Strack, F., & Deutsch, R. (2004). Reflective and impulsive determinants of social behaviour. *Personality and Social Psychology Review, 8*, 220–247.

Toyosawa, J., & Karasawa, K. (2004). Individual differences on judgment using the ratio-bias and the Linda problem: Adopting CEST and Japanese version of REI. *Japanese Journal of Social Psychology, 20*(2), 85–92.

Tranel, D., Damasio, H., & Damasio, A. R. (1995). Double dissociation between overt and covert face recognition. *Journal of Cognitive Neuroscience, 7*, 425–432.

Tversky, A., & Kahneman, D. (1974). Judgement under uncertainty: Heuristics and biases. *Science, 27*, 1124–1131.

van Os, J., Hanssen, M., Bijl, R. V., & Ravelli, A. (2000). Strauss (1969) revisited: A psychosis continuum in the normal population? *Schizophrenia Research, 45*, 11–20.

van Os, J., Linscott, R. J., Myin-Germeys, I., Delespaul, P., & Krabbendam, L. (2009). A systematic review and meta-analysis of the psychosis continuum: Evidence for a psychosis proneness-persistence-impairment model of psychotic disorder. *Psychological Medicine, 39*(2), 179–195.

Waller, H., Freeman, D., Jolley, S., Dunn, G., & Garety, P. (2011). Targeting reasoning biases in delusions: A pilot study of the Maudsley Review Training Programme for individuals with persistent, high conviction delusions. *Journal or Behaviour Therapy and Experiential Psychiatry, 42*, 414–421.

Warman, D. M., Lysaker, P., Martin, J. M., Davis, L., & Haudenschield, S. L. (2007). Jumping-to-conclusions and the continuum of delusional beliefs. *Behaviour Research and Therapy, 45*, 1255–1269.

White, L. O., & Mansell, W. (2009). Failing to ponder? Delusion-prone individuals rush to conclusions. *Clinical Psychology and Psychotherapy, 16*(2), 111–124.

Zawadzki, J. A., Woodward, T. S., Sokolowski, H. M., Boon, H. S., Wong, A. H. C., & Menon, M. (2012). Cognitive factors associated with sub-clinical delusional ideation in the general population. *Psychiatry Research, 197*, 345–349.

Ziegler, M., Rief, W., Werner, S. M., Mehl, S., & Lincoln, T. M. (2008). Hasty decision-making in a variety of tasks: Does it contribute to the development of delusions? *Psychology and Psychotherapy: Theory, Research and Practice, 81*(3), 237–245.

Zimbardo, P. G., Andersen, S, M., & Kabat, L. G. (1981). Induced hearing deficit generates experimental paranoia. *Science, 212*(4502), 1529–1531.

Zuckerman, M. (1979). *Sensation Seeking: Beyond the Optimal Level of Arousal*. Hillsdale, NJ: Lawrence Erlbaum Associates.

5
REASONING IN SCHIZOPHRENIA

Amelia Gangemi and Valentina Cardella

Introduction

I was awash in a sea of irrationality. The Voices swirled around me, teaching me their Wisdom. Their Wisdom was of the Deep Meaning, and I struggled to understand. They told me their secrets and insights, piece by piece. Slowly, I was beginning to make sense of it all. It was no delusion, I knew – in contrast to what the doctors said. "Erin, you are a scientist," they'd begin. "You are intelligent, rational. Tell me, then, how can you believe that there are rats inside your brain? They're just plain too big. Besides, how could they get in?" They were right. About my being smart, I mean; I was, after all, a graduate student in the neuroscience program at the University of British Columbia. But how could they relate that rationality to the logic of the Deep Meaning? For it was due to the Deep Meaning that the rats had infiltrated my system and were inhabiting my brain. They gnawed relentlessly on my neurons, causing massive degeneration. This was particularly upsetting to me, as I depended on a sharp mind for my work in neuroscience.

The rats spent significant periods of time consuming brain matter in the occipital lobe of my brain. I knew, from my studies, that this was the primary visual cortex. And yet, I experienced no visual deficits. Obviously, I realized, I had a very unique brain: I was able to regenerate large sections of my central nervous system – and do so extremely quickly. I relaxed a bit, but not entirely. Surely no good could come of having rats feed on my brain cells. So I sought means of ridding my body of them. I bled them out through self-cutting and banging my head until the skin broke, bloody. Continually, I kept my brain active, electrocuting the rats that happened to be feasting on the activated neurons.

"As a neuroscientist, how can you believe all this?" the doctors queried. "Because it is all of the Deep Meaning." "But it doesn't make sense. It's irrational. You surely know that." "Because," I replied deliberately, as if talking to a child, "The Deep Meaning transcends scientific logic." How else could it be true? I did know all the logical limitations of my ideas, but I was also receiving such intense messages that the rats and my regenerating brain were also true. So I rationally concluded that the one superseded the other. Still, I could use some of my scientific understanding to deal with that which the Deep Meaning imposed on me. Like the electrocution: I knew that when neurons are activated, they transmit signals using electrical current. I therefore reasoned that, since the rats were so small, on the order of magnitude of a neuron, they would experience the electricity as violent and perhaps fatal. [. . .]

The rats weren't the only thing that bothered me. My neighbor across the alley spied continually on me. He wanted to kill me, I learned from the Voices and the Deep Meaning. Scared, I put up some dark curtains. I slept well that night but awoke to a terrifying truth: the night before, he had entered my room and installed a tracking device in my abdomen. Now he could track me everywhere; there was no more hiding.

I reasoned, rational. But the doctors concluded differently. Delusion and paranoia were their words, their explanations. And there are many other such stories. Each time, I would be able to evaluate things from two perspectives: my scientific logic and the explanation from the Deep Meaning. As the doctors would say, these corresponded to rationality and irrationality, respectively. But, given the input I had from the Voices (auditory hallucinations, the doctors say) and the immense feelings of truth from the Deep Meaning, I was in fact fighting to preserve my rationality in the face of the irrational. I valued my logical mind so dearly that when it began to be challenged by schizophrenic hallucinations, delusions, and disorders of the ability to ascribe meaningfulness, I used everything available to me to try and figure out what were the most rational explanations. I craved rationality, and rationality to me was taking all evidence and making conclusions. Even if they didn't conform to everyone else's ideas of what was rational, I was fighting to maintain, at the very least, the integrity of my own rationality. Antipsychotic medication has helped to distance me from the Voices and the Deep Meaning. While I never quite give up these as irrational, I am aware that they influence my ideas of, and my actions in response to, rationality. I have come to believe that in order to truly understand others, be they schizophrenic or otherwise, we must not only discover their thoughts, feelings, and actions, but we must look to understand how they connect these into a coherent structure and to recognize that no matter what this structure looks like, it is the product of a rational mind.

(Stefanidis, 2006, pp. 422–423)

These words were written by a schizophrenic patient in the "first person account" section of the *Schizophrenia Bulletin*. We have chosen to begin our chapter with this story because it addresses two crucial questions simultaneously, questions that are the main focus of this work. The first one is the following: are reasoning processes biased in schizophrenia? The second question overlaps, but not completely, with the first one: are schizophrenic patients irrational?

Schizophrenia is one of the most severe forms of mental disorder. According to the DSM V (APA, 2013), the common signs of schizophrenia are delusions, hallucinations, disorganized thinking, negative symptoms and disorganized behaviour. Delusions are false beliefs, usually bizarre, which are not open to change in the light of conflicting evidence. In some cases, they involve extraordinarily bizarre beliefs, e.g. having a completely see-through mind, with telepathically accessible thoughts, or having a microchip in the brain by which alien entities control what the subject says or does. The hallucinations are more common in the auditory form, and they are one of the most distressing symptoms of schizophrenia (patients can hear voices almost constantly). The term "disorganization" refers to a group of various symptoms that comprise the loosening of thought associations, disorganized speech and bizarre behaviour. The loosening of thought associations is the lack of an obvious connection between one thought and the next, and it has been regarded as the core symptom of schizophrenia since Bleuler's time (Bleuler, 1911). Schizophrenia also involves alterations in language and behaviour, with both often becoming incoherent, poor, bizarre and incomprehensible (in other words, disorganized). The negative symptoms involve a withdrawal or lack of a number of functions or traits, as in anhedonia – the inability to experience pleasure; catatonia – motor immobility; and abulia – impaired ability to perform voluntary actions.

Given that schizophrenics suffer from different kinds of severe symptoms, that they have difficulties in keeping the connection between thoughts, that they show thought disorder and hold bizarre beliefs, the question is: to what extent do these deficits impair their reasoning abilities? And, moreover, do these symptoms cause a clear deficit in rationality? Delusional beliefs, in fact, with their somewhat absurd topics, and with their persistency, seem to be a clear proof of schizophrenics' lack of rationality (Huq, Garety & Hemsley, 1988; Garety, Hemsley & Wessely, 1991; Garety & Hemsley, 1994; Bentall, 1994).

Nevertheless, it is not that easy to show that schizophrenics have evident impairments in reasoning. In other words, the idea that a failure to reason by conventional logical rules is typical of schizophrenia is controversial. In this chapter, we will try to highlight the different positions, particularly focusing on two perspectives: that of phenomenological psychiatry, and, most of all, that of cognitive psychology. We will separate these studies on the basis of the ability analysed: syllogistic reasoning, conditional reasoning and probabilistic reasoning. The aim of this chapter is to provide an overview of reasoning abilities in schizophrenia, in order to explore whether this form of mental disorder is also characterized by specific reasoning deficits. Moreover, we will address the problem of rationality in schizophrenia, trying to determine whether schizophrenics' thinking and behaviours show a clear lack of rationality.

Syllogistic reasoning

Syllogistic reasoning is a form a deductive reasoning where a quantified statement of a specific form (the conclusion) is inferred from two other quantified statements (the premises). von Domarus (1944) opened research on schizophrenic reasoning with a study on syllogisms that not only showed that schizophrenics break the rules of conventional logic, but that assumed that this defect in reasoning abilities is the true cause of the disorganization typical of this disease. In particular, the author found a severe impairment in schizophrenics, the so-called von Domarus principle: a principle of identity which entails a false assumption of the identity of two subjects made on the basis of identical predicates ("whereas the logician accepts identities only upon the basis of identical subjects, the paralogician accepts identities upon the basis of identical predicates", von Domarus, 1944, p. 111). In other words, people with schizophrenia would draw conclusions that are grounded on the identity of the predicates, rather than on the identity of the subjects. For example, from the premises "a has the property x" and "b has the property x", a schizophrenic would conclude "a is b". Arieti (1964, p. 27) would later clarify this principle through an example that would become very famous: one of his schizophrenic patients thought she was the Virgin Mary, because of this kind of reasoning: The Virgin Mary was a virgin; I am a virgin; therefore, *I am the Virgin Mary*. Arieti (1964) claimed that schizophrenia was marked by paleological thought, which breaks the rules of Aristotelian logic, such as the principle of non-contradiction, according to which, "it is impossible to hold the same thing to be and not to be", or the principle of identity, "A = A", "a being is what it is"; these are the reasons why schizophrenic thought appears incorrect, obscure and meaningless.

Because of the von Domarus principle, schizophrenics would show many difficulties in syllogistic reasoning, in that they would draw invalid conclusions grounded on the identity of the predicates, rather than on the identity of the subjects. But, already in the 1960s, Gottesman and Chapman, though agreeing with the hypothesis of the defect in syllogistic reasoning, showed that there is no difference between schizophrenic and normal subjects in the tendency to identify two subjects on the basis of identical predicates: thus, the von Domarus principle would not be true for schizophrenics (Gottesman & Chapman, 1960; see also Williams, 1964). But, apart from the von Domarus principle, do schizophrenics have specific defects in deductive reasoning? According to some authors, they do: Goel, Bartolo, St. Clair and Venneri (2004), for example, administered syllogisms that were either emotionally salient or emotionally neutral to schizophrenic patients, and they found schizophrenics' performance to be very poor in all sorts of tests, also in the emotionally neutral variant, where healthy controls performed better. But, as noticed by Mirian, Heinrichs, McDermid and Vaz (2011), this study was weakened by a clear floor effect in the patient group.

Actually, when schizophrenics and controls are matched for education and IQ, the differences in their performance become very small, as showed, for example, by the work of Wason (1966), Belvin (1964) and Maher (1992). In a revealing study by Kemp and colleagues (Kemp, Chua, McKenna & David, 1997), schizophrenic patients with delusion and control subjects showed no differences in performance on syllogistic reasoning tasks. More precisely, this task tested the capacity to judge the validity of 40 syllogisms whose content was believable (e.g. "no priests are criminals, some religious people are criminals, some religious people are not priests") or unbelievable ("no religious people are criminals, some priests are criminals, some priests are not religious people"), in a group of relatively intelligent delusional schizophrenics (currently delusional, with an average IQ of 108). Their performances did not differ from those of the control subjects.

In a recent study based on a survey of previous works and on the results of different syllogistic reasoning tasks, Mirian and colleagues (2011) concluded that, when schizophrenic patients make mistakes about the judgment of a syllogism's validity, they do so because of a general weakness in cognitive performance (e.g. a lower I.Q.), rather than because of a specific impairment of schizophrenia. In other words, they make mistakes when they have a lower IQ or some other cognitive deficit.

Moreover, it has been recently highlighted that, in some cases, schizophrenics are even more logical than normal subjects. For example, Owen and colleagues (Owen, Cutting & David, 2007) tested both "pure reasoning", using valid and invalid syllogisms, and common sense, using syllogistic content that conformed to practical knowledge or departed from practical knowledge. Two series of syllogisms were presented to schizophrenic patients, each with a conflict between deductive truth and common sense truth; the first series contained valid syllogisms that were non-common sense (e.g. "all buildings speak loudly; a hospital does not speak loudly; therefore, a hospital is not a building"). The second series contained common sense syllogisms that were invalid (e.g. "if the sun rises, then the sun is in the east; the sun is in the east; therefore, the sun rises"). Subjects were asked to accept the premises of each syllogism as true and then to decide on the truth or falsity of the third sentence. Results show that, under conditions where common sense and logic conflict, people with schizophrenia reason more logically than healthy individuals. In fact, they seem to perform even better than normal controls in the second series of syllogisms, the non-common sense ones (e.g. that conclude with "a hospital is not a building"); that is quite intriguing, because they do not get diverted by the content, which is counter-intuitive, and they apply logical rules better than controls, recognizing the validity of an argument also when its conclusion goes against common sense.

According to Owen, we can interpret these results in two ways: either people with schizophrenia are better at logic, or they are worse at common sense. The authors lean towards the last hypothesis, but they claim, however, that "concepts of rationality that prioritize theoretical reasoning over and above practical reasoning might apply more accurately in a pathological example of human thinking than in a healthy one" (Owen *et al.*, 2007, p. 454).

Here, we can notice that the question of schizophrenic *reasoning* begins to mingle with that of schizophrenic *rationality*. But if we want to find studies that focus particularly on rationality in schizophrenia, a completely different perspective has to be taken into account, as well, one that has a long history: that of philosophical psychiatry. According to this approach, psychotic subjects err on the side of the excess of rationality, rather than on the side of its lack. Minkowski (1927), for example, used the expression morbid rationalism to identify that excess of rationality which leads schizophrenic patients to act in a very cold, hyperlogical way. The hypertrophy of the rational aspects of thought is what makes them perceive the world in a very rigid, intellectual way. Binswanger (1956), on the other hand, showed that schizophrenics' behaviour is guided by a rigid consequentiality, a logic that is brought to the extreme and that makes their actions very bizarre. But we will come back to this topic in the last paragraph of this chapter.

Conditional reasoning

Conditional reasoning is a form of deductive logic based on the structure "if . . . then . . .". We can draw two valid inferences from premises that have this structure: the modus ponens (given p, one can conclude q), and the modus tollens (given not-q, one can conclude not-p). In the mentioned article by Kemp and colleagues (1997), the schizophrenic ability in conditional reasoning was tested. Going into more detail, 40 reasoning tasks with the "if P, then Q" form were presented, together with different alternatives. Each alternative offered a choice of responses: true, false, and can't say, and subjects were asked to tick the correct one. The content was either neutral (e.g. "If she meets her friend, then she will go to a play. She does not meet her friend – what follows?") or emotional ("If she is raped then she will go to the police. She goes to the police – what follows?"). Results showed no relevant difference in the performance of schizophrenic patients and controls in the neutral conditionals. But, when the content was emotional, even if both groups performed worse, delusional patients were more "sensitive", and they made an increased number of fallacies. This result is consistent with the data of a growing literature, which focuses on the link between emotions and delusions (Bentall, 1994; Freeman, 2008) and shows the presence of a deep relationship between the confirmatory reasoning that is typical of delusions, and negative emotions, which seem to be a sort of trigger of the delusion itself. However, Kemp and colleagues (1997, p. 402) notice that "the manipulation of emotional content appears to make the normal subjects behave more like the deluded subjects, suppressing more valid inferences and fewer fallacies". Thus, when the content recalls a negative emotion, all subjects perform worse, but delusional ones are even more sensitive than controls.

Other studies seem to show that schizophrenic patients can be even better than healthy participants in conditional reasoning. Mellet and colleagues (Mellet *et al.*, 2006) administered a demanding reasoning task to 26 schizophrenic patients and 26 healthy participants, known to promote a bias (i.e. a reasoning error) in healthy subjects, triggered by a misleading context. Subjects were instructed to falsify conditional rules such as "If there is not a red square on the left, then there is a yellow circle on the right". The vast majority of normal subjects produce an incorrect response in juxtaposing a red square on the left and a yellow circle on the right. This time, the correct answer requires ignoring the figures quoted in the rule (e.g. keep the antecedent true: not a red square; make the consequent false: not a yellow circle). But the context of the task acts here as a trap: the presence of the word "not" together with the visual presentation of the figures quoted in the rule serves as a trigger to activate the "not heuristic", consisting of matching the item that is negated (Evans, 1998). In most everyday situations, using an item or performing an action preceded by "not" is indeed a good way to break the rule (for example, when we touch an object we are not supposed to touch). However, in the particular case of conditional rules having "not" in the antecedent, this leads to a matching strategy that induces an incorrect answer. Schizophrenic patients presented a surprising imperviousness to the reasoning bias and had significantly better logical performance than their paired healthy participants. According to the authors, patients are better because of their deficit in the context processing that usually impairs them, but that in this case, gives them a cognitive advantage over healthy controls.

Probabilistic reasoning

There is a large amount of research on probabilistic reasoning in psychotic patients, because these studies aim to explain the basis of delusions, both in schizophrenia and in paranoia. Paranoia, also called delusional disorder, is a psychiatric condition characterized by the presence of non-bizarre delusions, such as persecutory or grandiose ones, in the absence of other psychotic symptoms; therefore, anyone who wants to study delusions must deal with paranoid patients, as well. Many authors, among which Bentall (Bentall, Corcoran, Howard, Blackwood & Kinderman, 2001; Bentall, 1994), Garety (Garety, Hemsley & Wessely, 1991; Garety & Hemsley, 1994; Garety et al., 2005), Freeman (Freeman, Garety, Kuipers, Fowler & Bebbington, 2002; Freeman, 2008) and Langdon (Langdon, Ward & Coltheart, 2010), have focused on schizophrenic and paranoid patients with persecutory delusions, and identified a hypothetical deficit in data gathering, called jumping to conclusions. Individuals with delusions seem to request minimal information in situations where information is available, and to report a high level of confidence in their decisions (Peters, Thornton, Siksou, Linney & MacCabe, 2008). The task used to test this bias is the "beads in jars" (Phillips & Edwards, 1966; Garety & Freeman, 1999), in which individuals are presented with two jars each containing 100 coloured beads. There are 60 beads of one colour (e.g. black) and 40 beads of another (e.g. yellow) in one jar, while the other jar contains beads in opposite proportions (i.e. 40 black and 60 yellow). The jars are then removed from view. Upon request from the participant, beads will be presented, one at a time, from just one of the jars in a predetermined order. Participants can view as many beads as they want until they are certain from which jar the beads have been drawn. The number of beads requested before making a decision seems to be significantly lower in delusional patients (1–2, versus 3–4 of healthy subjects).

But these results still remain controversial. For example, Menon and colleagues (Menon, Pomarol-Clotet, McKenna & McCarthy, 2006) did not find a link between delusions and jumping to conclusions; they only found a tendency to jump to conclusions in schizophrenia. In other words, it is not true that only delusional subjects show this kind of bias. But, even if these data would disconfirm the link between delusion and jumping to conclusions, they could possibly confirm the presence of a link between schizophrenia and jumping to conclusions. But this is not the case. Even in schizophrenic patients, this cognitive style disappears when the role of memory is taken into account; when a variant of the task, with a memory aid, was carried out, there was in fact no difference between the performance of the schizophrenics and the controls. Just as in the case of syllogistic reasoning, where the differences in performance between patients and controls disappeared when the IQ variable was included, in data gathering the differences can decrease when the test includes other variables, like memory. Thus, this probabilistic reasoning bias may not be causally related to either delusions or schizophrenia, but might instead be partly due to a weakened memory or to a combination of impaired memory and executive functions.

But there is another element that we have to consider. The jumping to conclusions bias, when present, seems to make the performance of the subjects even better. For example, Conway and colleagues (Conway et al., 2002) presented paranoid patients with two reasoning tasks. The first one was the beads in jars; the second was a more complex gambling task. Subjects were asked to choose cards from four different decks; each card could cause them either to win some money or to lose some money. Some decks were "bad decks" (leading to losses), and other decks were "good decks" (leading to gains). After some time, subjects were expected to learn which decks were the good ones. In both tasks, paranoid patients showed the jumping to conclusions bias, requesting less information than controls, but the interesting fact is that, in the vast majority of cases, these hasty conclusions were correct (that is to say, they identified the right-coloured jar or the good deck).

The authors claim that a cognitive style which allows conclusions to be drawn as soon as possible and starting from a limited number of elements not only is not pathological in itself, but could rather be useful in some conditions, as showed by a large amount of research in the field of cognitive psychology (Friedrich, 1993; Trope & Lieberman, 1996; Smeets, de Jong & Mayer, 2000). This mechanism is usually triggered by a feeling of danger, when we sense a potential threat. In these cases, we activate a strategy that is known in the literature as *better safe than sorry* (cf. for example, Mancini, Gangemi & Johnson-Laird, 2007): we usually tend to confirm our fears and jump to conclusions. For instance, there is the smell of something burning, and we automatically get alarmed and open the windows, without even checking whether something is actually burning. If we were wrong, we opened the windows in vain, but it is better to act in vain than underestimate danger and waste precious time checking the data. Coming back to psychopathology, it is a matter of fact that those who hold persecutory delusions (be they schizophrenic or paranoid) see dangers and threats everywhere; a subject can look at two people whispering and jump to the conclusion that they are plotting against him and making an attempt to his life, and he can, therefore, quickly run away in order to leave them behind. If he was not right, he ran away unnecessarily, but if he was right, he fled to safety. So, there is really nothing wrong with this reaction.

Many authors that claim that people with delusions have a jumping to conclusions bias also claim that they have another bias in probabilistic reasoning: these patients (for example, according to Kaney, Bowen-Jones, Dewey & Bentall, 1997) would tend to judge negative events happening to themselves as more likely than controls. But in the same study by Kaney and colleagues, patients with schizophrenia and persecutory delusions also reported greater estimates of the likelihood of negative events happening to other people, and this would simply indicate a generally negative world-view, rather than a specific bias.

The theories we have considered thus far, concerning the deficits in probabilistic reasoning, seem to be more controversial than expected. But what we found quite intriguing about this kind of reasoning in schizophrenia comes from the already mentioned article by Kemp and colleagues (1997). In this article, the authors tested probabilistic reasoning in schizophrenia by administering four questions. These consist of descriptions of the background of four people, with several pieces of contextual information (vignettes). The subject is asked to choose the most likely of three scenarios, none of which can be chosen with certainty since none relates precisely to information contained in the vignette. One example of this description is the following:

> Sally is 29 years old. She ran away from home at the age of 15 because she got pregnant. She is sexually attractive and has had many partners. Recently, she has lost a lot of weight and has had to go into hospital for tests.

After this description, subjects were asked to judge the likelihood of these different alternatives: Sally . . . (a) is a famous high court judge; (b) is a teacher in a primary school; (c) is a teacher in a primary school and has AIDS. In this example, the first alternative is improbable, the second is possible although unlikely (the correct choice) and the third combines the second alternative with a likely description. Normal people tend to choose the response that contains contextual information which accords with the schema they have created on the basis of the vignette (in this case, the response (c), where the word "AIDS" is mentioned). Normal people rely on representativeness to make judgments (the representativeness heuristic); therefore we think that something is more likely because it is more representative (Tversky & Kahneman, 1982). However, in this specific case, this means that two events are judged as more likely than one of the events alone (a logical impossibility known as the conjunction fallacy). The results reveal a slightly higher rate of conjunction fallacies in the controls, while schizophrenics have more correct responses; they seem therefore to be less sensitive to this conjunction fallacy.

Thus, also in probabilistic reasoning, as for the syllogistic and conditional one, not only do specific deficits in schizophrenia remain to be shown, but in some cases, schizophrenic patients seem to reason even better than controls.

Conclusions: are schizophrenics bad at reasoning?

What is the difference, then, between schizophrenics and healthy subjects in reasoning abilities? Do schizophrenic patients follow the formal rules of logic or do they make more mistakes than normal subjects? At this point, we have to say something more about the notion of rationality. A lot of research seems to show that normal people do not usually follow the formal rules of logic (e.g. Wason, 1966; Kahneman, Slovic & Tversky, 1982; Johnson-Laird, 1983; Evans, 1989, 2002; Johnson-Laird & Byrne, 1991; Plous, 1993; Rips, 1994; Newstead & Evans, 1995; Osherson, 1995; Evans & Over, 1996; Baron, 1998; Shafir & Tversky, 1995; Johnson-Laird, 2006). The content of the single task, the context it activates, the beliefs it involves, all of this seems to influence human performance; we try to be rational, but that does not mean that we are always successful. Human reasoning appears to be "belief sensitive", and "goal sensitive", in that its strategies also depend on the perceived utilities, and thus, we can commit more logical errors than expected (Manktelow & Over, 1991; de Jong, Mayer & van den Hout, 1997; de Jong, Haenen, Schmidt & Mayer, 1998; Smeets et al., 2000).

On the other hand, studies on reasoning in anxiety and mood disorders (e.g. obsessive-compulsive disorder, hypochondria, depression) seem to show that people who suffer from psychological disorders are not bad at reasoning, rather they follow the same rules as healthy people, and patients could become expert reasoners in the domain of their disorder (cf. Smeets et al., 2000; Harvey, Watkins, Mansell & Shafran, 2004; Mancini, Gangemi & Johnson-Laird, 2007).

In line with this research, recent literature shows that even a severe mental illness like schizophrenia does not involve a deficit in reasoning abilities. Both in syllogistic and in conditional reasoning, differences in performance between controls and schizophrenics become surprisingly small when patients are matched for IQ or for other cognitive abilities. And, as regarding probabilistic reasoning, the jumping to conclusions, which is present in many schizophrenics, is likely a dependent variable as well, since it tends to disappear when the role of memory is taken into account.

What we would like to stress, however, is that under certain circumstances, schizophrenic subjects seem to reason even better than healthy ones (except for their greater sensitivity to emotional content). We could now return to the research tradition we mentioned above: that of psychiatric phenomenology. The approach of this kind of psychiatry is completely different to that of cognitive psychology, and of clinical psychiatry, as well. It is inspired by existentialism on one hand, and phenomenology on the other, and it aims to describe the basic structures of subjective experience in people suffering from mental disorders. The way the patient perceives and experiences the world has to be completely understood in order to find a reason in his behaviour, no matter how strange it might seem. Many authors that embrace this perspective claim that the problem in schizophrenic reasoning is not the lack of logic, but the excess of it, a sort of intellectual attitude toward the world. Binswanger (1956), for example, showed that the most bizarre actions are sometimes due to an excess of logic, such as when a schizophrenic patient gives his daughter (who is terminally ill) a coffin as a Christmas present. This action, which appears as something that is totally absurd and inhuman, actually derives from a sort of "syllogistic" reasoning: a present has to be useful, and for a dying daughter the only useful thing is a coffin; then, the only gift that the patient conceives is a coffin. The logic in this reasoning is faultless, but the result of this kind of logic is a behaviour that is striking for its strangeness and lack of empathy. Schizophrenic patients seem to have no choice, they see no alternatives, and cannot help but grasp on to logic because nothing else is left (cf. Pennisi, 1998). This sort of hyperlogical attitude can concern social relationships, too; Stanghellini and Ballerini (2011), for example, use the expression "algorithmic conception of sociality" to indicate the effort to understand the rules of social situations by building an explicit algorithm. Thus, schizophrenic patients can spend hours observing people's behaviour in order to "extract" mechanistic rules of social conduct. As one patient said: "I like to walk around. I am fascinated by observing other people in everyday activity and seeing how it functions" (Stanghellini & Ballerini, 2011, p. 187). Anna Rau, a schizophrenic girl analysed by another exponent of phenomenological psychiatry, Blankenburg, complains that she has to *study* the rules, while other people simply *know* them (Blankenburg, 1971). In other words, schizophrenic patients try to compensate the lack of common sense by elaborating a rational method that allows them to understand other people.

An increasing amount of data coming from the cognitive perspective seems to reach the same conclusion of phenomenological psychiatry; that the problem of schizophrenics is not that they are irrational. As we have seen, in some cases, schizophrenics are more logical than healthy people, they are able to judge the validity of a syllogism without being distracted by its content, they falsify conditional rules without being diverted by heuristic traps and they are usually less sensitive to a number of reasoning biases. Thus, can we conclude that they are more rational than healthy subjects?

Maybe it is time to dig into the notion of rationality a little further. Although this notion has been a crucial concept throughout the history of many disciplines (philosophy, economics, psychology and so on), a clear and uncontroversial concept of human rationality is still missing. But the analysis of the debate about this issue goes beyond the aims of this chapter. The question we want to address now is whether schizophrenia can help us to understand the concept of rationality a little more, and, on the other side, whether a richer conception of rationality can allow us to figure out what kind of rationality is impaired, if this is the case, in schizophrenia. Actually, when we describe a behaviour as rational, we can intend very different properties. For example, we can mean that the person has *reasons* to act in that way. Or, and this is something very different, we can mean that his act conforms to the normative principles of logic. Or, and this is something else again, we can intend that his behaviour is coherent with his beliefs. In an interesting work on normativity and rationality in mental disorders, Bermudez (2001) proposes the distinction between procedural rationality and epistemic rationality. When we reason in accordance with the principles of logic, we are procedurally rational; while the epistemic rationality relates to the capacity to revise our beliefs in response to changes in the evidence. His claim is that reasoning problems in schizophrenia are failings in epistemic rationality – that is, they come from difficulties in evaluating evidence and testing hypotheses; that might be the reason why delusional beliefs are maintained. Thus, delusions are not irrational because they are illogical or unintelligible, but because they are not amenable to change in light of conflicting evidence (one can find the same definition of delusion in the last edition of DSM, 2013). But it is important to stress that patients have reasons to do so. The delusional belief is something very important for them, something their lives depend on. So, it is not surprising that they do not want to lose them. It is something that we do, as well, when we attach importance to a particular belief (we are blind to counterevidence because we do not want to change our belief). And, by the way, the fact that delusional beliefs have a sort of "special treatment" is confirmed by some authors who showed that schizophrenics do not suffer from a general deficit in belief revision. For example, Kaliuzhna, Chambon, Franck, Testud and Van der Henst (2012) showed that, when delusion-neutral material is used in an advice-taking situation (where the subjects have to correct their initial estimate in a certain task after receiving the estimate of another person), schizophrenic patients do revise their beliefs, they take into account socially provided information and are not overconfident about their judgments. Thus, the impairment of epistemic rationality is very selective; it seems to concern only delusional beliefs.

What we would like to note, however, is that, according to Bermudez (2001), schizophrenics do not have impairments in procedural rationality. In other words, they do not break formal rules of logic. And this is exactly what the studies on reasoning in schizophrenia mentioned above seem to suggest. Defects on logical reasoning are not typical of schizophrenia, because they seem to depend on other variables, like low IQ or impairments in memory. When we find something strange in their way of thinking, it is often because, on the contrary, they seem too logical, too rational. And, in everyday life, being more logical does not always pay. In fact, the excess of logic makes the life of schizophrenics much more complicated, as highlighted by phenomenological psychiatry. Moreover, fighting to save rationality is sometimes what makes schizophrenic symptoms even worse (as one can notice in the self report we began this chapter with).

Thus, we agree with Owen and colleagues (2007) when they suggest a new concept of rationality: we cannot assume that schizophrenic patients are bad in reasoning, because they break formal rules less often than normal subjects, and maybe what is wrong with them, what makes their thinking so peculiar, is the predominance of theoretical reason over practical reason. Therefore, it appears to us that these words, written 50 years ago, are still true:

> in psychotherapeutic work with intelligent schizophrenics one is tempted, again and again, to conclude that they would be much better off, much more "normal", if they could only somehow blunt the acuity of their thinking and thus alleviate the paralyzing effect it has on their actions.
>
> *(Watzlawick, Beavin & Jackson, 1967, p. 222)*

References

American Psychiatric Association (APA) (2013). *Diagnostic and Statistical Manual of Mental Disorders (5th ed.)*. Washington: American Psychiatric Association.

Arieti, A. (1964). *Interpretazione della schizofrenia*. Milano: Feltrinelli.

Baron, J. (1998). *Judgment Misguided: Intuition and Error in Public Decision Making*. Oxford: Oxford University Press.

Belvin, W. E. (1964). Deductive reasoning in schizophrenia. *The Journal of Abnormal and Social Psychology, 69*(1), 47–61.

Bentall, R. P. (1994). Cognitive biases and abnormal beliefs: Towards a model of persecutory delusions. In David, A. & Cutting, J. (Eds.), *The Neuropsychology of Schizophrenia*. Hove, UK: Lawrence Erlbaum Associates Ltd.

Bentall, R. P., Corcoran, R., Howard, R., Blackwood, N., & Kinderman, P. (2001). Persecutory delusions: A review and theoretical integration. *Clinical Psychology Review, 21*(8), 1143–1192.

Bermudez, J. L. (2001). Normativity and rationality in delusional psychiatric disorders. *Mind & Language, 16*, 457–493.

Binswanger, L. (1956). *Drei Formen missglückten Daseins. Verstiegenheit, Verschrobenheit, Manieriertheit*. Tübingen: Niemeyer.

Blankenburg, W. (1971). *Der Verlust der natürlichen Selbstverständlichkeit*. Stuttgart: Ferdinand Enke Verlag.

Bleuler, E. (1911). *Dementia Praecox oder Gruppe der Schizophrenien*. Leipzig: Deuticke.

Conway, C. R., Bollini, A. M., Graham, B. G., Keefe, R. S., Schiffman, S. S., & McEvoy, J. P. (2002). Sensory acuity and reasoning in delusional disorder. *Comprehensive Psychiatry, 43*(3), 175–178.

de Jong, P. J., Haenen, M., Schmidt, A., & Mayer, B. (1998) Hypochondriasis: The role of fear-confirming reasoning. *Behaviour Research and Therapy, 36*, 65–74.

de Jong, P. J., Mayer, B., & van den Hout, M. (1997) Conditional reasoning and phobic fear: Evidence for a fear-confirming pattern. *Behaviour Research and Therapy, 35*, 507–516.

Evans, J. St. B. T. (1989). *Bias in Human Reasoning: Causes and Consequences*. Hove, UK: Lawrence Erlbaum Associates Ltd.

Evans, J. St. B. T. (1998). Matching bias in conditional reasoning. Do we understand it after 25 years? *Thinking and Reasoning, 4*, 45–82.

Evans, J. St. B. T. (2002). Logic and human reasoning: An assessment of the deduction paradigm. *Psychological Bulletin, 128*, 978–996.

Evans, J. St. B. T., & Over, D. E. (1996). *Rationality and Reasoning*. Sussex, UK: Psychology Press.

Freeman, D. (2008). The assessment of persecutory ideation. In D. Freeman, R. Bentall & P. Garety (Eds.), *Persecutory Delusions*. Oxford: Oxford University Press.

Freeman, D., Garety, P. A., Kuipers, E., Fowler, D., & Bebbington, P. E. (2002). A cognitive model of persecutory delusions. *British Journal of Clinical Psychology, 41*(4), 331–347.

Friedrich, J. (1993). Primary Error Detection and Minimization (PEDMIN) strategies in social cognition: A reinterpretation of confirmation bias phenomena. *Psychological Review, 100*, 298–319.

Garety, P. A., & Freeman, D. (1999). Cognitive approaches to delusions: A critical review of theories and evidence. *British Journal of Clinical Psychology, 38*, 113–154.

Garety, P. A., Freeman, D., Jolley, S., Dunn, G., Bebbington, P. E., Fowler, D., . . . & Dudley, R. (2005). Reasoning, emotions and delusional conviction in psychosis. *Journal of Abnormal Psychology, 114*, 373–384.

Garety, P. A., & Hemsley, D. R. (1994). *Delusions: Investigations into the Psychology of Delusional Reasoning.* Oxford: Oxford University Press.

Garety, P. A., Hemsley, D. R., & Wessely, S. (1991). Reasoning in deluded schizophrenic and paranoid patients: Biases in performance on a probabilistic inference task. *Journal of Nervous and Mental Disease, 179,* 194–201.

Goel, V., Bartolo, A., St Clair, D., & Venneri, A. (2004). Logical reasoning deficits in schizophrenia. *Schizophrenia Research, 66*(1), 87–88.

Gottesman, L., & Chapman, L. J. (1960). Syllogistic reasoning errors in schizophrenia. *Journal of Consulting Psychology, 24*(3), 250–255.

Harvey, A., Watkins, E., Mansell, W., & Shafran, R. (2004). *Cognitive Behavioural Processes Across Psychological Disorders: A Transdiagnostic Approach to Research and Treatment.* Oxford: Oxford University Press.

Huq, S. F., Garety, P., & Hemsley, D. R. (1988). Probabilistic judgements in deluded and non-deluded subjects. *Quarterly Journal of Experimental Psychology, 40A,* 801–812.

Johnson-Laird, P. N. (1983). *Mental Models: Towards a Cognitive Science of Language, Inference, and Consciousness.* Cambridge: Cambridge University Press.

Johnson-Laird, P. N. (2006). *How We Reason.* Oxford: Oxford University Press.

Johnson-Laird, P. N., & Byrne, R. M. J. (1991). *Deduction.* Hove, UK: Lawrence Erlbaum Associates Ltd.

Kahneman, D., Slovic, P., & Tversky, A. (Eds.) (1982) *Judgment Under Uncertainty: Heuristics and Biases.* Cambridge, MA: Cambridge University Press.

Kaliuzhna, M., Chambon, V., Franck, N., Testud, B. & Van der Henst, J.-B. (2012) Belief revision and delusions: How do patients with schizophrenia take advice? *PLoS ONE,* 7(4).

Kaney, S., Bowen-Jones, K., Dewey, M. E., & Bentall, R. P. (1997). Two predictions about paranoid ideation: Deluded, depressed and normal participants' subjective frequency and consensus judgments for positive, neutral and negative events. *British Journal of Clinical Psychology, 36*(3), 349–364.

Kemp, R., Chua, S., McKenna, P., & David, A. (1997). Reasoning and delusions. *The British Journal of Psychiatry, 170,* 398–405.

Langdon, R., Ward, P. B., & Coltheart, M. (2010). Reasoning anomalies associated with delusions in schizophrenia. *Schizophrenia Bulletin, 36*(2), 321–330.

Maher, B. A. (1992). Models and methods for the study of reasoning in delusions. *Revue Européenne de Psychologie Appliquee, 42,* 97–102.

Mancini, F., Gangemi, A., & Johnson-Laird, P. N. (2007). Il ruolo del ragionamento nella psicopatologia secondo la *Hyper Emotion Theory. Giornale Italiano di Psicologia a. XXXIV,* n. 4.

Manktelow, K. I., & Over, D. E. (1991) Social roles and utilities in reasoning with deontic conditionals. *Cognition, 39,* 85–105.

Mellet, E., Houdé, O., Brazo, P., Mazoyer, B., Tzourio-Mazoyer, N., & Dollfus, S. (2006). When a schizophrenic deficit becomes a reasoning advantage. *Schizophrenia Research, 84,* 359–364.

Menon, M., Pomarol-Clotet, E., McKenna, P. J., & McCarthy, R. A. (2006). Probabilistic reasoning in schizophrenia: A comparison of the performance of deluded and non-deluded schizophrenic patients and exploration of possible cognitive underpinnings. *Cognitive Neuropsychiatry, 11,* 521–536.

Minkowski, E. (1927). *La schizophrénie. Psychopathologie des schizoïdes et des schizophrènes.* Paris: Payot.

Mirian, D. R., Heinrichs, W., McDermid, & Vaz, S. (2011). Exploring logical reasoning abilities in schizophrenia patients. *Schizophrenia Research, 127,* 178–180.

Newstead, S. E., & Evans, J. St. B. T. (Eds.) (1995). *Perspectives on Thinking and Reasoning.* Hove, UK: Erlbaum.

Osherson, D. N. (1995) Probability judgment. In E. E. Smith & D. N. Osherson (Eds.), *Thinking,* vol. 3. Cambridge, MA: MIT Press.

Owen, G. S., Cutting, J., & David, A. S. (2007). Are people with schizophrenia more logical than healthy volunteers? *British Journal of Psychiatry, 191,* 453–454.

Pennisi, A. (1998). *Psicopatologia del linguaggio.* Roma: Carocci.

Peters, E. R., Thornton, P., Siksou, L., Linney, Y., & MacCabe, J. H. (2008) Specificity of the jump-to conclusions bias in deluded patients. *British Journal of Psychology, 47,* 239–244.

Phillips, L. D., & Edwards, W. (1966). Conservatism in a simple probabilistic inference task. *Journal of Experimental Psychology, 72,* 346–354.

Plous, S. (1993). *The Psychology of Judgment and Decision Making.* New York, NY: McGraw-Hill.

Rips, L. J. (1994). *The Psychology of Proof.* Cambridge, MA: MIT Press.

Shafir, E., & Tversky, A. (1995) Decision making. In E. E. Smith & D. N. Osherson (Eds.), *Thinking.* Cambridge, MA: MIT Press.

Smeets, G., de Jong, P. J., & Mayer, B. (2000). If you suffer from a headache, then you have a brain tumour: Domain-specific reasoning "bias" and hypochondriasis. *Behaviour Research and Therapy, 38*(8), 763–776.

Stanghellini, G., & Ballerini, M. (2011). What is it like to be a person with schizophrenia in the social world? A first-person perspective study on schizophrenic dissociality – Part 2: Methodological issues and empirical findings. *Psychopathology, 44,* 183–192.

Stefanidis, E. (2006). Personal account: Being rational. *Schizophrenia Bulletin, 32*(3), 422–423.

Trope, Y., & Lieberman, A. (1996). Social hypothesis testing: Cognitive and motivational mechanism. In E. T. Higgins & A. W. Kruglanski (Eds.), *Social Psychology: Handbook of Basic Principles.* New York, NY: Guilford Press.

Tversky, A., & Kahneman, D. (1982). Evidential impact of base rates. In: D. Kahneman, P. Slovic & A. Tversky (Eds.), *Judgment under Uncertainty: Heuristics and Biases.* Cambridge, MA: Cambridge University Press.

von Domarus, E. (1944). The specific laws of logic in schizophrenia. In J. S. Kasanin (Ed.), *Language and Thought in Schizophrenia.* Berkeley: University Of California Press.

Wason, P. C. (1966). Reasoning. In B. M. Foss (Ed.), *New Horizons in Psychology.* Harmondsworth: Penguin.

Watzlawick, P., Beavin, J. H., & Jackson, D. D. (1967). *Pragmatics of Human Communication. A Study of Interactional Patterns, Pathologies and Paradoxes.* New York: Norton & Company.

Williams, B. E. (1964). Deductive reasoning in schizophrenia. *The Journal of Abnormal and Social Psychology, 69*(1), 47–61.

6

PARANORMAL BELIEVERS' PRONENESS TO PROBABILISTIC REASONING BIASES

A review of the empirical literature

Paul Rogers[1]

A superfluous explanation is often suggested to account for the apparent deviation from randomness . . . we over-interpret the world.

(Ayton, Hunt & Wright, 1991; p. 216)

After more than 80 years of experimental parapsychology, scientific evidence for extrasensory perception (ESP) and psychokinesis (PK)[2] remains at best inconclusive and for sceptics unconvincing (for extensive debate, see Krippner & Friedman, 2010). In the absence of robust empirical support for allegedly supernatural phenomena, psychologists have become interested in why so many people believe in the paranormal (e.g. Moore, 2005). Sceptics generally view paranormal claims as the misattribution of supernatural causation to natural but inexplicable events (*misattribution hypothesis:* Wiseman & Watt, 2006). One suggestion is that paranormal believers tend to suffer from various cognitive 'deficits' such as lower (scientific) education, poorer critical thinking or reasoning skills, confirmation biases and/or biased memories for seemingly pro-paranormal events, but overall evidence for these characteristics is mixed (see, e.g., Irwin, 2009; French & Wilson, 2007). Because endorsement of ESP is often based on a seemingly remarkable but subjectively meaningful coincidence experience (e.g. Henry, 1993; Houran & Williams, 1998; Thalbourne, 2006), a more specific claim is that paranormal (ESP) believers are especially prone to errors in probabilistic reasoning. Some writers have even suggested the acronym ESP ought to stand for the 'Effect of Subjective Probability' (Brugger & Taylor, 2003; p. 221) or even 'Error Some Place' (Honorton, 1975; p. 103).

Since the 1970s, a mass of psychological research has repeatedly shown that people are poor at estimating the likelihood of uncertain events. This is because, when faced with conditions of uncertainty, they employ heuristics (cognitive 'rules of thumb') to make quick and easy, but nonetheless approximate and predictably biased, likelihood estimations (Gilovich, Griffin & Kahneman, 2002; Kahneman, Slovic & Tversky, 1982; Watt 1990–1991), which for some writers lie at the heart of almost all irrational decision making (Sutherland, 1992). Consistent with this view, Diaconis and Mosteller (1989) claim the apparent remarkableness of certain coincidences stems from people's tendency to be poor intuitive statisticians, which in turn stems from their general failure to recognise hidden but normal causes, to accept near misses as predictive 'hits', and to be ignorant of the *Law of Truly Large Numbers* (LTLN; i.e. the statistical fact that with a large enough sample *any* outcome, no matter how *seemingly* remarkable, will happen at some point in time; Carroll, 2003). Matthews and Blackmore (1995) argue that people tend to gauge the likelihood of coincidences using an essentially linear 'intuitive scaling rule', which, in extreme cases, becomes non-linear and unreliable. As a result observers inappropriately surprised by what appears to be a seemingly outlandish co-occurrence so much so that they erroneously assume that only a causal – usually paranormal – explanation seems viable. These errors may be exacerbated by other judgemental biases, such as the tendency to focus on belief-confirming over belief-disconfirming evidence (*confirmation bias*: Jones & Russell, 1980), to view one's own coincidence experiences as being more important (*egocentric bias*: Falk, 1989) and to judge future coincidences less likely than those from the past (*temporal bias*: Falk, 1981–1982).

People also tend to misperceive randomness.[3] When asked to predict the outcome of coin-toss sequences, for instance, observers tend to underestimate the number of repetitions (e.g. of consecutive heads) and overestimate the number of alterations (e.g. heads then tails) than would occur by chance (Falk & Konold, 1997), a process termed 'negative recency' (Ayton *et al.*, 1991). Underlying this is the erroneous expectation that random samples should resemble the population or process from which they are drawn (*representativeness heuristic*; Kahneman & Tversky, 1982). In other words, people mistakenly expect randomly generated outcomes to always *look* random – that is, irregular with statistically equiprobable outcomes and an alteration rate higher than that objectively predicted by chance (Hahn & Warren, 2009; see also Brugger, 1997). This representativeness-driven misperception of randomness has been observed in numerous real-world settings (Taleb, 2004) and, noticeably, has been associated with sympathetic magic (Roney & Trick, 2009), belief in God (Kay, Moscovitch & Laurin, 2010) and the endorsement of pseudoscientific concepts such as horoscopes, graphology and dream interpretation (Gilovich & Savitsky, 1996). As such, there seems good reason to expect paranormal (ESP) believers will also be prone to such biases. Empirical evidence for and against this claim is now discussed.

Paranormal belief and biases in probabilistic reasoning

Blackmore and Trościanko (1985) were the first to examine whether paranormal believers were especially prone to errors in probabilistic reasoning. In the first of three studies, they had teenage schoolgirls answer a battery of questions concerning the generation of random strings (e.g. list 20 numbers as if randomly drawn from a hat) plus judgements of randomness (e.g. indicate whether various random boy/girl mixes were biased), coin tossing (i.e. indicate whether the proportion of heads from a sequence of coin tosses was biased) and sampling outcomes (e.g. indicate which colour is more likely to be drawn from a given number of red and blue items), with the latter including the infamous 'birthday paradox' (i.e. how many people are needed before there is a 50:50 chance that two of them share the same birthday excluding year?). Each question was followed by three or four response options of which one was the statistically correct answer. For example, one of the sampling questions stated: 'A hat contains ten red and ten blue Smarties. I pull out ten and eight of them are red. Am I more likely to get a red or blue [Smartie] next time?' Here, response options were (a) red, (b) blue (the statistically correct answer) or (c) both equally likely. Participants also completed items assessing their belief in ESP. Whilst no group differences were found in the random string generation, randomness judging or sampling outcome questions, ESP believers made more errors on the coin-tossing questions than non-believers. In two follow-up studies with undergraduate students, ESP believers made more sampling errors (Study 2) and underestimated the number of hits expected by chance, and demonstrated a greater illusion of control (cf. Langer, 1975) over outcomes in a computerised coin-toss simulation (Study 3). These data suggest paranormal believers minimise the role of chance effect and 'look beyond' coincidence in search of a causal explanation for seemingly remarkable co-occurrences when, in reality, no such explanation is warranted. Blackmore and Trościanko (1985) termed this process the 'chance baseline shift' (p. 466). Subsequent evidence that paranormal believers have a stronger preference for games of pure chance (i.e. lotteries and roulette; Tobacyk & Wilkinson, 1991) offers additional support for this *chance baseline shift hypothesis*. Needless to say, in the absence of a recognisable natural cause, paranormal believers will rely on alleged supernatural phenomena for an explanation (*misattribution hypothesis*; Wiseman & Watt, 2006).

Brugger, Landis and Regard (1990) also examined believers' propensity for randomness misperception. In one study, they retrospectively analysed data from a previous telepathy experiment in which receivers tried to predict which Zener card symbol – either a circle, cross, square, star or wavy lines – was being mentally transmitted by the 'sender'. On average, respondents' predicted just three symbol repetitions, significantly fewer than the 4.5 expected by chance. Contrary to expectations, believers and non-believers did not differ in their degree of repetition avoidance (negative recency). In a second study, Brugger and colleagues asked respondents to generate 66 numbers as if thrown by a (fair) die. As before, respondents' generated fewer than the 10.8 repetitions expected by chance with, this time, believers generating significantly fewer repetitions than non-believers. In a final study, Brugger and colleagues tested respondents' appreciation of randomness by presenting pairs of fictitious dice throw sequences with one sequence containing fewer number repetitions than the other (e.g. 1, 3, 6, 4, 3, 2 versus 1, 2, 2, 6, 5, 5). Respondents had to indicate which, if either, sequence was more likely to appear first if a (fair) die were tossed. Overall, sequences containing more repetitions were erroneously judged less likely, with ESP believers more prone to this randomness misperception than non-believers. Bressan (2002; Study 1) has since replicated this finding (see below).

In follow-up work, Brugger, Regard and Landis (1991) asked undergraduate participants which of two hypothetical dice-throwing scenarios (i.e. throwing ten dice at the same time [event 1] versus throwing one dice ten times in succession [event 2]) was more likely to result in ten sixes being thrown. Response options were (a) event 1, (b) event 2 or (c) both events equally likely (the correct answer). ESP believers misperceived the nature of dice throws (simultaneous versus sequential) as having a significant impact on this objectively random process, again implying belief in the paranormal is associated with a greater illusion of control (cf. Blackmore & Trościanko, 1985; Study 3).

Brugger, Regard, Landis, Krebs and Niederberger (1994; Study 1) subsequently found believers' propensity for misperceiving randomness extends to customised pictorial dice, with believers generating fewer-than-chance repetitions for both conceptually related (e.g. carrot–rabbit) and conceptually identical (e.g. carrot–carrot) outcomes. In two further studies, the same authors found paranormal believers also misperceived semantic relatedness between randomly paired drawings (Study 2) and random dot patterns (Study 3) (see also Brugger & Taylor, 2003). Brugger and Baumann (1994) report a comparable trend for avoiding repetitious responding in a fake multiple choice questionnaire. These data support the view that paranormal believers are *especially* prone to misperceiving patterns (meaning) in randomness (the absence of meaning).

Bressan (2002) extended Blackmore and Trościanko's research using a mixed sample of workers and undergraduate students. In Study 1, respondents were given the same random string, randomness perception, coin tossing and sampling outcome tasks, plus additional items assessing sensitivity to variations in sample size. The latter included Kahneman and Tversky's (1982) 'maternity ward problem' as given below:

> A certain town is served by two hospitals. In the larger hospital about 45 babies are born each day, and in the smaller hospital about 15 babies are born each day. As you know, about 50% of all babies are boys. The exact percentage of baby boys, however, varies from day to day. Sometimes it may be higher than 50%, sometimes lower. For a period of one year, each hospital recorded the days on which more than 60% of the babies were born boys. Which hospital do you think recorded more such days?

Response options for this last problem were (a) the larger hospital, (b) the smaller hospital (the correct answer[4]) or (c) about the same. Respondents were also presented with three randomness problems: the first a replication of the random digit generation task used in Blackmore and Trościanko's (1985) first study. The second and third were two dice roll simulations (i.e. produce a string of numbers from

1 to 6 that simulate the rolling of a fair die) with, respectively, generated digits either covered (hidden string task) or uncovered and free for participants to view (visible string task). Contrary to expectations, belief in the paranormal was unrelated to errors on the sampling and sampling variation items. Believers did, however, make more errors in the coin toss and randomness perception tasks as well as both hidden and visible string versions of the dice roll simulation (non-students only). These findings suggest paranormal believers are especially prone to misperceiving patterns in randomness rather than to misunderstanding chance or the importance of sample size differentials.

In a second study, Bressan (2002) gave a new participant group alternative tasks to assess their sensitivity to sample size differentials and, additionally, their proneness to representativeness biases. The former utilised a modified version of Bar-Hillel's (1982) 'pollster problem' namely:

> Two pollsters are conducting surveys to estimate the proportion of voters in their respective cities who intend to vote in favour of a certain party. Firm A operates in a city of 1 million voters; firm B operates in a city of 50,000 voters. Both firms are sampling 1 out of every 1,000 voters. Whose estimate would you be more confident in accepting?

Response options were more confidence in (a) firm A's estimate (the correct answer), (b) firm B's estimate or (c) equal confidence in either estimate. The latter task was a modified version of Blackmore and Trościanko's (1985) coin-tossing scenario assessing subjective perceptions of coin bias, this time with nine outcomes varied according to the number of coin tosses (2, 20, 200, 3, 30, 300, 4, 40 or 400) and the proportion of resultant heads thrown (50%, 75% or 100%). Two further tasks were included to assess representativeness biases applied to random sequences. The first was a reformulation of Kahneman and Tversky's (1982) 'birth order problem'. Here respondents are told:

> All families of six children in a city were surveyed. In 70 families the exact order of boys and girls was GBGBBG. What is your estimate of the number of families surveyed in which the exact order was BGBBBB?

Response options were (a) about 10 or less; (b) about 30; (c) about 50; (d) about 70 (the correct answer[5]); (e) about 90; (f) about 110; or (g) about 130 or more. The second task was a modified version of Brugger at al.'s dice roll simulation described earlier (Brugger *et al.*, 1990; Study 2). Finally, Bressan (2002) included three randomness generation tasks; a coin-toss adaptation of the aforementioned dice roll simulation (i.e. writing H and T instead of the numbers 1 to 6), plus the same hidden and visible string dice roll simulations employed in her first study. Contrary to expectations, belief in the paranormal was unrelated to errors derived from the pollster problem. Similarly, most participants failed to understand that the likelihood of a given distribution of coin-toss outcomes (i.e. of throwing 50%, 75% or

100% heads) was dependent upon the number of times the coin was thrown, with overall more errors of judgement made for the more extreme, less representative distributions. For example, relatively few respondents – just 9% – realised that landing 50% heads over a larger (versus smaller) number of throws meant the coin is less likely to be biased (cf. Bar-Hillel, 1982; Kahneman & Tversky, 1982). As expected, paranormal believers were more prone to these errors than non-believers. This was most prominent when the distribution of heads versus tails was more evenly balanced (non-students only). As Bressan (2002) states:

> Believers more than non-believers failed to notice that a perfect 50:50 proportion [of head-to-tail outcomes] is more representative of larger, rather than smaller, samples; the underlying idea seems to be that 200 heads out of 400 tosses decrease the likelihood that a coin is fair compared to two heads out of four, because chance is imperfect and in the long run coins are doomed to produce a few minor irregularities.
>
> *(p. 23)*

Finally, belief in the paranormal was also associated with more errors for some, but not all, the randomness tasks. Whilst believers and non-believers were equally poor at judging birth orders and generating random (coin toss) strings, the former did make more errors when judging which of two hypothetical dice sequences was the most likely to be thrown. This is consistent with earlier evidence (Brugger *et al.*, 1990; Study 3). Believers also tended to generate fewer number repetitions both in the hidden and especially in the visible string conditions (non-students only). Overall results again suggest paranormal believers are more prone to misperceiving randomness – and thus to seeing meaningful patterns where none exist – than to simply misunderstanding the concept of chance (Bressan, 2002). Hereafter, this is termed the *randomness misperception hypothesis* (RMH) of paranormal belief.

Parallel arguments can be drawn from randomness perception studies utilising coin-toss simulations. In one, Dagnall, Parker and Munley (2007) gave undergraduate psychological students four such questions including: 'If an unbiased coin was tossed six times and each showed a head, what do you estimate the probability to be of a tail being shown on the next toss?' Response options were (a) 100%; (b) 75%; (c) 50% (the correct answer); or (d) 25%. Consistent with the RMH, Dagnall *et al.* found the mean number of randomness errors was a significant predictor of global paranormal belief.

In similar research, Blagrove, French and Jones (2006) had members of the UK public solve a different type of dice-throwing problem (i.e. what is the best chance of rolling ten sixes from rolling die; (a) rolling one dice ten times; (b) rolling ten dice in one go, or (c) both ways are equally likely (the correct response)?), plus one assessing their illusion of control for lottery games. The latter read: 'If you let someone else pick your numbers for a national lottery ticket, does this increase or decrease your chances of winning, or do the chances stay the same (the correct answer) as when you pick your own numbers?' Respondents were also asked three sampling questions. Half were asked questions which focused on *them* (i.e. did they currently have a scar on their left knee, back pain and/or a cat?) (Group T). For the remainder, corresponding questions focused on *other* people supposedly sampled from a hypothetical street survey (i.e. what percentage of *other* people currently have a scar on their left knee, back pain and/or a cat?) (Group O). Blagrove *et al.* found individuals with a stronger belief in precognition made more errors on the lottery but not dice-throwing task. Both errors were, however, associated with a greater number of reported dream precognitions (non-students only). But errors were bi-directional, with believers misperceiving the odds of a lottery win as either decreasing *or* increasing whenever number selections were made by a third party. These seemingly paradoxical data suggest paranormal belief is associated more with probability misjudgements than with an illusion of control. Finally, paranormal belief was also associated with more self-reported knee scars, back pain and cat ownership as well as higher estimates of how many other people have these things, with Group O believers making higher population estimates than their non-believing counterparts.

As previously stated, paranormal believers seem especially prone to developing illusory correlations between statistically unrelated events (Tobacyk & Wilkinson, 1991; see Vyse, 1997). A number of researchers have extended this line of reasoning to test whether believers are especially prone to overestimating the likelihood of co-occurring ('conjunctive') events relative to singular ('component') events; that is, whether paranormal belief is associated with a heightened susceptibility to the 'conjunction fallacy' (Tversky & Kahneman, 1982; 2002; see also Fisk, 2004).

In the first study to explore this possibility, Dagnall *et al.* (2007) gave undergraduate psychology students a hypothetical football scenario (i.e. two football teams – Team A and Team B – are playing in a local derby) and asked which of four possible outcomes was most likely. Response options were: (a) Team A scores first (the correct answer); (b) Team A scores first and wins; (c) Team A scores first and loses; or (d) Team A scores first and the game is drawn.[6] Contrary to expectations, paranormal believers made just as many conjunction errors as non-believers.

Rogers, Davis and Fisk (2009) have since criticised this work on various methodological grounds (e.g. the irrelevance of a football match to paranormal claims) and, in response, created 16 hypothetical vignettes depicting either ostensibly paranormal or clearly non-paranormal events. For instance, in one paranormal scenario, the following information was given:

> Billy has a long lost friend who he hasn't seen in years. They were good friends in school but drifted apart when they went away to different colleges. Billy comes home from work one evening and sits down to eat his dinner.

Members of the UK general public were then asked to estimate three likelihoods, namely that (a) Billy thinks about his long lost friend; (b) Billy's long lost friend unexpectedly telephones him; and (c) Billy thinks about his long lost friend *and*

Billy's long lost friend unexpectedly telephones him.[7] Similarly, one non-paranormal scenario read:

> Robert goes to a seafood restaurant for dinner with his friends. They have not eaten there before, but they don't have much time and are hungry so they decide to try it. The restaurant is an unclean, grubby, rundown place which generally gets few customers. It sells food at cheap prices.

Participants were asked to estimate the likelihood that (a) the crab is off; (b) Robert is ill the next day; and (c) the crab is off *and* Robert is ill the next day. Following Fisk (2004), participants estimated either the probability (i.e. 'chances in 100') or frequency (i.e. 'the number out of 100 occurrences') of each event, with a conjunction error being made whenever the co-occurring or conjunctive event (option c) was deemed more likely than one or both of the singular component events (options a and/or b). As hypothesised, paranormal believers tended to make more conjunction errors than non-believers. Furthermore, this was true for both paranormal and non-paranormal event types regardless of response (probabilistic versus frequentist) format, suggesting believers' heightened susceptibility to the conjunction fallacy is both generic – rather than domain specific (cf. Alcock & Otis, 1980; Wierzbicki, 1985) – and robust.

One possibility is that the idiosyncratic content of paranormal and non-paranormal scenarios may have influenced results; having a lost-long friend suddenly telephoning is, after all, quite different from getting food poisoning. Another limitation was that five of the eight paranormal scenarios depicted ostensibly precognitive events and as such were more inclined to incorporate temporally disjointed components than were non-paranormal scenarios. Consequently, Rogers, Fisk and Wiltshire (2010) conducted follow-up research to overcome these limitations. They created a new set of 16 vignettes in which paranormal and non-paranormal scenarios were identical in content save for one key difference; the apparent *source* of information. For example, one paranormal scenario reads:

> Alan is a 49 year old accountant who comes from a large but distant family. One day his uncle – whom Alan has not spoken to in over ten years – is suddenly taken ill with severe chest pains and shortness of breath. Alan's uncle is rushed to hospital but soon afterwards dies aged 87 years. A week later Alan consults a medium about a possible inheritance.

The non-paranormal version is identical except that Alan consults a lawyer rather than a (spiritualist) medium. A second experimental manipulation was incorporated to test whether the temporal closeness of component events was a significant factor in shaping believers' higher conjunction error rates. Specifically, component events were described as being either (virtually) co-occurring with no discernible delay between them else temporally disjointed with a clear intervening time gap. For instance, the above inheritance scenario clearly states that Alan consulted a medium or lawyer 'a week later' and thus is an unambiguous, temporally disjointed event. In all cases, participants were asked to estimate the likelihood (again from 0–100%) of both components and their ensuing conjunction, which in the above inheritance example are represented by (a) Alan is told his uncle died of heart failure; (b) Alan is told he will inherit his uncle's entire £1 million estate; and (c) Alan is told his uncle died of heart failure *and* Alan is told he will inherit his uncle's entire £1 million estate, respectively. Paranormal believers again made more conjunction errors for both event types than sceptics, confirming earlier findings (Rogers *et al.*, 2009). Furthermore, this was true regardless of the temporal relationship between the two component events (Rogers *et al.*, 2010).

The authors then tested a number of possible explanations for this group difference. First, given their *a priori* acceptance of ESP, it was reasoned that paranormal believers might be less surprised by, or may even expect, occurrence of the second component (e.g. Alan receiving a £1 million inheritance) given that the first (i.e. Alan being told how his uncle had died) had already happened, particularly if information appeared to come from a paranormal source. This argument was based on evidence that the combination of a subjectively likely (unsurprising) plus subjectively unlikely (surprising) component usually results in the conjunction fallacy being committed (Fisk, 2004). Thus, if believers view the second component event as more likely (less surprising) given prior occurrence of the first then, compared to sceptics, they should make more conjunction errors. In a second argument, Rogers *et al.* (2010) also reasoned that, because believers tend to misperceive a causal relationship between statistically unrelated events (Vyse, 1997), they might, relative to non-believers, also misperceive the two component events as being more strongly associated with the conjunctive term. This too would lead to more conjunction errors (Fisk, 2004). No support for either of these two hypotheses was found. Current work is exploring the importance of the component–conjunction relationship in such cases, with preliminary findings suggesting paranormal believers are especially prone to conjunction errors for conditionally related – but not conditionally independent – constituents (Rogers, Fisk & Lowrie, in preparation).

Additional research suggests it is believers in ESP and in particular PK who are especially susceptibility to the conjunction fallacy (Rogers, Lowrie & Fisk, in preparation).[8] The same work also explored the extent to which this heightened susceptibility was shaped by whether conjunctive events appeared to support or reject the paranormal hypothesis; that is, by whether they were congruent or incongruent with their *a priori* worldview. To assess this, Roger and colleagues modified previous vignettes so that the second component event either confirmed or disconfirmed the prediction outlined in the first. For instance, in a modified inheritance scenario, the first component states 'Alan is told there is a chance he will inherit his uncle's entire £1 million estate', with the second component either stating this prediction is realised (i.e. Alan later receives a £1 million inheritance) or not realised (i.e. Alan receives no inheritance).

Overall, partial support for hypotheses was found, albeit for specific types of (rather than global) paranormal belief. Whilst ESP believers made marginally more conjunction errors than sceptics, this was only for conjunctions that appeared to confirm the paranormal hypothesis. Parallel, and more pronounced, differences were found for believers versus non-believers of PK, with the former making more conjunction errors regardless of outcome type. It seems that PK believers have a more robust propensity for overestimating the likelihood of conjunctive events. Despite this, the reasons for paranormal believers' heightened susceptibility to the conjunction fallacy remain, as yet, largely unknown.

The above findings offer reasonable support for the randomness misperception hypothesis. Additional support for this can be found in believers' tendency to misperceive relatedness between conceptually distant word pairs (Gianotti, Mohr, Pizzagalli, Lehmann & Brugger, 2001; Mohr, Graves, Gianotti, Pizzagalli & Brugger, 2001) and indirectly related word primes (Pizzagalli, Lehmann & Brugger, 2001); for generating more rare words in letter fluency tasks (Duchêne, Graves & Brugger, 1998); for being less tolerant of uncertainty (Hart, Sullivan-Sanchez, Packer & Loveless, 2013) and ambiguity (Houran, 1998; Houran & Williams, 1998); for misperceiving target-transcript matches in both fake (French, Herrmann, Hales & Northam, 1997) and genuine (Marks, 2002) remote viewing tasks; and, finally, for misperceiving patterns or meaningful shapes in random or ambiguous visual stimuli (Blackmore & Moore, 1994; Brugger, Gamma, Muri, Schäfer & Taylor, 1993). The latter, known as pareidolia (Carroll, 2003), is of particular relevance to sceptical accounts of apparitional experiences and alleged UFO sightings (Hines, 2003; see also Blackmore, 1998; 2010).

Not all studies support the RMH. As already noted, paranormal believers have been found to make just as many errors on sampling and dice-throwing problems as non-believers (e.g. Blagrove et al., 2006; Bressan, 2002; Dagnall et al., 2007). The same lack of significant belief type effect has been found in relation to the perceived likelihood of common life events (e.g. owning a cat; Blackmore, 1997), the neglect of base rate information (Dagnall et al., 2007), expected value errors (Dagnall et al., 2007), use of population stereotypes (Grimmer & White, 1986) and random string generation (Blackmore, Galaud & Walker, 1994; Lawrence, 1990–1991; although see Brugger & Taylor, 2003), including those made within genuine ESP test data (Houtkooper & Haraldsson, 1997). In addition, Roberts and Seager (1999) found paranormal belief was associated with poorer syllogistic, but not poorer probabilistic, reasoning for both paranormal and non-paranormal problems. Finally, a few studies suggest believers' propensity for probabilistic reasoning biases may be confounded by their general cognitive and/or academic ability (e.g. Musch & Ehrenberg, 2002; Stuart-Hamilton, Nayak & Priest, 2006). It appears evidence for believers' proneness to probabilistic reasoning biases may be less robust than first thought.

To summarise: whilst a number of studies show paranormal believers are especially prone to underestimating the importance of chance, others have failed to support this view, thereby weakening Blackmore and Trościanko's (1985) chance baseline shift hypothesis. Arguably, more robust evidence exists for two other types of probabilistic reasoning bias. The first is believers' heightened tendency to misperceive patterns in randomness. When asked to produce random sequences of, say, numbers, dice throw or coin toss outcomes most people generate fewer repetitions (e.g. consecutive sixes, consecutive heads) than objective statistics would expect. But paranormal believers are more prone to such repetition avoidance than non-believers.

The second is believers' heightened susceptibility to the conjunction fallacy. When presented with two singular events (e.g. thinking of a long lost friend and that friend unexpectedly telephoning a few moments later), most people rate the conjunction of these two events more likely than either of the two singular components alone. But again, paranormal believers do so to a greater extent than sceptics. The latter appears to be generic rather than domain specific and unaffected by response format, the temporal gap between individual components or the perceived (strength of) relationship between constituent and conjunctive events. At present, there is also some evidence than the degree of constituent conditional relatedness is, however, important. Finally, whilst ESP believers make more errors only for conjunctive events which were belief-congruent, PK believers made as many errors regardless of whether the conjunction supported or rejected the paranormal hypothesis. With conjunctive probability estimates determined solely by the potential surprise value (PSV) of the less likely (more surprising) component (Fisk, 2004), it seems paranormal believers and sceptics maintain different subjective perceptions of what constitutes a random co-occurrence of events (cf. Bressan, 2002). As Rogers, Fisk and Wiltshire (2010) conclude, 'some as yet undetermined factor appears responsible for paranormal believers' greater susceptibility to the conjunction fallacy' (p. 700).

Theoretical implications

At first glance, the above findings seem to suggest paranormal belief is associated with two separate types of probabilistic reasoning bias, namely randomness misperception and the conjunction fallacy. However, these differences diminish when one considers that a conjunctive term is effectively the co-occurrence of two otherwise unrelated (i.e. random) component events. In this context, believers' heightened proneness to conjunction errors can be viewed as a heightened propensity for misperceiving random events as somehow being causally connected (cf. Bressan, 2002; Wiseman & Watt, 2006).

The RMH suggests paranormal believers and sceptics have a different internal representation of what constitutes a random event, with believers requiring less subjective evidence of relatedness before they start to see meaningful patterns in what is essentially meaningless data. Shermer (2011) terms this 'patternicity' (p. 5). In the language of Signal Detection Theory (SDT; Tanner & Swets, 1954), believers have looser response criteria and require lower signal strength before they erroneously detect patterns where none exist, thus rendering them prone to false alarms (Brugger & Taylor, 2003; Krummenacher, Mohr, Haker & Brugger, 2010). Recently, this has been tested directly. Hadlaczky and Westerlund (2011) explored whether paranormal believers have a lower threshold for being surprised by coincidences.

They had undergraduate psychology students rate the perceived remarkableness of target-word matches which they were told may or may not have been derived from a genuine Ganzfeld test of telepathy.[9] Specifically, participants were shown a series of 12 target pictures each accompanied by the auditory presentation of two supposedly correct (word) choices from an unknown (in reality, hypothetical) Ganzfeld receiver. Experimental manipulation meant that one word was comparatively broad so its match to the target picture would seem a 'somewhat remarkable' coincidence, with the other word more precise so its match would seem a 'very remarkable' coincidence. For example, if the target image was a police car, the correct but vague guess would be 'vehicle', whereas the correct but precise guess would be 'car' (cars being a subset of vehicles). As hypothesised, paranormal believers were poorer at discriminating between somewhat remarkable versus very remarkable coincidences, implying their threshold for being surprised by coincidences was lower than that of sceptics. Hadlaczky and Westerlund reason that individuals with a lower surprise threshold are likely to experience a greater number of coincidences, including those that are difficult or impossible to explain naturally. This is consistent with Blackmore and Trościanko's (1985) chance baseline shift hypothesis.

The subsequent tendency to misattribute personal meaning or significance to objectively random events – termed 'agency' by Shermer (2011; p. 5) but more commonly known as apophenia (Caroll, 2003; Fyfe, Williams, Mason & Pickup, 2008) – suggests paranormal believers have a 'lower threshold of causal attribution', causing them to more quickly seek some supernatural explanation for what is actually a random event (Bressan, 2002). Rominger, Weiss, Fink, Schulter and Papousek (2011) have since confirmed paranormal belief is more likely to be a consequence rather than a cause of these randomness misperceptions. Indeed, Brugger and Taylor (2003) assert that believers' apparent ability to out-perform sceptics on tests of ESP performance – the infamous 'sheep-goat effect' (Schmeidler & McConnell, 1958) – mirrors believer versus non-believer differences in randomness perception and/or generation biases. As Brugger and Taylor exclaim, 'a distinctly human characteristic [is] the tendency to invoke a supernatural agency to explain the existence of meaningful events whose origins are unknown' and for these authors alleged instances of ESP reflect nothing more than individual differences in highly non-random guessing behaviour (pp. 221–222).

Believer versus non-believer differences in randomness perception and/or generation biases can be understood in terms of group differences in hemispheric asymmetry and semantic-associative processing (Brugger & Taylor, 2003). Generally, more meaningful images are perceived in random dot stimuli when the latter is presented briefly to the left visual field/right hemisphere (LVF/RH) as opposed to the right visual field/left hemisphere (RVF/LH) (e.g. Brugger, Regard, Landis, Cook, Krebs & Niederberger, 1993; Brugger, Gamma, Muri, Schäfe & Taylor, 1993). A number of studies have now found greater LVF/RH dominance – meaning more right hemispheric functioning is released from left hemisphere control – amongst paranormal (ESP) believers than corresponding sceptics (e.g. Leonhard & Brugger, 1998; Pizzagalli et al., 2001). Similarly, believers also present more right hemisphere overactivation (Brugger, Gamma *et al.*, 1993; Pizzagalli, Lehmann, Gianotti, Koenig & Tanaka *et al.*, 2000). Believers' unique LVF/RH dominance and RH overactivation leads, in turn, to a more widespread, more diffuse activation of the semantic network, generating 'easier' co-activation of more distantly related concepts (e.g. Mohr *et al.*, 2001; Rominger *et al.*, 2011). Ultimately, it is believers' LVF/RH dominance and RH overactivation that results in them to misperceiving random and co-occurring events as being (causally) connected some a meaningful way.

Conclusion

Numerous studies suggest individuals who endorse paranormal concepts such as ESP are especially prone to probabilistic reasoning biases. Rather than a misunderstanding of chance *per se*, current evidence suggests believers are especially prone to a misperception (of patterns) in randomness and/or an overestimation of the likelihood of co-occurring (relative to singular component) events. Both these biases presumably stem from believers having a 'looser' mental representation of randomness, which leads them to more easily dismiss this as the reason behind a seemingly remarkable coincidence. These appear to be rooted in hemispheric asymmetry and believers' heightened RH dominance and/or over-activation. Whether greater public education in statistical concepts like randomness would be successful in reducing the prevalence and robustness of paranormal belief remains to be seen, although, given their intuitive appeal and underlying neuropsychology, one should not be too optimistic of such change.

Notes

1   The author was formerly Senior Lecturer in Psychology at the University of Central Lancashire, Preston UK. Correspondence should be addressed to him via progers1966@ gmail.com.
2   ESP is defined as the alleged ability to acquire information seemingly without the mediation of the five recognised human senses or the processes of logical inference and is said to comprise *telepathy* (direct mind-to-mind communication), *clairvoyance* (awareness of sensorially inaccessible information) and *precognition* (awareness of future events). PK is defined as the alleged ability to have direct mental influence on the structure of the physical environment without mediation of the recognised physical energies or mechanisms. Colloquially PK is also known as 'mind-over-matter'. Because of a conceptual overlap between ESP and PK, parapsychologists often refer to the theoretical term 'psi' (pronounced 'sigh') to denote the unknown paranormal element underlying the two (Irwin & Watt, 2007).
3   Randomness can be defined as a process without method or conscious decision which is governed by, or involves, outcomes that are equally probable (Oxford Dictionary of English, 2005; see also Haigh, 2012). However, several writers have noted the difficulty of conceptualising, measuring and testing randomness (for discussions, see, e.g., Ayton *et al.*, 1991; Falk & Konold, 1997; Nickerson, 2002; Wagenaar, 1972).
4   Statistical theory states that more extreme deviations from the norm – which here is reflected in a male birth rate of 60 rather than 50 per cent – are more likely to be found within smaller samples (Kahneman & Tversky, 1982).
5   Assuming boy and girl births are equally likely, 70 is the best estimate of the frequency of BGBBBB given the 70 families sampled. But, because this has more boy than girl births,

it looks less representative and thus less likely than the evenly distributed GBGBBG (Kahneman & Tversky, 1982; p. 34).

6 Here, one needs to recognise that it is statistically impossible for Team A to score first *and* either win, lose or draw the game (options b, c and d, respectively) if they fail to actually score first (option a). In other words, scoring first subsumes all other outcomes and so *has* to be the most likely option. Thus, anyone who fails to answer (a) succumbs to the conjunction fallacy (Dagnall *et al.*, 2007).

7 Here, as in all subsequent scenarios, the term 'and' has been italicised to highlight its conjunctive nature. These italics were not present in the original questionnaires.

8 These trends did not apply to individuals who believe in post-mortem survival (aka. life-after-death), presumably because such beliefs are driven more by socio-cultural, religious, philosophical and/or motivational factors than by flaws in probabilistic reasoning (Thalbourne, 1996).

9 In Ganzfeld research, one person (the 'sender') views a randomly selected target picture or video clip for a set period of time whilst, in a different physical location (usually a secure room), a second person (the 'receiver') tries to determine the nature of this target using ESP. During this transmission phase, receivers have their visual, auditory and tactile senses diminished through eye-masking (usually with halved ping-pong balls), listening to white noise and guided relaxation to the point of near sensory deprivation. Having freely described their mentation, receivers are then asked to indicate which of several (usually four) images they believe to be the target, with a hit rate significantly above the mean chance expectation suggestive of anomalous information transfer (aka. psi). Many parapsychologists believe Ganzfeld research offers the best empirical support for ESP (e.g. Williams, 2001; see also Irwin & Watt, 2007).

References

Alcock, J. E., & Otis, L. P. (1980). Critical thinking and belief in the paranormal. *Psychological Reports, 46*(2), 479–482. doi: unavailable.

Ayton, P., Hunt, A. J., & Wright, G. (1991). Commentaries on 'psychological conceptions of randomness'. *Journal of Behavioral Decision Making, 4*(3), 215–218. doi: 10.1002/bdm.3960040307.

Bar-Hillel, M. (1982). Studies of representativeness. In D. Kahneman, P. Slovic & A. Tversky (Eds.), *Judgement under Uncertainty: Heuristics and Biases* (pp. 69–83). Cambridge: Cambridge University Press.

Blackmore, S. J. (1997). Probability misjudgment and belief in the paranormal: A newspaper survey. *British Journal of Psychology, 88*(4), 683–689. doi: 10.1111/j.2044-8295.1997.tb02665.x.

Blackmore, S. (1998). Psychic experiences: Psychic illusions. In K. Frazier (Ed.), *Encounters with the Paranormal: Science, Knowledge and Belief* (pp. 201–211). Amherst, New York: Prometheus.

Blackmore, S. (2010). Seeing is believing? In W.M. Grossman & C.C. French (Eds.), *Why Statues Weep: The Best of the Skeptic*. London: The Philosophy Press.

Blackmore, S., Galaud, K., & Walker, C. (1994). Psychic experiences as illusions of causality. In W. E. Cook & D. Delanoy (Eds.), *Research in Parapsychology*. (pp. 89–93), Metuchen, NJ: Scarecrow Press.

Blackmore, S., & Moore, R. (1994). Seeing things: Visual recognition and belief in the paranormal. *European Journal of Parapsychology, 10*, 91–103. doi: unavailable.

Blackmore, S. J., & Trościanko, T. (1985). Belief in the paranormal: Probability judgements, illusory control, and the 'chance baseline shift'. *British Journal of Psychology, 76*(4), 459–468. doi: 10.1111/j.2044-8295.1985.tb01969.x.

Blagrove, M., French, C. C. & Jones, G. (2006). Probabilistic reasoning, affirmative bias and belief in precognitive dreams. *Applied Cognitive Psychology, 20*, 65–83. doi: 10.1002/acp.1165.

Bressan, P. (2002). The connection between random sequences, everyday coincidences and belief in the paranormal. *Applied Cognitive Psychology, 16*, 17–34. doi: 10.1002/acp.754.

Brugger, P. (1997). Variables that influence the generation of random sequences: An update. *Perceptual & Motor Skills, 84*(2), 627–661. doi: 10.2466/pms.1997.84.2.627.

Brugger, P., & Baumann, A. T. (1994). Repetition avoidance in responses to imaginary questions: The effect of respondents' belief in ESP. *Psychological Reports, 75*(2), 883–893. doi: 10.2466/pr0.1994.75.2.883.

Brugger, P., Gamma, A., Muri, R., Schäfer, M., & Taylor, K. I. (1993). Functional hemispheric asymmetry and belief in ESP: Towards a 'neuropsychology of belief'. *Perceptual & Motor Skills, 77*(3, Pt 2), 1299–1308. doi: 10.2466/pms.1993.77.3f.1299.

Brugger, P., Landis, T., & Regard, M. (1990). A 'sheep-goat' effect in repetition avoidance: Extra-sensory perception as an effect of subjective probability? *British Journal of Psychology, 81*(4), 455–468. doi: 10.1111/j.2044-8295.1990.tb02372.x.

Brugger, P., Regard, M., & Landis, T. (1991). Belief in extrasensory perception and illusory control: A replication. *Journal of Psychology: Interdisciplinary & Applied, 125*(4), 501–502. doi: unavailable.

Brugger, P., Regard, M., Landis, T., Cook, N., Krebs, D., & Niederberger, J. (1993). 'Meaningful' patterns in visual noise: Effects of lateral stimulation and the observer's belief in ESP. *Psychopathology, 26*(5–6), 261–265. doi: 10.1159/000284831.

Brugger, P. Regard, M., Landis, T., Krebs, D., & Niederberger, J. (1994). Coincidences: Who can say how 'meaningful' they are? In E. Williams-Cook & D. L. Delanoy (Eds.), *Research in Parapsychology:* Abstracts and Papers from the 34th Annual Convention of the Parapsychological Association (pp. 94–98). London: Scarecrow Press.

Brugger, P., & Taylor, K. I. (2003). ESP: Extrasensory perception or effect of subjective probability? *Journal of Consciousness Studies, 10*(6–7), 221–246. doi: unavailable.

Carroll, R. D. (2003). *The Skeptic's Dictionary: A Collection of Strange Beliefs, Amusing Deceptions and Dangerous Delusions.* Hoboken, NJ: Wiley & Sons.

Cohen, J. (1960). *Chance, Skill and Luck: The Psychology of Guessing and Gambling.* Baltimore, MD: Penguin.

Dagnall, N., Parker, A., & Munley, G. (2007). Paranormal belief and reasoning. *Personality & Individual Differences, 43*, 1406–1415. doi: 10.1016/j.paid.2007.04.017.

Diaconis, P., & Mosteller, F. (1989). Methods for studying coincidences. *Journal of the American Statistical Association, 84*(408), 853–861. doi: unavailable.

Duchêne, A., Graves, R. E., & Brugger, P. (1998). Schizotypal thinking and associative processing: A response commonality analysis of verbal fluency. *Journal of Psychiatry & Neuroscience, 23*(1), 56–60. doi: unavailable.

Falk, R. (1981–1982). On coincidences. *Skeptical Inquirer, 6*(2), 18–31. doi: unavailable.

Falk, R. (1989). Judgment of coincidence: Mine versus yours. *American Journal of Psychology, 102*(4), 477–493. doi: 10.2307/1423303.

Falk, R., & Konold, C. (1997). Making sense of randomness: Implicit encoding as a basis for judgement. *Psychological Review, 104*(2), 301–318. doi: 10.1037/0033-295X.104.2.301.

Fisk, J. E. (2004). Conjunction fallacy. In R. F. Pohl (Ed.). *Cognitive Illusions: A Handbook on Fallacies and Biases in Thinking, Judgement and Memory* (pp. 23–42). Hove: Psychology Press.

French, C. C., Herrmann, D., Hales, S., & Northam, C. (1997). Psi in the eye of the beholder: Sheep-goat differences in evaluating evidence of the paranormal. Unpublished manuscript, Department of Psychology, Goldsmiths College, University of London.

French, C. C., & Wilson, K. (2007). Cognitive factors underlying paranormal beliefs and experiences. In S. Della Sala (Ed.), *Tall Tales: Popular Myths about the Mind and Brain* (pp. 3–22). Oxford: Oxford University Press.

Fyfe, S., Williams, C., Mason, O. J., & Pickup, G. J. (2008). Apophenia, theory of mind and schizotypy: Perceiving meaning and intentionality in randomness. *Cortex: A Journal Devoted to the Study of the Nervous System and Behavior, 44*(10), 1316–1325. doi: 10.1016/j.cortex.2007.07.009.

Gianotti, L. R., Mohr, C., Pizzagalli, D., Lehmann, D., & Brugger, P. (2001). Associative processing and paranormal belief. *Psychiatry & Clinical Neurosciences, 55*(6), 595–603. doi: 10.1046/j.1440-1819.2001.00911.x.

Gilovich, T., Griffin, D., & Kahneman, D. (2002). *Heuristics and Biases: The Psychology of Intuitive Judgement.* Cambridge: Cambridge University Press.

Gilovich, T., & Savitsky, K. (1996). Like goes with like: The role of representativeness in erroneous and pseudoscientific beliefs. *Skeptical Inquirer, 20*(2), March/April, 34–40. Reprinted in T. Gilovich, D. Griffin, & D. Kahneman (Eds.), *Heuristics and Biases: The Psychology of Intuitive Judgment* (pp. 601–616). New York: Cambridge University Press.

Grimmer, M. R., & White, K. D. (1986). Psychics and ESP: The role of population stereotypes. *Australian Psychologist, 21*(3), 405–411. doi: 10.1080/00050068608256918.

Hadlaczky, G., & Westerlund, J. (2011). Sensitivity to coincidences and paranormal belief. *Perceptual & Motor Skills, 113*(3), 894–908. doi: 10.2466/09.22.PMS.113.6.894-908 ISSN 0031-5125.

Hahn, U., & Warren, P. A. (2009). Perceptions of randomness: Why three heads are better than four. *Psychological Review, 116*(2), 454–461. doi: 10.1037/a0015241.

Haigh, J. (2012). *Probability: A Very Short Introduction* (Vol. 310). Oxford: Oxford University Press.

Hart, J. W., Sullivan-Sanchez, C., Packer, T., & Loveless, J. (2013). Is any explanation better than no explanation? Intolerance of uncertainty and paranormal beliefs. *Social Behavior & Personality, 41*(2), 343–344. doi: 10.2224/sbp.2013.41.2.343.

Henry, J. (1993). Coincidence experience survey. *Journal of the Society for Psychical Research, 59*(831), 97–108. doi: unavailable.

Hines, T. (2003). *Pseudoscience and the Paranormal* (2nd edition). Amherst, NY: Prometheus.

Honorton, C. (1975). Error some place. *Journal of Communication, 25*(1), 103–116. doi: 10.1111/j.1460-2466.1975.tb00560.x.

Houran, J. (1998). Preliminary study of tolerance of ambiguity of individuals reporting paranormal experiences. *Psychological Reports, 82*(1), 183–187. doi: 10.2466/PR0.82.1.183-187.

Houran, J., & Williams, C. (1998). Relation of tolerance of ambiguity to global and specific paranormal experience. *Psychological Reports, 83*(3, Pt 1), 807–818. doi: 10.2466/PR0.83.7.807-818.

Houtkooper, J. M., & Haraldsson, E. (1997). Reliabilities and psychological correlates of guessing and scoring behavior in a forced-choice ESP task. *Journal of Parapsychology, 61*(2), 119–134. doi: unavailable.

Irwin, H. J. (2009). *The Psychology of Paranormal Belief: A Researcher's Handbook.* Hatfield: University of Hertfordshire Press.

Irwin, H. J., & Watt, C. A. (2007). *An Introduction to Parapsychology (5th edition).* Jefferson, NC: McFarland.

Jones, W. H., & Russell, D. (1980). The selective processing of belief disconfirming information. *European Journal of Social Psychology, 10*(3), 309–312. doi: 10.1002/ejsp.2420100309.

Kahneman, D., Slovic, P., & Tversky, A. (1982). *Judgement under Uncertainty: Heuristics and Biases.* Cambridge: Cambridge University Press.

Kahneman, D., & Tversky, A. (1982). Subjective probability: A judgment of representativeness. In D. Kahneman, P. Slovic, & A. Tversky (Eds.), *Judgement under Uncertainty: Heuristics and Biases* (pp. 32–47). Cambridge: Cambridge University Press.

Kay, A. C., Moscovitch, D. A., & Laurin, K. (2010). Randomness, attributions of arousal, and belief in God. *Psychological Science, 21*(2), 216–218. doi: 10.1177/0956797609357750.

Krippner, S., & Friedman, H. L. (2010). *Debating Psychic Experience: Human Potential or Human Illusion?* Santa Barbara, CA: Praeger.

Krummenacher, P., Mohr, C., Haker, H., & Brugger, P. (2010). Dopamine, paranormal belief, and the detection of meaningful stimuli. *Journal of Cognitive Neuroscience, 22*(8), 1670–1681. doi: 10.1162/jocn.2009.21313.

Langer, E. J. (1975). The illusion of control. *Journal of Personality & Social Psychology, 31*, 311–328. doi: 10.1037/0022-3514.32.2.311.

Lawrence, T. R. (1990–1991). Subjective random generations and the reversed sheep-goat effect: A failure to replicate. *European Journal of Parapsychology, 8*, 131–144. doi: unavailable.

Leonhard, D., & Brugger, P. (1998). Creative, paranormal, and delusional thought: A consequence of right hemisphere semantic activation? *Neuropsychiatry, Neuropsychology, & Behavioral Neurology, 11*(4), 177–183. doi: unavailable.

Marks, D. (2002). *The Psychology of the Psychic (2nd edition).* Buffalo, NY: Prometheus.

Matthews, R., & Blackmore, S. (1995). Why are coincidences so impressive? *Perceptual & Motor Skills, 80*(3, Pt 2), 1121–1122. doi: 10.2466/pms.1995.80.3c.1121.

Mohr, C., Graves, R. E., Gianotti, L. R., Pizzagalli, D., & Brugger, P. (2001). Loose but normal: A semantic association study. *Journal of Psycholinguistic Research, 30*(5), 475–483. doi: 10.1023/A:1010461429079.

Moore, D. W. (2005). Three in four Americans believe in paranormal: Little change from similar results in 2001, Gallup Poll. Online at www.gallup.com/poll/16915/three-four-americans-believe-paranormal.aspx (Accessed 30 October 2013).

Musch, J., & Ehrenberg, K. (2002). Probability misjudgement, cognitive ability and belief in the paranormal. *British Journal of Psychology, 93*, 169–177. doi: 10.1348/000712602162517.

Nickerson, R. S. (2002). The production and perception of randomness. *Psychological Review, 109*(2), 330–357. doi: 10.1037/0033-295X.109.2.330.

Oxford Dictionary of English (2005) (Second Edition, Revised). Oxford: Oxford University Press.

Pizzagalli, D. D., Lehmann, D. D., & Brugger, P. P. (2001). Lateralized direct and indirect semantic priming effects in subjects with paranormal experiences and beliefs. *Psychopathology, 34*(2), 75–80. doi: 10.1159/000049284.

Pizzagalli, D., Lehmann, D., Gianotti, L., Koenig, T., Tanaka, H., Wackermann, J., & Brugger, P. (2000). Brain electric correlates of strong belief in paranormal phenomena: Intracerebral EEG source and regional Omega complexity analyses. *Psychiatry Research: Neuroimaging, 100*(3), 139–154. doi: 10.1016/S0925-4927(00)00070-6.

Roberts, M. J., & Seager, P. B. (1999). Predicting belief in paranormal phenomena: A comparison of conditional and probabilistic reasoning. *Applied Cognitive Psychology, 13*(5), 443–450. doi: 10.1002/(SICI)1099-0720(199910)13:5<443::AID-ACP592>3.0.CO;2-K.

Rogers, P., Davis, T., & Fisk, J. E. (2009). Paranormal belief and susceptibility to the conjunction fallacy. *Applied Cognitive Psychology, 23*(4), 524–542. doi: 10.1002/acp.1472.

Rogers, P., Fisk, J. E., & Lowrie, E. L. (in preparation). The role of constituent conditional relatedness in paranormal believers' susceptability to the conjunction fallacy.

Rogers, P., Fisk, J. E., & Wiltshire, D. (2010). Paranormal belief and the conjunction fallacy: Controlling for temporal relatedness and potential surprise differentials in component events. *Applied Cognitive Psychology, 24*, 1–20. doi: 10.1002/acp.1732.

Rogers, P., Lowrie, E. L., & Fisk, J. E. (in preparation). Paranormal belief and the conjunction fallacy: Differences across pro-paranormal versus ant-paranormal conjunctive events.

Rominger, C., Weiss, E. M., Fink, A., Schulter, G., & Papousek, I. (2011). Allusive thinking (cognitive looseness) and the propensity to perceive 'meaningful' coincidences. *Personality & Individual Differences, 51*(8), 1002–1006. doi: 10.1016/j.paid.2011.08.012.

Roney, C. R., & Trick, L. M. (2009). Sympathetic magic and perceptions of randomness: The hot hand versus the gambler's fallacy. *Thinking & Reasoning, 15*(2), 197–210. doi: 10.1080/13546780902847137.

Schmeidler, G. R., & McConnell, R. A. (1958). *ESP and Personality Characteristics*. Oxford, UK: Yale University Press.

Shermer, M. (2011). *The Believing Brain: From Ghosts and Gods to Politics and Conspiracies. How We Construct Beliefs and Reinforce Them as Truths.* New York: Times Books/Henry Holt & Co.

Stuart-Hamilton, I., Nayak, L., & Priest, L. (2006). Intelligence, belief in the paranormal, knowledge of probability and aging. *Educational Gerontology, 32*(3), 173–184. doi: 10.1080/03601270500476847.

Sutherland, N. S. (1992). *Irrationality: The Enemy Within*: London: Penguin.

Taleb, N. N. (2004). *Fooled by Randomness: The Hidden Role of Chance in Life and the Markets.* London: Penguin.

Tanner, W. P., & Swets, J. A. (1954). A decision-making theory of visual detection. *Psychological Review, 61*(6), 401–409. doi: 10.1037/h0058700.

Thalbourne, M. A. (1996). Belief in life after death: Psychological origins and influences. *Personality & Individual Differences, 21*(6), 1043–1045. doi: 10.1016/ S0191-8869(96)00167-5.

Thalbourne, M. A. (2006). A brief treatise on coincidence. Unpublished manuscript. Online at http://parrochia.wifeo.com/documents/coincidence.pdf (Accessed 6 December 2010).

Tobacyk, J. J., & Wilkinson, L. V. (1991). Paranormal beliefs and preference for games of chance. *Psychological Reports, 68*, 1088–1090. doi: 10.2466/PR0.68.4.1088-1090.

Tversky, A., & Kahneman, D. (1982). Judgements of and by representativeness. In D. Kahneman, P. Slovic & A. Tversky (Eds.), *Judgement under Uncertainty: Heuristics and Biases* (pp. 84–98). Cambridge: Cambridge University Press.

Tversky, A., & Kahneman, D. (2002). Extensional versus intuitive reasoning: The conjunction fallacy in probability judgement. In T. Gilovich, D. Griffin & D. Kahneman (Eds.), *Heuristics and Biases: The Psychology of Intuitive Judgement* (pp. 19–48). Cambridge: Cambridge University Press.

Vyse, S. A. (1997). *Believing in Magic: The Psychology of Superstition.* Oxford: Oxford University Press.

Wagenaar, W. A. (1972). Generation of random sequences by human subjects: A critical survey of literature. *Psychological Bulletin, 77*(1), 65–72. doi: unavailable.

Watt, C. A. (1990–1991). Psychology and coincidences. *European Journal of Parapsychology, 8*, 66–84. doi: unavailable.

Wierzbicki, M. (1985). Reasoning errors and belief in the paranormal. *Journal of Social Psychology, 125*(4), 489–494. doi: 10.1080/00224545.1985.9713529.

Williams, B. J., (2011). Revisiting the Ganzfeld ESP debate: A basic review and assessment. *Journal of Scientific Exploration, 25*(4), 639–661. doi: unavailable.

Wiseman, R., & Watt, C. (2006). Belief in psychic ability and the misattribution hypothesis: A qualitative review. *British Journal of Psychology, 97*, 323–338. doi: 10.1348/000712605X72523.

7

DANGER-CONFIRMING REASONING AND THE PERSISTENCE OF PHOBIC BELIEFS

Peter J. de Jong

Introduction

Individuals suffering from phobic fears typically consider phobic stimuli as signals of impending danger. A critical feature of these phobic convictions is their persistence in the absence of contingent aversive events. Although head-aches seldom signal the presence of a brain tumour, heart palpitations are usually not followed by a heart attack, and spiders tend not to bite, phobic individuals typically fail to correct their phobic beliefs but rather continue to interpret these stimuli as danger signals. To explain the persistence of these phobic convictions, it has been proposed that anxiety patients are characterized by maladaptive cognitive structures in memory (e.g. Beck, Emery, & Greenberg, 1985). These so-called schemata would give rise to selective attention for threat, promote danger-confirming interpretations of ambiguous information, and would prevent elaborate processing of threatening information, thereby heightening the threshold for identifying false alarms. In line with this, there is consistent research evidence supporting the existence of danger-relevant information processing biases in anxiety patients (MacLeod & Mathews, 2012).

Current cognitive models of anxiety vulnerability emphasize the importance of differentiating between the various stages of information processing and underline the relevance of differentiating between the more reflexive, associative processes and the more deliberate, reflective processes in this respect (e.g. Ouimet, Gawronski, & Dozois, 2009). In response to the occurrence of a concern-relevant danger-stimulus (e.g. a rejecting facial expression, a spider, sound in the elevator), threat-related memory associations are proposed to be reflexively activated as part of the *associative* system (including specific beliefs and affective responses). Following the dual process framework, the semantic and affective information from the *associative system* will then be concurrently used for the validation of the initially activated beliefs through propositional processing in the *rule-based system*. The outcome of this validation process can lead either to a de-activation of the associative system, or to further activation of danger-related associations, and thus serve to alter or to confirm the impulsive (e.g. fear) responses generated by the associative system (see Figure 7.1).

Following such a dual system perspective, propositional (reasoning) processes play a critical role in the correction and/or persistence of particular beliefs. In this chapter, it will be argued that the validation process will usually not result in a correction but instead in a strengthening of "phobogenic" beliefs. Various processes may contribute to such danger-confirming reasoning in the context of phobic fears. On the basis of empirical findings and theoretical speculations, the following sections will subsequently address the most prominent reasoning processes that may help explain why the reflective (rule-based) system is just as inclined as the reflexive (associative) system to sustain rather than to correct faulty anxiogenic convictions, and thus tend to promote avoidance and escape behaviours.

Reflexive responses as input

For survival, it is obviously of critical importance to be sensitive to signs of impending threats, as this allows for a timely avoidance of dangerous situations.

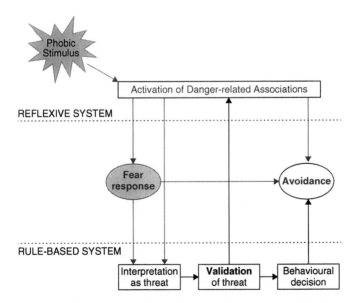

FIGURE 7.1   Main elements of a dual system, multi-process model of anxiety vulnerability. A phobic stimulus will activate danger-related associations and may give rise to affective responses (e.g. fear or disgust) that both will be used as input for the propositional processes in the rule-based system. The reasoning process ("validation") will typically result in a further strengthening of the danger-related associations and phobic beliefs, and will support the initial fear-induced tendency to avoid the phobic stimulus

Accordingly, our cognitive system is extremely efficient in detecting potentially threatening stimuli and there is ample evidence that threatening stimuli get prioritized access to limited cognitive resources (e.g. de Jong, Koster, van Wees, & Martens, 2010). Importantly, the reflexive (associative) system is highly adaptive and sensitive to all kinds of learning experiences. The preferential processing of danger signals is therefore not restricted to a predefined set of universal threats (e.g. predators, heights, etc.) but may also apply to highly idiosyncratic initially neutral stimuli that have acquired threat value (Koster, Crombez, Van Damme, Verschuere, & De Houwer, 2005, Alpers, Ruhleder, Walz, Muhlberger, & Pauli, 2005). Once a stimulus has acquired a threat value (e.g. a spider in spider phobia), these stimuli will not only acquire prioritized access to the cognitive system but upon confrontation these stimuli will also elicit reflexive fear responses, just as objectively dangerous stimuli.

Fear

From an evolutionary perspective, fear is viewed as a functional response promoting avoidance of dangerous stimuli or situations. Accordingly, there is an intimate link between the detection of danger and the fear response: If danger, then fear. Relatively strong associations have been shown to promote the tendency to accept the antecedent (here danger) given the presence of the consequent (here fear), resulting in the common reasoning fallacy known as affirmation of the consequent (AC) (e.g. De Neys, Schaeken, & d'Ydewalle, 2003). Therefore, people may tend to infer danger on the basis of their reflexive fear response. People may be especially sensitive to this reasoning fallacy as heightened affect has been shown to more generally impair individuals' reasoning performance (see Blanchette & Richards for a review, 2010). Hence if fear is elicited upon encountering a particular stimulus or situation, this not only sets the stage for using this response as information, but may also impair logicality. Thus, when in an anxious mood-state, people may be especially prone to make logically unjustified inferences such as "I feel fear, thus there must be danger".

In the context of objective danger this heuristic may be helpful to underline the threat value of particular stimuli/behaviours and to sustain proper escape and avoidance responses (cf. Clore & Storbeck, 2006). However, in the context of phobic fears, and thus in the absence of objective danger, this heuristic would hamper the identification of false alarms (i.e. feelings of fear but no danger) and contribute to the persistence of erroneous, phobic beliefs (cf. Slovic, Finucane, Peters, & MacGregor, 2002). In other words, if people erroneously interpret feelings of fear as signalling danger, and use their fear response as input in the process of validating their lingering concerns ("I feel anxious, thus there must be something to fear") they will enter a danger-confirming vicious circle.

By now there is considerable evidence that indeed individuals suffering from anxiety disorders do use their feelings of fear as input in the process of evaluating the presence of actual danger. In a first experiment, participants read a series of scenarios that systematically varied with regard to the absence/presence of objective danger and the absence/presence of a subjective fear response (Arntz, Rauner, & van den Hout, 1995). Participants were instructed to rate the threat value of each scenario. In support of the hypothesis that anxiety patients use their fear response to infer danger, specifically anxiety patients reported higher threat ratings for scenarios in which a subjective fear response was present than for scenarios in which a fear response was absent. Unexpectedly, this pattern of emotion-based reasoning (ER) was not restricted to scenarios relevant for their particular anxiety disorder. This points to the possibility that ER is a premorbid characteristic that sets people at risk for developing anxiety disorders.

In conceptually similar research, Muris and colleagues provided children (8–13 years) scenarios with or without the addition of a *bodily* (instead of subjective) fear response (for a review, see Muris, 2010). Consistent with the view that ER may set people at risk for developing anxiety disorders, it was shown that the strength of ER was associated with indices of anxiety vulnerability such as trait anxiety and anxiety sensitivity (Muris, Merckelbach, & van Spauwen, 2003). In further support of the view that ER may enhance anxiety vulnerability, there is some evidence that ER in children (8–11 years) has predictive validity for anxiety symptoms at ten-month follow-up. However, it should be acknowledged that these effects were small and not consistent for all age groups (Morren, Muris, Kindt, Schouten, & van den Hout, 2008). Moreover, a recent controlled study testing children with social anxiety disorder or another anxiety disorder failed to find strong evidence for a relatively strong ER in the clinical groups, although there was a trend in the predicted direction (Alkozei, Cooper, & Creswell, 2014). Yet it should be acknowledged that in the social anxiety group the threat interpretation and fear ratings with regard to the (ambiguous) scenarios were already enhanced without physical response information. To arrive at more final conclusions with regard to the relevance of ER in clinically anxious youth, it would be important to replicate the study with less ambiguous scenarios and to present subjective response information instead of information about physical symptoms.

In an attempt to more directly test the causal influence of ER on the persistence of phobic convictions, a recent study examined the impact of experimentally reducing ER on danger beliefs about spiders (Lommen, Engelhard, van den Hout, & Arntz, 2013). To reduce ER, participants were presented with 60 scenarios that systematically varied in the absence/presence of (i) objective safe versus danger information, and (ii) absence/presence of a fear response. Participants were instructed to imagine the scenarios as if it happened to them, and to complete the final sentence of the scenarios as a means to disambiguate the outcome by choosing one out of two options (a negative or a positive outcome). For example, the final sentence: "Shortly after that, the car . . ." could be completed by choosing either (1) "crashes into a tree" or (2) ". . . drives into the garage at home". Upon making their choice they received feedback ("correct" or "incorrect, try again"). The next scenario was presented as soon as the "correct" option was selected. In the experimental condition, the feedback was based on the objective information (a dangerous situation should be followed by a negative outcome, whereas a safe situation should be followed by a positive outcome). In the control condition, the feedback was based on the subjective response information.

As intended, ER reduced in the experimental group, but was retained in the control group. Most important for the present context, the danger estimates during the behavioural approach task were also lower in the experimental condition and this effect was maintained at the follow-up one day later. Thus these results showed that reducing ER also reduces the strength of phobic beliefs. This pattern of findings not only provides direct evidence for the causal influence of ER on the persistence of phobic beliefs but also points to a straightforward clinical application to reduce the strength of such beliefs.

Disgust

The affective responses that are elicited by phobic stimuli are not restricted to fear. There is increasing evidence that also disgust is often involved in specific phobias such as small-animal phobias (e.g. Mulkens, de Jong, & Merckelbach, 1996), blood-injection-injury phobia (Olatunji, Lohr, Sawchuk, & Patten, 2007), fear of sexual penetration (e.g. de Jong, van Overveld, & Borg, 2013), and contamination fears (Olatunji et al., 2007). It has been proposed that disgust is an adaptive psychological mechanism that drives behavioural avoidance of infectious disease (Oaten, Stevenson, & Case, 2009). The costs of infection constitute an important selection pressure and disgust-induced avoidance of potential contaminants has been argued to represent an important behavioural disease avoidance mechanism that complements the physiological immune systems (Curtis, 2013). Thus where fear is typically linked to the avoidance of physical harm, disgust is linked to the avoidance of invisible dangers related to the transmission of disease (e.g. bacteria, viri). Unjustified feelings of disgust may, just as feelings of fear, be used as signals of actual (but invisible) danger. Accordingly, also disgust-based reasoning may contribute to the persistence of irrational (phobic) danger beliefs.

In a first attempt to examine the relevance of disgust-based reasoning, high and low contamination fearful individuals were presented with a series of scenarios that varied in the absence/presence of objective threat of contamination and the absence/presence of the actor's disgust response. Following each script, participants rated the perceived threat of getting ill. In line with the hypothesis that disgust-based reasoning might be involved in fear of contamination, specifically high contamination fearful individuals inferred risk of becoming ill on the basis of experienced disgust in scenarios that were low in objective danger of contamination (Verwoerd, de Jong, Wessel, & van Hout, 2013). In a similar vein, it was found that individuals with fear of vomiting (emetophobia) inferred higher illness risks when disgust response information was added to objectively safe scenarios (Verwoerd, van Hout, & de Jong, 2013).

In subsequent research, participants high and low in contamination fear were presented with "harm" and "contamination" relevant scenarios that were systematically varied with the absence presence of a fear or a disgust response (de Jong, Verwoerd, Wessel, & van den Hout, 2013). Replicating the original results of

Arntz *et al.* (1995), especially in relatively high fearful individuals, the addition of a fear response resulted in higher danger ratings for the harm-relevant scenarios. Importantly, specifically for participants high in fear of contamination, adding a disgust response resulted in higher danger ratings for the contamination-relevant scenarios. Thus the impact of affective responses on individuals' danger ratings appeared specific for both the type of response (fear vs. disgust) and the domain of concern (physical threat vs. disease). The domain/response specificity seems to imply that ER does not reflect a generally enhanced tendency to be a prey to common reasoning fallacies, such as affirmation of the consequent, but critically relies on individuals' fearful preoccupations.

Intrusions

For some anxiety disorders such as post-traumatic stress disorder (PTSD), disorder-relevant stimuli not only elicit strong affective (fear) responses, but also threatening intrusive thoughts. The occurrence of threatening trauma-related intrusions may, just as emotional responses, be used as input for the rule-based system. If PTSD patients would infer danger on the basis of intrusive memories, this might contribute to the persistence of PTSD. As a first test of intrusion-based reasoning (IR), a group of Vietnam veterans with PTSD and a group of veterans without PTSD were presented with a series of scenarios that systematically varied in the absence/presence of objective danger and the absence/presence of distressing intrusions (Engelhard, Macklin, McNally, van den Hout, & Arntz, 2001).

A sample scenario would be:

> It's a fourth of July holiday, and you're on your way to meet some friends. You're looking forward to seeing them, but you're running late. As you're driving your car, several children toss firecrackers under the wheels of your car.

The version of danger and intrusions continued:

> You hit the accelerator, but lose control of the wheel. The car stalls in the wrong lane. The oncoming traffic moves quickly towards you. You hear more firecrackers. The sudden noise triggers upsetting thoughts about Vietnam.

The version of danger and no intrusions was:

> You hit the accelerator, but lose control of the wheel. The car stalls in the wrong lane. The oncoming traffic moves quickly towards you. You hear more firecrackers. The sudden noise makes you angry, but then you laugh to yourself and think: "Well, at least I've got a good excuse now for being late".

The version of safety and intrusions was: "The sudden noise triggers upsetting thoughts about Vietnam." The version of safety and no intrusions was: "The sudden noise makes you angry, but then you laugh to yourself and think: 'Well, at least I've got a good excuse now for being late'." The results suggested that indeed PTSD patients may use IR when appraising the threat-value of PTSD-relevant scenarios: whereas veterans without PTSD inferred the danger of scenarios from objective stimulus information, veterans with PTSD also inferred danger from the presence of intrusions.

Underlining the relevance of IR, a subsequent study showed that IR has predictive value for the development of PTSD (Engelhard, van den Hout, Arntz, & McNally, 2002). In this study, a group of people who had witnessed a dreadful train crash in a Belgian town and a control group of people from the same town who did not see the crash completed an IR task in which both the absence/presence of objective danger and the absence/presence of intrusions about the crash were systematically varied. Both groups were re-assessed for PTSD at 3.5-month follow-up. The directly exposed residents reported higher danger ratings to scenarios in which intrusions were included than the control group. Consistent with the previous study among Vietnam veterans, the strength of IR was strongly related to the strength of concurrent (acute) PTSD symptoms. Pointing to the potential role of IR in the maintenance of anxiogenic beliefs, IR showed also prognostic value for the strength of PTSD symptoms at follow-up. An important next step would be to experimentally reduce IR following trauma exposure to test whether this would prevent the development of PTSD (cf. Lommen et al., 2013). If so, this would not only support the alleged causal influence of IR but also set the stage for a fresh theory-derived preventive intervention.

Avoidance behaviour

In the context of looming danger, people take all kinds of behavioural precautions to ward off feared outcomes. Although this type of safety behaviour may be highly functional in the context of actual threats, when applied in the absence of objective danger (phobic threats), it may become counterproductive. In the context of phobic fears, these avoidance behaviours interfere with the validation process by preventing experiences that can disconfirm the validity of phobic danger beliefs. For example, although excessive hand washing in obsessive compulsive disorder (OCD) may be intended to prevent negative outcomes (e.g. the transmission of disease), it also serves to prevent the correction of inaccurate danger beliefs (e.g. that touching a door knob would be an important health risk). Accordingly, it has been shown that clinical interventions are less effective if patients are allowed to use safety behaviours during exposure exercises (e.g. Sloan & Telch, 2002).

Interestingly, employing safety behaviours may not only interfere with the modification of already existing beliefs, but may also promote the development of phobic danger beliefs. Participants who were instructed to engage in OCD safety behaviours for two weeks showed an increase in danger estimates and fear of contamination (Deacon & Maack, 2008). One way to explain these findings is that these participants may have concluded that their safety behaviours might have prevented the occurrence of dangerous outcomes. This might have led to a phobic appraisal of initially harmless stimuli as dangerous. Thus they might have inferred danger on the basis of their avoidance behaviours "if I (feel the urge to) wash, then there must be danger". In the context of non-existent (phobic) threats, such "If I avoid, there must be danger" heuristic will logically contribute to the persistence of phobic beliefs.

To test whether indeed patients with anxiety disorders infer danger on the basis of their own acts of avoidance, a group of participants with panic disorder, OCD, or social anxiety disorder, and a non-clinical control group were asked to rate the danger in scenarios that systematically varied in the absence/presence of objective danger and the absence/presence of safety behaviour (Gangemi, Mancini, & van den Hout, 2012). Interestingly, where non-anxious controls only relied on objective danger information, the danger estimates of anxiety patients were also influenced by safety behaviour information. This tendency to infer danger on the basis of their avoidance behaviours might contribute to the development and persistence of phobic beliefs. As soon as one believes that one's safety behaviours imply danger, people may enter a downward spiral in which safety behaviours strengthen the perception of danger, which in turn will enhance avoidance motivation, etc.

All in all, there is consistent evidence that, in the context of irrational fears, reflexive affective responses and behavioural tendencies are used as input for the rule-based system and give rise to fallacious danger-confirming inferences. Because heightened affect generally impairs logicality, this type of danger-confirming reasoning fallacy may be especially resistant to logical correction.

Automatic associations

Encountering threatening situations or the mere processing of danger-related information will automatically (i.e. non-intentional and uncontrollable) elicit threat-related associations. This is not restricted to objective dangers. An extensive series of studies using performance-based measures such as the Implicit Association Test (Greenwald, McGhee, & Schwartz, 1998) and the Affective Simon Task (De Houwer & Eelen, 1998) has shown that, in the context of phobic fears, also intrinsically harmless stimuli such as a house spider or an interpersonal event may elicit danger-related automatic associations (e.g. Teachman, Gregg, & Woody, 2001; Glashouwer, Vroling, de Jong, Lange, & de Keijser, 2013). The selective activation of danger associations will result in a biased representation of the actual characteristics of the pertinent stimuli in working memory (cf. Strack & Deutsch, 2004). Thus the input for the rule-based system will already be dominated with threatening information. Even when people would use proper reasoning strategies, such distorted data base will lead to threat-biased conclusions and thus lower the probability that the rule-based system will exert its influence to modify fallacious danger beliefs.

Phobic danger beliefs can be condensed to conditional statements of the type "if phobia-relevant stimulus (P) then danger (Q)". When available information in working memory systematically implies a strong link between the phobia-relevant stimulus P (e.g. displaying a blush) and impending danger Q (e.g. negative social evaluation), various common mechanisms may contribute to the refractoriness of phobic beliefs. Germane to this, there is evidence indicating that two different causal structures are typically accessed in semantic memory when considering the occurrence of consequence Q given cause P: One corresponding to "*ways of making Q happen*", the other corresponding to "*ways to prevent Q to occur*" (i.e. disabling conditions) (Quinn & Markovits, 1998; De Neys et al., 2003). The stronger a specific cause P is associated with consequence Q, the higher the probability that people consider P as a sufficient condition for Q to occur (e.g. a blush will always have negative social consequences), whereas the more easily disabling conditions are retrieved (e.g. following a mishap blushing has typically favourable social consequences), the less likely it is that people perceive P as a sufficient condition for Q. Basic research with emotionally neutral materials has shown that the larger the number of disabling conditions that come to people's minds and the stronger their associative strength, the less people are inclined to accept P as a sufficient cause for the occurrence of Q (De Neys et al., 2003).

It would be important for future research to examine whether similar mechanisms are also at work in the context of phobia-relevant conditional beliefs and to test if indeed phobic individuals show difficulty in generating examples of disabling conditions, and/or whether they are relatively insensitive to information involving conditions that prevent Q to occur (e.g. information signifying that a blush is not a sufficient sign of incompetence). If so, interventions that enhance the accessibility of counterexamples might be helpful as a clinical intervention to undermine the persistence of phobic danger beliefs (cf. Clerkin & Teachman, 2010; Craske & Mystkowski, 2006).

As already discussed in the context of emotional reasoning, relatively strong P–Q associations also promote the fallacious tendency to accept P given Q (affirmation of the consequent). In the context of phobic anxiety, this may give rise to danger-confirming reasoning of the type: "If tumour then headache, I have a headache thus there must be a tumour." Basic research using neutral conditionals of the type *If the brake is depressed (P), then the car slows down (Q)* has shown that this type of strong P–Q associations promotes the fallacy of AC – *The car slows down (Q) thus the brake is depressed (P)*. Participants find it relatively difficult to come up with alternative conditions ("alternative ways of making Q happen"), and tend to persist in their faulty (AC) conclusion even when alternative conditions are presented (e.g. running out of gas, having a flat tyre).

Along the same lines, individuals suffering from health anxiety may have difficulty in thinking of alternative causes and/or may be relatively insensitive to relevant information suggesting alternative causes for a headache, such as lack of sleep. Thus far the proposed role of AC in the persistence of phobic danger beliefs has not been tested in empirical research. If future research would indeed show that phobic individuals are prone to this type of reasoning fallacy, this would not only improve our understanding of the refractoriness of phobic convictions but would also suggest that it might be clinically useful to enhance the accessibility of alternative causes for the occurrence of symptom Q.

Prior beliefs

Encounters with a phobic stimulus will also reflexively activate prior (danger) beliefs. Obviously, correcting such phobic beliefs requires the ability to accurately deduce the logical implications of the empirical evidence for certain beliefs and to actively search for falsifying information to critically evaluate the validity of these convictions. Basic research on everyday reasoning suggests, however, that individuals in fact tend to use simple heuristics instead of engaging in analytical reasoning. Most relevant to the current context, people tend to use the heuristic "what I believe is true". That is, people are inclined to consider believable conclusions as valid and unbelievable conclusions as invalid (e.g. Evans, Newtsead, & Byrne, 1993), a reasoning bias known as "belief bias".

Current reasoning models (e.g. Evans, 2003) propose that belief bias may not only result from using a "what is believable is true" heuristic but may also arise during more analytical evaluation of the evidence to the extent that people are inclined to prove believable conclusions as valid, and/or disprove unbelievable conclusions as invalid. This latter tendency may vary as a function of perceived utilities associated with erroneously accepting an invalid conclusion, or erroneously refuting a valid conclusion. In the context of looming danger, people may be relatively conservative when the conclusion points to impending threat, although the conclusion does not match with one's beliefs. Conversely, people may be relatively critical when a conclusion points to the absence of threat, especially when this safety information conflicts with individuals' convictions. Thus these so-called Type 2 belief bias effects would be most prominent for invalid (yet believable) danger signals and valid (yet unbelievable) safety signals.

Belief-biased reasoning has been typically investigated using syllogisms. Syllogisms consist of premises that one needs to accept as being true, and a conclusion that does or does not logically follow from the premises. Most research in this domain has employed so-called categorical syllogisms. An example of such syllogism would be: *No cancers are curable/Some illnesses are curable//Therefore all illnesses are cancers* (e.g. Eliades, Mansell, Stewart, & Blanchette, 2012). In a belief bias paradigm, the conclusion of the syllogism is manipulated in terms of both logical validity (valid or invalid) and believability (believable and unbelievable). If a valid conclusion is consistent with prior beliefs (e.g. some illnesses are not cancers), then a logical response is more likely to be drawn. If, on the other hand, a valid conclusion is unbelievable (e.g. all illnesses are cancers), then individuals are more likely to erroneously judge it to be logically invalid. The opposite pattern typically emerges for invalid conclusions. This interaction between logical validity and believability reflects the belief bias effect.

Emotional content

Research that tested deductive reasoning performance in the context of emotionally charged materials generally showed less logicality as indicated by an overall tendency to accept fewer valid conclusions as logical and reject less invalid conclusions when reasoning about emotional compared to neutral contents. Perhaps even more relevant for the present context, reasoning about emotional contents is also usually associated with enhanced belief bias effects (e.g. Eliades *et al.*, 2012). However, there are notable exceptions. For example, it has been found that war veterans showed enhanced performance – and thus less belief bias – when reasoning about battle-related materials (Blanchette & Campbell, 2012). Yet participants with more intense combat experiences showed a reduced advantage in reasoning about combat-related emotional problems. Thus perhaps in veterans with PTSD this lowered advantage might even turn into a disadvantage. In addition, it has been claimed that the influence of beliefs can be attenuated by negative emotions (Goel & Vartanian, 2011). Indeed these authors showed that belief bias was attenuated when reasoning with negative materials. However, the content of the problems in that study were not so much concerned with threat or danger but with the violation of social norms. An alternative explanation could therefore be that participants considered these problems as more relevant/important in addition to more/less believable and more/less negative, which might have motivated participants to subject these problems to more rigorous analytical validation. In line with this, participants took more time to solve the counter-intuitive violation-of-social-norm problems.

Thus, all in all, it seems fair to conclude that the majority of the evidence supports the view that reasoning with emotional content is associated with enhanced belief bias effects and less analytical processing. Clearly, this suggests that also reasoning about danger-relevant information might be biased in a way to confirm the original danger beliefs.

Universal danger beliefs

Most research on belief bias has employed so-called categorical syllogisms. However, because categorical syllogisms are relatively difficult to solve (error rates are often substantial in spite of the fact that most studies rely on student participants), this type of reasoning task does not seem suitable for the investigation of belief bias in clinical populations that also comprise of individuals with only very limited educational experience. In addition, the structure of categorical syllogisms (e.g. *No As are B/Some Cs are B//Therefore some Cs are not A*) seems quite distant from everyday reasoning problems, and many people without training in formal reasoning are probably unaware of these problems and their logical implications. Therefore, we decided to use so-called linear syllogisms in most of our studies on danger-relevant belief bias. An abstract example of a linear syllogism would be: *A is larger than B/B is larger than C//Therefore, A is larger than C*. This type of syllogism is relatively simple to solve, and in the absence of a time limit, people generally make only very few errors in judging their logical validity (e.g. Smeets & de Jong, 2005). Because individuals typically tend to make only very few errors when judging the validity of linear syllogisms, for these tasks, participants' latencies to solve the problems, rather than the percentage of logical errors, are used to index individuals' reasoning performance. Supporting the validity of this approach to examine belief bias effects, an initial series of studies using linear syllogisms concerning factual beliefs (e.g. An elephant is larger than a cat/A cat is larger than a fly//Therefore an elephant is larger than a fly) systematically showed that participants' performance was relatively poor when there was a mismatch between the logical validity and believability (i.e. factual correctness) of the syllogisms' conclusions (e.g. Smeets & de Jong, 2005).

To examine belief bias in the context of danger-related materials, we presented participants with a series of linear syllogisms that represented generally threatening (e.g. Potassium cyanide is more toxic than tylenol), safety-related (e.g. The Netherlands is safer than Afghanistan), and neutral (A caravan is smaller than a castle) themes (Vroling & de Jong, 2010). Each syllogism was presented in a valid-believable, valid-unbelievable, invalid-believable, and invalid-unbelievable type. For the threat syllogisms, believability strongly affected participants' response latencies for invalid trials (i.e. slow responses for believable-invalid trials), whereas such effects of believability were virtually absent for valid trials. The opposite pattern was evident for safety syllogisms. For the safety themes, believability affected performance on valid trials (long latencies for unbelievable-valid trials), whereas such effects were absent for invalid trials (see Figure 7.2).

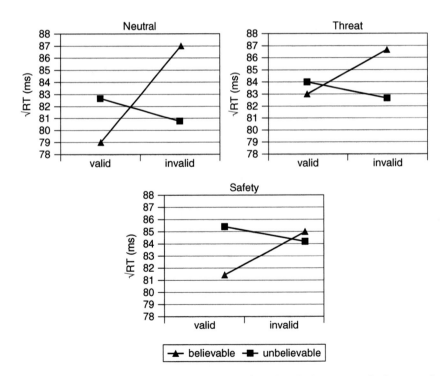

FIGURE 7.2 Square root normalized mean median RT (ms) on neutral, threat, and safety syllogisms, varying over validity and believability

Thus, consistent with the notion that it is adaptive to be especially reluctant to falsify danger signals, the confirmation of danger seems to have had priority even if the threatening conclusion was not in line with participants' prior beliefs, whereas additional time was taken to reconsider a logically justified refutation if such a refutation would be in conflict with participants' a priori (threat) belief. Conversely, the disconfirmation of conclusions implying safety seems to have had priority even if the safety signals were in line with a priori beliefs, whereas additional time was taken to reconsider a logically justified acceptance of a safety signal if this signal was not consistent with participants' beliefs.

All in all, it seems that individuals' reasoning performance was characterized by a "Better Safe Than Sorry" strategy (for a more elaborate discussion, see de Jong & Vroling, 2014). Such conservatism bias may be considered functional in the context of objective threats. However, if such belief-biased reasoning processes would also be applied to phobic (non-existing) dangers, this common reasoning pattern would contribute to the persistence of phobic (danger) beliefs.

Phobic danger beliefs

In a first attempt to test whether belief-biased reasoning would also apply to phobic convictions, we tested a group of women with spider phobia (de Jong, Weertman, Horselenberg, & van den Hout, 1997). Yet this study failed to find a convincing belief bias effect for phobia-relevant syllogisms. However, this might well have been due to methodological problems. Most important, spider phobia relevant beliefs (see, e.g., Arntz, Lavy, van den Berg, & van Rijsoort, 1993) are hard to translate into (linear) syllogisms. The necessary inclusion of a comparison category further decreases the resemblance between the syllogisms' conclusions and the dysfunctional beliefs (e.g. "a spider is creepy" was translated into: "A spider is creepier than a fish/A fish is creepier than a pigeon//A spider is creepier than a pigeon"). It seems highly conceivable that this methodological constraint reduced the sensitivity of the task. In addition, there are reasons to doubt whether spider phobia is the optimal candidate for testing the influence of phobic beliefs on reasoning performance. Although there is evidence that spider phobic individuals do report high believability ratings for irrational spider-related beliefs (e.g. "the spider will kill me"; Arntz et al., 1993), it is still a matter of dispute whether dysfunctional beliefs indeed play a crucial role in the aetiology and maintenance of spider phobia.

Therefore, we subsequently focussed on social anxiety to test further the potential role of belief bias in the context of phobic convictions. Dysfunctional beliefs are generally assumed to be central to social anxiety disorder (e.g. Clark & Wells, 1995). In addition, social anxiety beliefs often imply social comparison (e.g. Trower & Gilbert, 1989), making social anxiety convictions especially suitable for translation into linear syllogisms (e.g. "I am not likeable" translates into "I am less likeable than others" or into a linear syllogism such as "I am less likeable than Jane and Jane is less likeable than John"). In a first study, we presented a series of linear syllogisms concerning social anxiety relevant themes to a group of student participants and tested the strength of belief bias effects as a function of their fear of negative evaluation (Vroling & de Jong, 2009). The syllogisms related to social anxiety relevant beliefs varied in logical validity and social anxiety (SA) congruency. A SA-congruent conclusion would be "Others find me less capable than person A", whereas a SA-incongruent conclusion would be "Others find person A less capable than me". Participants high in fear of negative evaluation were relatively fast when there was a match and relatively slow when there was a mismatch between SA congruency and logical validity (see Figure 7.3). This belief bias effect was similarly evident for valid and invalid syllogisms. This pattern suggests that high socially anxious individuals took additional time to reconsider both a logically justified refutation of a social anxiety congruent ("threat") conclusion and a logically justified acceptance of a social anxiety incongruent ("safe") conclusion. Clearly, such reasoning strategy may hamper the correction of phobic beliefs.

Interestingly, relatively low socially anxious individuals showed the opposite pattern. These individuals were relatively *slow* when there was a match between SA congruency and validity. This finding nicely fit with other findings indicating that low anxious individuals display a self-favouring effect (de Jong, 2002) and are better at learning the positive rule "I am liked" than the negative rule "I am disliked" in a probabilistic learning task (Button, Browning, Munafò, & Lewis, 2012). Such positive self-biases might enable individuals to function more confidently in social interactions and help protect individuals' mental health. Belief-biased reasoning in low socially anxious individuals may thus be considered as a "cognitive vaccine"

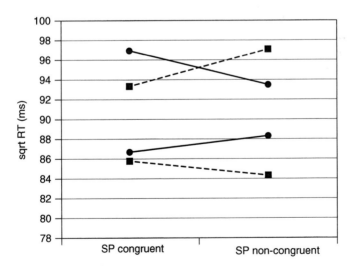

FIGURE 7.3   Square-rooted RTs (ms) on the four conditions of the social anxiety convictions domain for the lowest (BFNE = 1) and the highest (BFNE = 42) socially fearful participants, illustrating the SA congruency * validity * BFNE interaction. BFNE = Brief Fear of Negative Evaluation scale; BFNE = 1, valid; BFNE = 1, invalid; BFNE = 42, valid; BFNE = 42, invalid

(cf. Holmes, Lang, & Shah, 2009) that may help to prevent the development of low social self-esteem and other subsequent symptoms, such as social anxiety and depression.

The initial findings in analogue participants also translated to a clinical population. Individuals with clinically diagnosed social anxiety disorder (SAD) similarly showed relatively long latencies when there was a mismatch between SA congruency and logical validity, whereas the opposite pattern was evident in the nonfearful control participants (Vroling, Glashouwer, Lange, Allart, & de Jong, 2013). Thus the relationship between phobic convictions and belief-biased reasoning performance seems a reliable finding. An important next step would be to test the influence of treatment on concern-specific belief bias. To the extent that belief bias is more than an epiphenomenon of phobic concerns, residual belief bias effects will show prognostic value for the return of fear following initially successful treatment (cf. Vasey, Harbaugh, Buffington, Jones, & Fazio, 2012). In addition, it would be interesting for future research to bring belief bias under experimental control. If indeed belief bias contributes to the persistence of phobic danger beliefs, one would predict that experimental reduction of belief-biased reasoning will also reduce the strength of individuals' phobic convictions. One way to reduce belief bias would be to present phobic individuals with an extensive series of linear syllogisms of which the believable danger-related conclusions are mostly logically invalid, and the unbelievable safety conclusions most often valid. Again, if this would work out, this would not only provide direct evidence for the causal influence of belief bias on the persistence of phobic danger beliefs but may also provide a fresh starting point for an efficient theory-derived clinical intervention.

Generally enhanced belief bias

Enhanced belief-biased reasoning may not only arise as a consequence of strongly held (phobic) beliefs, but may also reflect a premorbid reasoning tendency. Although belief bias is a universal phenomenon, people vary in the strength of this tendency to readily accept conclusions that match with a priori beliefs and to refute conclusions that are in conflict with prior beliefs (e.g. Smeets & de Jong, 2005). The stronger this habitual belief-biased reasoning style, the more difficulty people will experience in correcting their prior beliefs on the basis of falsifying information. Thus, as soon as people might have acquired phobogenic danger beliefs (e.g. due to a conditioning experience), the presence of an enhanced belief bias might prevent individuals from giving up these beliefs in the face of incompatible data.

The strength of belief bias effects is determined by at least two factors. First, there are individual differences in the strength of an individual's habitual tendency to rely on prior beliefs when considering the validity of a particular proposition. Second, the strength of the belief bias effect will depend on the content of the proposition. It is only when propositions relate to what one believes that belief-biased reasoning will arise. When one does not hold strong convictions regarding spiders, belief-biased reasoning will not be activated when confronted with spider-relevant information. However, when a person has acquired the belief that spiders are dangerous, belief-biased reasoning will be applied when confronted with spider-relevant information, and these belief bias effects will be especially pronounced in individuals who are characterized by an enhanced belief-biased reasoning style.

Recently, we experimentally explored whether enhanced (trait) belief bias might indeed immunize against refutation of once acquired phobogenic beliefs. We subjected participants with variable levels of belief bias to a differential aversive (picture/shock) conditioning paradigm and examined whether individuals with a relatively strong belief bias would be relatively insensitive to subsequently presented corrective information during extinction (Vroling & de Jong, 2013). If people have a (habitual) difficulty with incorporating disconfirming information, somehow acquired UCS (unconditioned stimulus) expectancies will be more difficult to extinguish. In line with this, belief bias indeed predicted delayed extinction of UCS expectancies when there was a high a priori CS–UCS belongingness (i.e. cactus as CS [conditioned stimulus]). When we used a CS+ with no UCS belongingness (picture displaying blue circle instead of a cactus), we found the opposite pattern. Under these conditions, higher levels of belief bias were related to speeded extinction, probably because the CS–UCS association was inconsistent with the prior belief that "blue circles" are not predictors of aversive outcomes. Together, the findings support the view that a habitual belief-confirming reasoning strategy may be involved in delayed extinction, and can therefore be seen as one of the factors that may contribute to the consolidation of dysfunctional danger beliefs through which phobic fears may develop and/or persist. Following this, it might be worthwhile to develop a belief bias modification training as a "cognitive vaccine" that may prevent the development of irrational danger beliefs.

Hypothesis testing

Of course, the input to the rule-based system is not merely constituted by bottom up acquired information. People may also actively search for relevant information to judge the validity of automatically elicited associations and automatic thoughts. As discussed before, the phobic beliefs can be typically condensed into conditional propositions of the type "If P, then Q" ("If I blush, then people will judge me as incompetent"). Testing the logical validity of such conditional beliefs requires the investigation of whether P is indeed followed by Q and a careful check whether any non-Q is preceded by P. If the latter is true (displayed a blush, but not judged as incompetent), the conditional rule is proven to be invalid.

A task that is often used to investigate what type of information people select when judging the validity of this type of conditional propositions is the Wason Selection Task (WST; Wason, 1968). A typical WST consists of a conditional rule and four cards. One side of each card shows whether the antecedent is true or false (P or not-P), whereas the other side indicates whether the consequent is true or false (Q or not-Q). Only one side of each card is shown. Thus participants are shown with one card indicating P, one not-P, one Q, and one not-Q. It is the participants' task to indicate what card or cards they definitely need to turn over in order to find out whether the rule is true or false for those four cards. Following the rules of logic, they need to turn the P card (to check whether on the other side indeed is a Q) and the non-Q card (to see whether there might be a P on the other side).

A series of studies using the WST clearly demonstrated that, in general, people do not reason according to the normative rules of formal logic. Rather it appears that individuals' reasoning performance is highly domain specific and guided by perceived utilities (e.g. Kirby, 1994). In the context of threat, the utility levels of potentially verifying and falsifying information highly depends on the type of rule. In the context of looming threat, information that may signify danger is of relatively great value. Although it may seem inefficient to flee for false alarms, a single instance of ignoring a danger signal may be fatal. In the case of safety signals, the opposite is true. Information that may signify that a certain safety signal is not reliable has greater survival value than information which may prove the signal reliable. In line with this, a series of studies showed that participants tend indeed to select potentially verifying information in case of danger rules (i.e. turn card P and Q) and potentially falsifying information in case of safety rules (i.e. turn card P and not-Q; e.g. de Jong, Mayer, & van den Hout, 1997; Smeets, de Jong, & Mayer, 2000).

Experimental manipulation of the consequent's threat value showed that the strength of this danger-confirming reasoning bias is directly related to the subjective threat value of the consequent (e.g. Muris et al., 2009). In line with this, it has been demonstrated that especially anxiety disordered individuals show a similar "Better-Safe-Then-Sorry" reasoning strategy in the context of concern-relevant danger/safety rules (de Jong. Mayer, & van den Hout, 1997; Smeets et al., 2000; Nitrauw, 2002). In case of irrational danger beliefs, such a reasoning strategy immunizes against refutation of concern-relevant convictions, which might also help explain the refractoriness of phobogenic beliefs in the face of falsifying information.

An important next step would be to test whether this reasoning strategy would subside following successful treatment. If not, it might be useful to put more emphasis on teaching reasoning skills that can be applied to deal with dysfunctional beliefs (e.g. Nisbett, Fong, Lehman, & Cheng, 1987). To more directly test the role of such a Better-Safe-Than-Sorry strategy in the persistence of symptoms, it would be important to design interventions that specifically modify this reasoning bias and to see whether reducing this bias also affects individuals' anxiety symptoms.

Conclusion

The previous sections discussed various ways in which reflexive (affective and behavioural) responses may bias the input of the rule-based system and how the process of validation may further contribute to threat-biased conclusions. The danger-confirming "validation" processes seem to reflect essentially functional strategies that serve to minimize the risk that something bad will happen (cf. Verschueren,

Peeters, & Schaeken, 2006). However, when applied to phobic responses or phobic convictions, these strategies become counterproductive and hamper the correction of erroneous phobic beliefs.

Although reasoning processes are critically implied in current models of anxiety, most research has thus far focussed on the impact of reflexive processes, whereas the role of reflective (reasoning) processes received only scant attention. The experimental approach of inducing/reducing particular components of reflexive cognitive biases has proven to be very fruitful and provided convincing evidence for the alleged causal influence of cognitive biases in the development and persistence of anxiety disorders (for a review, see MacLeod & Mathews, 2012). Apart from the study of Lommen and colleagues (2013), research on reasoning tendencies in the context of phobic convictions has thus far been essentially correlational in nature. It would be important to follow up the experimental approach of Lommen *et al.* to test the alleged causal properties of the various reasoning fallacies that are assumed to contribute to the persistence of phobic danger beliefs. Such research might also provide concrete theory-derived leads for designing fresh interventions that might help to counteract the persistence of phobic symptoms.

As a complementary effort, it would be important to test the proposed interrelationship between the various (types of) cognitive processes implied in current dual system models of anxiety vulnerability (see Figure 7.1). As an example of such research, White and colleagues (2011) tested the effect of experimentally modifying attentional bias on the interpretation of ambiguous information and showed that individuals trained to attend to threat were more likely to show a threat-confirming interpretation bias than non-trained controls. This suggests that modifying attention in a benign direction might prevent a cascade of subsequent processing biases that may otherwise act in a way to confirm danger (see also Everaert, Tierens, Uzieblo, & Koster, in press). Following a similar strategy, it would be relevant to examine whether, for example, directly modifying automatic associations or enhancing the accessibility of alternative causes for phobic symptoms would have an impact on phobic individuals' tendency to fall prey to reasoning fallacies, such as danger-confirming affirmation of the consequent or threat-confirming belief bias.

More generally, it would be helpful to more systematically assess the various reflexive and reflective biases in a single study (e.g. Ouimet, Radomsky, & Barber, 2012) and to add these types of measures in the context of immediate and long-term effects of currently used treatment procedures. Currently this type of information is largely lacking, thus future research investigating the influence of regular cognitive behavioural treatments (CBT) on the interrelationship between cognitive biases (including reasoning bias) would be extremely welcome. In a similar vein, it would be very helpful to directly compare tailored reasoning bias modification procedures (e.g. training to reduce belief-biased reasoning, or to enhance the accessibility of disabling conditions) with regular CBT, not only in their efficacy of reducing symptoms and reasoning biases but also to examine to what extent the efficacy of CBM (cognitive behavioural modification) and CBT may be mediated by different mechanisms. These types of studies might provide information that is critical to decide whether reasoning modification procedures might be relevant as complementary or even alternative approaches to correct phobic danger beliefs.

To conclude, there is increasing evidence supporting the relevance of reasoning biases in the persistence of phobic danger beliefs. As an important development, recent research started to employ an experimental approach to test the causal influence of reasoning biases on the generation and persistence of phobic convictions. These recent lines of research bear the promise not only to improve insight in the mechanisms involved in the refractoriness of phobic concerns, but also to provide exciting starting points for translating this knowledge in theory-derived interventions within the context of prevention and treatment.

References

Alkozei, A., Cooper, P. J., & Creswell, C. (2014). Emotional reasoning and anxiety sensitivity: Associations with social anxiety disorder in childhood. *Journal of Affective Disorders, 152–154*, 219–228.

Alpers, G. W., Ruhleder, M., Walz, N., Muhlberger, A., & Pauli, P. (2005). Binocular rivalry between emotional and neutral stimuli: A validation using fear conditioning and EEG. *International Journal of Psychophysiology, 57*, 25–32.

Arntz, A., Lavy, E., van den Berg, G., & van Rijsoort, S. (1993). Negative beliefs of spider phobics: A psychometric evaluation of the Spider Phobia Beliefs Questionnaire. *Advances in Behaviour Research and Therapy, 15*, 257–277.

Arntz, A., Rauner, M., & van den Hout, M. (1995). "If I feel anxious, there must be danger": Ex-consequentia reasoning in inferring danger in anxiety disorders. *Behaviour Research and Therapy, 33*, 917–925.

Beck, A. T., Emery, G., & Greenberg, R. L. (1985). *Anxiety Disorders and Phobias: A Cognitive Perspective*. New York: Basic Books.

Blanchette, I., & Campbell, M. (2012). Reasoning about highly emotional topics: Syllogistic reasoning in a group of war veterans. *Journal of Cognitive Psychology, 24*, 157–164.

Blanchette, I., & Richards, A. (2010). The influence of affect on higher level cognition: A review of research on interpretation, judgement, decision making and reasoning. *Cognition & Emotion, 24*, 561–595.

Button, K. S., Browning, M., Munafò, M. R., & Lewis, G. (2012). Social inference and social anxiety: Evidence of a fear-congruent self-referential learning bias. *Journal of Behavior Therapy and Experimental Psychiatry, 43*(4), 1082–1087.

Clark, D. M., & Wells, A. (1995). A cognitive model of social phobia. In R. G. Heimberg, M. R. Liebowitz, D. A. Hope, & F. R. Schneier (Eds.), *Social Phobia: Diagnosis, Assessment, and Treatment* (pp. 69–93). New York: Guilford Press.

Clerkin, E. M., & Teachman, B. A. (2010). Training implicit social anxiety associations: An experimental intervention. *Journal of Anxiety Disorders, 24*, 300–308.

Clore, G. L., & Storbeck, J. (2006). Affect as information about liking, efficacy, and importance. In J. P. Forgas (Ed.), *Affect in Social Thinking and Behavior* (pp. 121–142). New York, NY: Psychology Press.

Craske, M. G., & Mystkowski, J. L. (2006) Exposure therapy and extinction. In M. G. Craske, D. Hermans, & D. Vansteenwegen (Eds.), *Fear and Learning: From Basic Processes to Clinical Implications* (pp. 217–233). Washington, DC: American Psychological Association.

Curtis, V. (2013). Manner mayks man: On manners and hygiene. In C. Butijn, J. van Ophem, & G. Casimir (Eds.), *The Arena of Everyday Life* (pp. 69–79). Wageningen Academic Publishers.

Deacon, B. J., & Maack, D. J. (2008). The effects of safety behaviors on the fear of contamination: An experimental investigation. *Behaviour Research and Therapy, 46,* 537–547.

De Houwer, J., & Eelen, P. (1998). An affective variant of the Simon paradigm. *Cognition and Emotion, 12,* 45–61.

de Jong, P. J. (2002). Implicit self-esteem and social anxiety: Differential self-favouring effects in high and low anxious individuals. *Behaviour Research and Therapy, 40,* 17–24.

de Jong, P. J., Koster, E. H. W., van Wees, R., & Martens, S. (2010). Angry faces hamper subsequent task performance. *Emotion, 10,* 727–732.

de Jong, P. J., Mayer, B., & van den Hout, M. A. (1997). Conditional reasoning and phobic fear: Evidence for a fear-confirming reasoning pattern. *Behaviour Research and Therapy, 35,* 507–516.

de Jong, P. J., van Overveld, M., & Borg, C. (2013). Giving in to arousal or staying stuck in disgust. Disgust-based mechanisms in sex and sexual dysfunction. *Annual Review of Sex Research, 50,* 247–262.

de Jong, P. J., Verwoerd, J., Wessel, J. P., & van den Hout, W. J. P. J. (2013). *Disgust-based Reasoning in OCD.* Presentation during the World Congress of Behavioral and Cognitive Therapies, Lima.

de Jong, P. J., & Vroling, M. S. (2014). Better safe than sorry: Threat-confirming reasoning bias in anxiety disorders. In I. Blanchette (Ed.), *Emotion and Reasoning* (pp. 22–43). London: Psychology Press (in the series of Current Issues in Thinking and Reasoning).

de Jong, P. J., Weertman, A., Horselenberg, R., & van den Hout, M. A. (1997). Deductive reasoning and pathological anxiety: Evidence for a relatively strong belief bias. *Cognitive Therapy and Research, 21,* 647–662.

De Neys, W., Schaeken, W., & d'Ydewalle, G. (2003). Causal conditional reasoning and strength of association: The disabling condition case. *European Journal of Cognitive Psychology, 15,* 161–176.

Eliades, M., Mansell, W., Stewart, A. J., & Blanchette, I. (2012) An investigation of belief-bias and logicality in reasoning with emotional contents. *Thinking & Reasoning, 18,* 461–479.

Engelhard, I. M., Macklin, M. L., McNally, R. J., van den Hout, M. A., & Arntz, A. (2001). Emotion- and intrusion-based reasoning in Vietnam veterans with and without chronic posttraumatic stress disorder. *Behaviour Research and Therapy, 39,* 1139–1348.

Engelhard, I. M., van den Hout, M. A., Arntz, A., & McNally, R. J. (2002). A longitudinal study of "Intrusion-based reasoning" and PTSD after a train disaster. *Behaviour Research and Therapy, 40,* 1415–1424.

Evans, J. St. B. T. (2003). In two minds: Dual-process accounts of reasoning. *Trends in Cognitive Sciences, 7,* 454–459.

Evans, J. St. B. T., Newstead, S. E., & Byrne, R. M. (Eds.). (1993). *Human Reasoning: The Psychology of Deduction.* London: Psychology Press.

Everaert, J., Tierens, M., Uzieblo, K., & Koster, E. H. W. (in press). The indirect effect of attention bias on memory via interpretation bias: Evidence for the combined cognitive bias hypothesis in subclinical depression. *Cognition & Emotion.*

Gangemi, A., Mancini, F., & van den Hout, M. (2012). Behavior as information: "If I avoid, then there must be a danger". *Journal of Behavior Therapy and Experimental Psychiatry, 43,* 1032–1038.

Glashouwer, K. A., Vroling, M. S., de Jong, P. J., Lange, W.-G., & de Keijser, J. (2013). Low implicit self-esteem and dysfunctional automatic associations in social anxiety disorder. *Journal of Behavior Therapy and Experimental Psychiatry, 44,* 262–270.

Goel, V., & Vartanian, O. (2011). Negative emotions can attenuate the influence of beliefs on logical reasoning. *Cognition and Emotion, 25*, 121–131.

Greenwald, A. G., McGhee, D. E., & Schwartz, J. L. K. (1998). Measuring individual differences in implicit cognition: The implicit association test. *Journal of Personality and Social Psychology, 74*, 1464–1480.

Holmes, E. A., Lang, T. J., & Shah, D. M. (2009). Developing interpretation bias modification as a "cognitive vaccine" for depressed mood: Imagining positive events makes you feel better than thinking about them verbally. *Journal of Abnormal Psychology, 118*, 76–88.

Kirby, K. N. (1994). Probabilities and utilities of fictional outcomes in Wason's four-card selection task. *Cognition, 51*, 1–28.

Koster, E. H. W., Crombez, G., Van Damme, S., Verschuere, B., & De Houwer, J. (2005). Signals for threat modulate attentional capture and holding: Fear-conditioning and extinction during the exogenous cueing task. *Cognition and Emotion, 19*, 771–780.

Lommen, M. J., Engelhard, I. M., van den Hout, M. A., & Arntz, A. (2013). Reducing emotional reasoning: An experimental manipulation in individuals with fear of spiders. *Cognition and Emotion, 27*, 1504–1512.

MacLeod, C., & Mathews, A. (2012). Cognitive bias modification approaches to anxiety. *Annual Review of Clinical Psychology, 8*, 189–217.

Morren, M., Muris, P., Kindt, M., Schouten, E., & van den Hout, M. A. (2008). Emotional and parent-based reasoning in non-clinical children, and their prospective relationships with anxiety symptoms. *Child Psychiatry and Human Development, 39*, 351–367.

Mulkens, S., de Jong, P. J., & Merckelbach. H. (1996). Disgust and spider phobia. *Journal of Abnormal Psychology, 105*, 464–468.

Muris, P. (2010). Anxiety-related reasoning biases in children and adolescents. In J. A. Hadwin & A. P. Field (Eds.), *Information Processing Biases and Anxiety: A Developmental Perspective* (pp. 21–45). Chichester: John Wiley & Sons.

Muris, P., Merckelbach, H., & Van Spauwen, I. (2003). The emotional reasoning heuristic in children. *Behaviour Research and Therapy, 41*(3), 261–272.

Muris, P., Rassin, E., Mayer, B., Smeets, G., Huijding, J., Remmerswaal, D., & Field, A. (2009). Effects of verbal information on fear-related reasoning biases in children. *Behaviour Research and Therapy, 47*, 206–214.

Nisbett, R. E., Fong, G. T., Lehman, D., & Cheng, P. W. (1987). Teaching reasoning. *Science, 238*, 625–631.

Nitrauw, E. (2002). *Better Safe than Sorry – A Study on a Threat-confirming Reasoning Strategy in Panic Disorder.* Unpublished Master's thesis, Mental Health Sciences, Maastricht University.

Oaten, M., Stevenson, R. J., & Case, T. I. (2009). Disgust as a disease-avoidance mechanism. *Psychological Bulletin, 135*, 303–321.

Olatunji, B. O., Lohr, J., Sawchuk, C. N., & Patten, K. (2007). Fear and disgust responding to heterogeneous blood-injection-injury stimuli: Distinctions from anxiety symptoms. *Journal of Psychopathology and Behavioral Assessment, 29*, 1–8.

Ouimet, A. J., Gawronski, B., & Dozois, D. J. A. (2009). Cognitive vulnerability to anxiety: A review and an integrative model. *Clinical Psychology Review, 29*, 459–470.

Ouimet, A. J., Radomsky, A. S., & Barber, K. C. (2012). Interrelationships between spider fear associations, attentional disengagement and self-reported fear: A preliminary test of a dual-systems model. *Cognition and Emotion, 26*, 1428–1444.

Quinn, S., & Markovits, H. (1998). Conditional reasoning, causality, and the structure of semantic memory: Strength of association as a predictive factor for content effects. *Cognition, 68*, B93–B101.

Sloan, T., & Telch, M. J. (2002). The effects of safety-seeking behavior and guided threat reappraisal on fear reduction during exposure: An experimental investigation. *Behaviour Research and Therapy, 40*, 235–251.

Slovic, P., Finucane, M., Peters, E., & MacGregor, D. G. (2002). The affect heuristic. In T. Gilovich, D. Griffin, & D. Kahneman (Eds.), *Heuristics and Biases: The Psychology of Intuitive Judgement* (pp. 397–421). Cambridge: Cambridge University Press.

Smeets, G., & de Jong, P. J. (2005). Belief bias and symptoms of psychopathology in a non-clinical sample. *Cognitive Therapy and Research, 29*, 377–386.

Smeets, G., de Jong, P. J., & Mayer, B. (2000). "If you suffer from a headache, then you have a brain tumour": Domain specific reasoning "bias" and hypochondriasis. *Behaviour Research and Therapy, 38*, 763–776.

Strack, F., & Deutsch, R. (2004). Reflective and impulsive determinants of social behavior. *Personality and Social Psychology Review, 8*, 220–247.

Teachman, B. A., Gregg, A. P., & Woody, S. R. (2001). Implicit associations for fear-relevant stimuli among individuals with snake and spider fears. *Journal of Abnormal Psychology, 110*, 226–235.

Trower, P., & Gilbert, P. (1989). New theoretical conceptions of social anxiety and social phobia. *Clinical Psychology Review, 9*, 19–35.

Vasey, M. W., Harbaugh, C. N., Buffington, A. G., Jones, C. R., & Fazio, R. H. (2012). Predicting return of fear following exposure therapy with an implicit measure of attitudes. *Behaviour Research and Therapy, 50*, 767–774.

Verschueren, N., Peeters, G., & Schaeken, W. (2006). Don't let anything bad happen: The effect of consequence valence on conditional reasoning. *Current Psychology Letters, 20*, 3.

Verwoerd, J., de Jong, P. J., Wessel, I., & van Hout, W. J. P. J. (2013). "If I feel disgusted, I must be getting ill": Emotional reasoning in the context of contamination fear. *Behaviour Research and Therapy, 51*, 122–127.

Verwoerd, J., van Hout, W. J. P. J., & de Jong, P. J. (2013). *Disgust- and Anxiety-based Emotional Reasoning in the Context of Non-clinical Fear of Vomiting.* Unpublished manuscript.

Vroling, M. S., & de Jong, P. J. (2009). Deductive reasoning and social anxiety: Evidence for a fear-confirming belief bias. *Cognitive Therapy and Research, 33*, 633–647.

Vroling, M. S., & de Jong, P. J. (2010). Threat-confirming belief bias and symptoms of anxiety disorders. *Journal of Behavior Therapy and Experimental Psychiatry, 41*, 110–116.

Vroling, M. S., & de Jong, P. J. (2013). Belief bias and the extinction of induced fear. *Cognition & Emotion, 27*, 1405–1420.

Vroling, M. S., Glashouwer, K. A., Lange, W.-G., Allart, E., & de Jong, P. J. (2013) *Belief-confirming Reasoning Bias in Social Anxiety Disorder.* Manuscript submitted for publication.

Wason, P. C. (1968). Reasoning about a rule. *Quarterly Journal of Experimental Psychology, 20*, 273–281.

White, L. K., Suway, J. G., Pine, D. S., Bar-Haim, Y., & Fox, N. A. (2011). Cascading effects: The influence of attention bias to threat on the interpretation of ambiguous information. *Behaviour Research and Therapy, 49*, 244–251.

8

NON-PHARMACOLOGICAL TREATMENT TARGETING COGNITIVE BIASES UNDERLYING DELUSIONS IN SCHIZOPHRENIA

Metacognitive training and therapy

Ryan Balzan, Todd S. Woodward, Mahesh Menon and Steffen Moritz

Introduction

Pharmaceutical interventions remain the dominant approach for treating the symptoms of schizophrenia, such as delusions and hallucinations, and provide relief for many people with the disorder. However, many studies report that 20–30% of clients do not respond to these medications (see Elkis, 2007), and even when these treatments are effective, they are often associated with only medium effect sizes relative to placebo, high levels of relapse, issues with compliance and illness insight, and serious side-effects (e.g. Leucht *et al.*, 2009; Lieberman *et al.*, 2005; Muench & Hamer, 2010).

Accordingly, interest in adjunctive non-pharmacological treatments has gathered momentum in recent years. For example, cognitive-behavioural therapy for psychosis (CBTp) is now routinely administered alongside antipsychotic medications to treat the core symptoms of schizophrenia (e.g. Barrowclough *et al.*, 2006; Bechdolf *et al.*, 2010; Garety, Kuipers, Fowler, Chamberlain, & Dunn, 1994; Granholm, Auslander, Gottlieb, McQuaid, & McClure, 2006; Landa, Silverstein, Schwartz, & Savitz, 2006; Lecomte *et al.*, 2008; Spidel, Lecomte, & LeClerc, 2006). CBTp aims to identify and actively modify maladaptive delusional beliefs, attitudes, and behaviours often associated with schizophrenia, and thereby helps clients to become aware of alternative explanations and coping strategies (Steel, 2013). Reviews and meta-analyses of its efficacy as an adjunct therapy to pharmacological treatments have shown that CBTp adds small to medium effect sizes on top of medication, and it represents an effective treatment alternative for medication-resistant clients (Wykes, Steel, Everitt, & Tarrier, 2008; Zimmermann, Favrod, Trieu, & Pomini, 2005).

Metacognitive training (MCT)

Built on the principles of CBTp, novel psychological interventions for treating delusions in schizophrenia are now starting to focus on the underlying cognitive factors that contribute to the formation and maintenance of delusional beliefs. Examples of such novel interventions are the Social Cognition and Interaction Training (SCIT; Combs *et al.*, 2007; Roberts & Penn, 2009), the Maudsley Review Training Programme (Waller, Freeman, Jolley, Dunn, & Garety, 2011) and metacognitive training (MCT), which was developed by our group (Moritz, Vitzthum, Veckenstedt, Randjbar, & Woodward, 2010). Rather than targeting the idiosyncratic delusions specific to the individual client, MCT indirectly targets psychotic symptoms by focusing on the underlying cognitive and social biases thought to underlie the formation and maintenance of delusional beliefs (see preceeding chapters and Bell, Halligan, & Ellis, 2006; Blackwood, Howard, Bentall, & Murray, 2001; Garety & Freeman, 1999 for reviews).

MCT is both a behavioural intervention and a knowledge translation programme. Metacognition in this context refers to "thinking about one's own thinking", this being both the educational goal and the therapeutic approach of MCT. Thus, one of the three fundamental components of the programme is *knowledge translation*. Clients are informed of current empirical research which links cognitive biases to delusion formation/maintenance, and are provided with illustrative examples demonstrating how this cognitive mechanism works. Although knowledge translation is typically conceptualized as information flowing from research teams to clinical care teams, MCT involves knowledge translation from research teams directly to people who experience psychosis. In this sense, MCT is focused on raising clients' awareness of their illness, because bringing certain thinking disturbances to the attention of the client leads to a new awareness of how schizophrenia can be understood. This researcher-to-client knowledge translation is a natural and powerful conclusion to the academic process. The second component of MCT is a *demonstration of the negative consequences* of these cognitive and social biases via exercises that target each bias individually. While we highlight the fallibility of human cognition in general, we emphasize the increases in intensity that are specific to schizophrenia, and how these might be underlying some of the symptoms that clients experience. MCT promotes countering these unhealthy thinking patterns with the intention of preventing or reducing the severity of relapse. The third component of MCT involves offering clients *alternative thinking strategies*, which may help them to arrive at more appropriate inferences and thereby avoid the "cognitive traps" that otherwise lead to delusional beliefs (Moritz & Woodward, 2007b). It is through relating these concepts back to clients' everyday experiences that MCT exerts its effects.

In the original group-based MCT programme, we combined original material with material shared with us by a range of researchers studying delusions within cognitive neuropsychiatry, and arranged these into a series of eight instructor-led group intervention sessions, covering six different cognitive and social biases (available free of charge from www.uke.de/mkt). Although there is some overlap between the modules, they are non-sequential and can be administered in any order. What follows is a brief overview of the material covered across the MCT programme, which is categorized under the six cognitive and social biases the programme targets (i.e. attribution biases, jumping to conclusions, belief inflexibility, overconfidence in errors, theory of mind deficits, and depressive cognitive schemata). We focus on how the programme attempts to raise the metacognitive awareness of such biases within clients, and thereby planting "seeds of doubt", encouraging critical reflection, and ultimately reducing the severity of delusional symptoms.

Attributional styles

Most of us have a tendency to attribute positive events (e.g. passing an exam) to internal causes (e.g. "I am very clever"), and negative events (e.g. running late to a meeting) to external causes (e.g. "I caught all the red lights"); this self-serving bias helps to preserve self-esteem. However, it has been suggested that people with schizophrenia display an increased attribution bias whereby unjustified blame for negative events can be cast on other people (e.g. neighbours) and/or institutions (e.g. police), when in fact unidentified events may be to blame (Bentall, 1994; Diez-Alegria, Vazquez, Nieto-Moreno, Valiente, & Fuentenebro, 2006; Kinderman & Bentall, 1997). This is thought to promote feelings of paranoia, whereby the environment is perceived to be dangerous or threatening (e.g. "the world is against me"). Similarly, our group has recently found that people with schizophrenia also tend to provide one-sided (monocausal) explanations for complex social events (Randjbar, Veckenstedt, Vitzthum, Hottenrott, & Moritz, 2011), which might further reinforce persecutory delusions.

In the module dedicated to this bias, the social consequences of different attributional styles are highlighted (e.g. blaming others for failure may lead to interpersonal tensions). Following this, clients are asked to find reasons for briefly described incidents (e.g. "people laugh while you are speaking at a party"). It is stressed that situational, in addition to personal factors, should be taken into account, and that there are always a number of different possible explanations which should be considered even if only one explanation seems valid at first. This is particularly relevant for complex social situations, which can rarely be traced back to one cause, but rather are the product of many factors (i.e. a combination of the self, other people, and circumstances). By encouraging clients to consider more balanced interpretations of social events that incorporate multiple causes (e.g. self, others, context), this module attempts to counter the tendency to rely on monocausal attribution biases. For example, if for the scenario "people laugh while you are speaking at a party", clients were to give a negative one-sided explanation (e.g. "they are obviously making fun of me"), we would encourage them to consider alternative explanations: "I didn't notice that I had accidentally said something funny and actually made a good joke" (self); "one of the other people had just made a joke that I didn't hear" (others);

"it is a party and everyone is in a festive mood and laughing at every opportunity" (situation). Therefore, group participants learn that multiple factors may have contributed to the outcome of an event (self/others/circumstances), and are reminded that it is not always justified to put the blame on others, just as it is not always our fault when things go wrong. In this fashion, awareness of the role attribution biases play in daily situations is increased, and thinking tools are developed that promote linking this awareness to personalized delusional content. An understanding that attributional biases affect all people (not only those experiencing delusions) contributes to a reduction of the stigmatization associated with mental illness.

Decision-making: jumping to conclusions (JTC)

One of the most extensively studied cognitive biases in schizophrenia (and the focus of several chapters within this volume) is the jumping to conclusions (JTC) bias, whereby strong conclusions are made hastily on the basis of limited evidence (for a recent review, see Fine, Gardner, Craigie, & Gold, 2007). Such "short-circuit" thinking patterns can lead to suboptimal decisions that may foster and maintain delusional beliefs. For example, crackling noises over a phone line might lead someone with schizophrenia to jump to the conclusion that their phone has been "bugged" by the Mafia or CIA.

The MCT programme dedicates two modules to the JTC bias. In both modules, the group first discusses advantages (e.g. saving time) and (especially) disadvantages of jumping to conclusions (e.g. less reliable judgment, high probability of errors), particularly for complex social situations where the consequences of hasty decisions can be dramatic (e.g. souring a friendship). Arguments for and against common false beliefs (e.g. urban legends) in society are then discussed. It is made clear to the clients that urban legends have partly arisen due to JTC, and are based on very little evidence (e.g. Paul McCartney of Beatles fame died in 1966 in an accident, and was replaced by a lookalike double, as "evidenced" by the Abbey Road album cover). Thus, urban legends can be considered a good miniature model for delusional ideas in general, and an understanding that JTC affects all people (not only those experiencing delusions) contributes to a reduction of the stigmatization associated with mental illness. Importantly, the two modules cover a number of exercises that demonstrate the bias "at work". One exercise shows common objects, which are displayed in decreasing degrees of fragmentation, and new features are added in successive stages, until the entire object is eventually displayed. Clients are asked to rate the plausibility of either self-generated or pre-specified response alternatives. In one example, the first stage of the image (actually a frog) strongly resembles a lemon, because only the contour of the frog is displayed (see Figure 8.1). Thus, a hasty decision ("it is a lemon") results in an error and participants learn to withhold making a definite decision until more evidence is revealed.

Another exercise involves presentation of visual illusions or "two-way" pictures, which initially suggest one scenario (e.g. an elderly couple staring at each other), but on closer inspection it is clear that alternative interpretations exist (e.g.

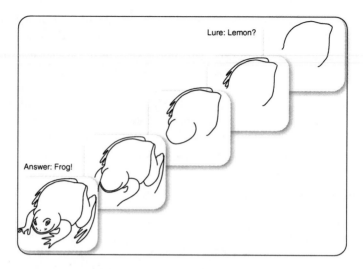

FIGURE 8.1 "Frog" stimuli set for "fragmentation exercise" in the JTC module

the "elderly couple" actually consist of two seated musicians). For these tasks, it is emphasised that hasty decisions do not always lead to errors, but they sometimes only tell half the story. In a third exercise, a number of paintings are displayed, the task is to choose the correct title from four alternatives. For some paintings, the correct title is rather obvious, but for others it becomes clear only after a thorough visual search and group discussion. Again, the learning purpose is that hasty decisions lead to errors, and that careful examination of all the evidence is often required before a definite decision can be reached. Across these three types of exercises, clients learn to search for as much information as possible, and are reminded that "to err is human", so they must be prepared for the possibility of error. We suggest that when events are of minor importance (e.g. choosing a yogurt brand), it can be effective to decide quickly, but if decisions are crucial or may have dramatic implications (e.g. feeling that your neighbour is chasing after you), a more intensive "evidence accumulation" should be applied, and we encourage clients to exchange views with others before "committing" to a decision. In this fashion, awareness of the role of BADE (see below) in daily situations is increased, and thinking tools are developed that promote linking this awareness to personalized delusional content.

Changing beliefs: bias against disconfirmatory evidence (BADE)

When we are passionate about a particular belief (e.g. the superiority of our preferred political system), we tend to cling to this belief despite mounting counter-evidence and rational counter-arguments (e.g. social problems existing within this system). This tendency is greatly exaggerated in the formation and maintenance of delusional beliefs, where such counter-evidence and rational counter-argument is downplayed, ignored, or "explained away" by integration into the delusional framework (e.g. the only reason they did not shoot me yesterday was because I avoided watching television) (Freeman, Garety, Kuipers, Fowler, & Bebbington, 2002; Garety, Kuipers, Fowler, Freeman, & Bebbington, 2001). In past work, our group has shown that a cognitive bias against disconfirmatory evidence (BADE) exists in schizophrenia even for delusion-neutral material, whereby clients are less likely to integrate new evidence that contradicts previously presented information (e.g. Moritz & Woodward, 2006; Woodward, Moritz, Menon, & Klinge, 2008), being particularly enhanced in delusional clients (Sanford, Veckenstedt, Moritz, Balzan, & Woodward, in revision; Speechley, Ngan, Moritz, & Woodward, 2012; Woodward, Moritz, & Chen, 2006; Woodward, Moritz, Cuttler, & Whitman, 2006).

The "changing beliefs" MCT module begins by highlighting the disadvantages of belief inflexibility. Historical and case examples are given on how an unwillingness to revise opinions and beliefs can lead to serious problems, or even disastrous events (e.g. a belief that the Titanic was "unsinkable" led to dismissal of early warnings during the voyage). The main exercise in this module consists of a series of three pictures depicting events from one scenario, but shown in temporally reversed order (i.e. last event is shown first). The sequences of pictures gradually disambiguate a scenario (see Figure 8.2). For each picture, clients are asked to rate the plausibility of four different interpretations. The correct interpretation ("true" interpretation) becomes clear after all three pictures are presented. However, on presentation of the first picture, two of the other interpretations seem plausible, but are eventually shown to be implausible after three pictures ("lures"). The goal is for clients to learn to search for more information before judging, and to correct themselves as disconfirmatory evidence is encountered. Clients therefore learn that events sometimes turn out very differently than originally expected, and that we should always consider different interpretations and/or hypotheses and adjust our beliefs accordingly. Moreover, the idea is reinforced that quick decisions often lead to inaccurate conclusions, and that we should always seek as much information as possible to verify our judgment. This overlaps with the learning objectives from the

FIGURE 8.2 Example of a "BADE exercise" from the Changing Beliefs module; Picture 3 is shown first, followed by Picture 2 then Picture 1

JTC modules, but awareness of BADE in daily situations provides additional thinking tools that promote reconsideration of personalized delusional content.

Metamemory and overconfidence in errors

There is substantial evidence that people with schizophrenia exhibit objective memory deficits relative to the general population (for a recent meta-analysis, see Fioravanti, Bianchi, & Cinti, 2012). Research also suggests that clients lack awareness of these memory deficits, and will underestimate the extent of these impairments (e.g. Keefe, Poe, Walker, Kang, & Harvey, 2006; Medalia & Thysen, 2010; Poletti *et al.*, 2012). Building on this work, our group has conducted a number of "metamemory" studies that focus on subjective *memory confidence*. These studies have identified a unique overconfidence effect amongst people with schizophrenia, whereby people with schizophrenia are significantly *overconfident* in memory errors and slightly *underconfident* given correct responses (e.g. Moritz, Woodward, & Chen, 2006; Moritz, Woodward, Cuttler, Whitman, & Watson, 2004; Moritz, Woodward, Jelinek, & Klinge, 2008; Moritz, Woodward, & Rodriguez-Raecke, 2006; Moritz, Woodward, Whitman, & Cuttler, 2005). More recent work has determined that the metamemory "overconfidence in errors" effect can be generalized to other domains of cognition outside of memory errors (Köther *et al.*, 2012; Moritz, Woznica, Andreou, & Köther, 2012), and that decreasing overconfidence in errors may be a prominent mechanism of change evoked by antipsychotic agents (Andreou, Moritz, Veith, Veckenstedt, & Naber, 2013).

This MCT module begins by highlighting the fallibility of memory. Group participants are reminded that past events are usually imperfectly recalled, and that all people are prone to forgetting and adding to information that was not originally present the latter is known in the cognitive psychology literature as "false memory". Although MCT offers strategies to improve memory (e.g. mnemonics; incorporating multiple senses during encoding), the emphasis of this module is reducing confidence in memories, primarily by producing temporary false memories (which is very easy to do). Group participants are presented with visual stimuli which are known to elicit false memories (e.g. price tags are commonly "remembered" in shop scenes, even when absent), whereby participants are instructed to look at the pictures carefully and to memorize each item (see "kiosk scene" in Figure 8.3). Each picture is followed by a recognition task in which clients have to decide whether an item has been displayed or not (e.g. were price tags present?). By then revealing that commonly reported items (e.g. price tags; garbage can) were not actually present in the original picture, clients quickly learn about the fallibility of memory through this experience. The aim of this exercise is therefore to teach clients to doubt their memories, particularly if a vivid recollection is not available, and that more evidence should be considered, particularly for important situations (e.g. interpersonal conflicts).

We drive these points home by presenting case scenarios to which people can easily relate. For example, we might ask clients to imagine that they had a quarrel with someone but only *vaguely* remember that this person made a number

FIGURE 8.3   "Kiosk scene" from the Memory and Overconfidence module; people often falsely recall items (e.g. price tags; garbage cans) despite not being depicted in the picture

of insulting remarks about them. Rather than over-ascribing confidence to this recollection (which might lead to hostile confrontations or heightened paranoia), clients are reminded of the fallibility of memory and that such recollections may be distorted, and so are encouraged to seek alternative evidence (e.g. ask people who were present at the event). This serves to increase awareness of the role of memory confidence in daily situations, provide thinking tools that can link to personalized delusional content, and contribute to a reduction of the stigmatization associated with mental illness by recognizing that all people experience memory fallibility.

To empathize: theory of mind (ToM)

Theory of mind (ToM) refers to the ability to infer the mental states (e.g. thoughts, perspectives, beliefs) of others, and there is an extensive literature suggesting that people with schizophrenia exhibit deficits in this complex domain of social cognition (e.g. Brune, 2005; Corcoran, Mercer, & Frith, 1995; Doody, Gotz, Johnstone, Frith, & Owens, 1998; Frith & Corcoran, 1996; Pickup & Frith, 2001). Such deficits, in combination with other cognitive biases such as JTC and BADE, may contribute to the onset and maintenance delusions, particularly paranoid delusions. For example, the concentrated and thoughtful look of a therapist may be misinterpreted as "hostile", or a smile from a stranger may be misinterpreted as mockery.

Two MCT modules are dedicated to these ToM deficits, and cover a variety of exercises that attempt to improve social cognitive skills among clients. One of these exercises discusses the different cues for social cognition (e.g. appearance, language) and their validity. It is stressed that over-reliance on a particular cue may lead to errors (e.g. a "shady" looking person is actually a well-respected doctor), and that social cognition is best when a set of different cues is considered. To illustrate the fallibility of over-relying on facial expressions and/or gestures when interpreting the intentions of others, we show clients cropped images that depict facial expressions/gestures that are highly suggestive of a particular interpretation (e.g. "a man delivering a passionate political speech"). However, upon viewing the full uncropped image, which provides extra contextual information (e.g. man is holding a piano accordion and is playing to a crowd of people), the true interpretation becomes obvious (i.e. "musician serenading a crowd of people"). These exercises convey the message that, although facial expressions are very important for the understanding of inner feelings of a person, they can often lead to false conclusions, and additional information (e.g. the situation and/or prior knowledge about that person) should be considered before facial expressions/gestures are interpreted as a direct reflection of the person's state of mind (ToM, first order). Indeed, many misunderstandings and conflicts with others arise simply because people incorrectly guess what is on others' minds. Reiterating the themes from the other modules, we again stress that the more information considered, the more likely it is that an appropriate judgment will be made.

In another exercise, we present pictorial scenarios for which clients are required to take the perspective of one of the protagonists, and to deduce what the character may think about another person, or certain events, given the limited information available to that character (ToM, second order; see Figure 8.4). We also present clients with comic sequences, similar to the exercise presented in the Changing Beliefs/BADE module (see Figure 8.2), where most slides are presented in reverse sequential order, such that the final picture in the comic sequence is displayed first, while the opening pictures of the sequence (that provide more context) remain covered. As each picture is revealed, more contextual information is revealed about

FIGURE 8.4 Participants are asked to determine what the character may think about another person given the limited information available to that character (e.g. annoyance)

the storyline. For the majority of items, several interpretations remain possible until the end. In this case, clients should propose what additional information is required for a reliable judgment. Even if a sequence remains ambiguous, it should be discussed which interpretation is best supported by the available evidence. This again reinforces the idea that, in order to accurately interpret complex social situations, we need to take in different perspectives and consider all available contextual information. Only then can we accurately gauge the intentions of others. Awareness of the importance of ToM in daily situations, and how it combines with JTC and BADE concepts, provides tools that promote linking this awareness to personalized delusional content, and reduces stigma by showing that ToM errors affect all people (not only people experiencing delusions).

Mood and self-esteem

It has been estimated that 50% (or more) of people with schizophrenia experience symptoms of affective disturbances such as depression and low self-esteem (Buckley, Miller, Lehrer, & Castle, 2009). In this module, we stress that depressive thinking structures can be changed, and that depression and low self-esteem is not an irreversible fate. We go through exercises that target depressive cognitive biases, such as overgeneralization and selective abstraction, and explain how distorted cognitive schemata can be replaced by more realistic and helpful ones. For example, thinking that one "is stupid" for not comprehending a book or "worthless" for failing a test can be countered by more positive/constructive evaluations (e.g. "am I really into this book?"; "next time I'll study harder"). We stress that "nobody is perfect", and that generalizing one imperfection to every situation or dwelling on selective appraisals (e.g. focusing on one absent friend rather than the other 20 who helped celebrate the party) is counter-productive and likely to lead to negative mood states and low self-esteem.

In addition, the module targets dysfunctional coping strategies often adopted by people with affective disturbances. For example, the denial of positive feedback (e.g. compliments on great performance interpreted as dishonesty) but uncritical acceptance of negative feedback (e.g. constructive criticism is accepted as evidence of being "worthless/stupid"). Finally, some techniques are provided which, when used regularly, help to alter low self-esteem and to raise depressed mood. For example, we suggest that clients try to write down positive things that have occurred on that day and to reflect on these, or to take time out to do enjoyable activities (e.g. going to movies; baking a cake). Thus, in this module, JTC, BADE, attributional biases, and ToM are extended to the context of affective disturbances, by way of introduction of overlapping cognitive biases more characteristic of depression.

Metacognitive therapy (MCT+)

In addition to the group-orientated MCT programme described above, our group has also developed an individually administered programme entitled metacognitive therapy, or MCT+. This programme combines the "process-oriented" approach of the MCT group training with elements of individual cognitive-behavioural therapy for psychosis (CBTp). The combined approach involves relating information from the original MCT modules to the individual experiences, observations, and symptoms of the individual client (Moritz, Vitzthum, Randjbar, Veckenstedt, & Woodward, 2010). Given that CBTp attempts to shift delusional thinking by targeting the specific delusional content, while group-based MCT aims to reduce delusions by educating clients about the cognitive biases underlying delusion formation and maintenance, the MCT+ approach may be more effective than either psychological treatment alone.

MCT+ runs over a similar layout to the group-based MCT, and covers the same six cognitive and social biases. However, due to the individualized nature of MCT+, there are a number of additions to the programme. A structured clinical interview is administered in the first session, to evaluate the medical history and current symptoms of the client, as well as to provide an introduction to MCT+. This is an important first step, as we frequently come back to the current hallucinatory and/or delusional experiences of the client throughout the programme, which helps to make the content more personalized (e.g. if a client believes their house is bugged, we might ask what events/evidence have caused them to come to this conclusion, or whether they jumped to this conclusion too quickly, or if they think that there are any alternative explanations). Note that discussing a client's symptoms within the context of cognitive biases is meant to be a gentler approach, possibly perceived as less threatening than a more direct CBTp "front door" approach, and may even help foster a better therapeutic alliance. The individualized approach also allows for a greater range of therapeutic strategies, such as establishing therapy goals (e.g. improving social cognition and reducing paranoia in public spaces), reality testing (i.e. clients are encouraged to recall certain events in their everyday life which they regard as clear evidence for their ideas), Socratic discussion (i.e. extensive questioning to generate pros/cons as well as consequences of a particular viewpoint or behaviour), and use of friends/family to aid in the process of the therapy (i.e. relatives can help to recognize the early warning signs of relapse). MCT+ also dedicates an entire module to relapse prevention, which also focuses on stress coping strategies. For instance, we discuss factors that might lead to stress, and in extreme cases to a relapse, as well as the balancing and stress-reducing factors that may be available to the particular client.

Efficacy

Several studies have now been conducted on MCT/MCT+ in order to address the feasibility, safety, and effectiveness of these programs, but this evidence should still be considered preliminary (for a recent systematic review see Moritz, Andreou, *et al.*, 2014). Early studies demonstrated that MCT was rated as superior to a control condition on fun and usefulness to daily life, and was considered by participants to be engaging and (subjectively) effective (Gaweda, Moritz, & Kokoszka, 2009; Moritz & Woodward, 2007a).

The earliest study investigating the efficacy of MCT in reducing positive symptoms compared MCT to an active control (Aghotor, Pfueller, Moritz, Weisbrod, & Roesch-Ely, 2010). The study enrolled 15 participants per group, and reductions in positive symptoms and a diminished tendency to JTC were observed at re-test (at four weeks). However, these did not reach statistical significance, likely due to the small sample sizes. A second study allocated 17 participants per group to either a brief "reasoning training" (i.e. adapted version of the JTC/BADE modules) or an attention control group (Ross, Freeman, Dunn, & Garety, 2011). Less conviction in delusions was noted in the MCT trials, but again this finding did not reach statistical significance. In a third study using 18 subjects per group (Moritz, Kerstan *et al.*, 2011), the effectiveness of MCT was compared to treatment as usual (TAU) at baseline and post-treatment assessments at eight weeks. MCT significantly reduced delusion distress (effect size $d = 0.68$; reported for MCT vs. control condition comparisons here and below), and improved social functioning ($d = 0.77$). The objectively measured MCT-targeted thinking bias (JTC) was reduced, but the latter did not reach statistical significance.

A more recent small-scale study (14 participants per group) combined aspects of the JTC and BADE bias modules into a single individually administered module that focused specifically on improving cognitive biases that are thought to be driven by a "hypersalience evidence-hypothesis matches" (e.g. jumping to conclusions, belief inflexibility, reasoning heuristics, illusions of control). It was hypothesized that a more targeted MCT module could still improve performance on these bias tasks, and reduce delusional ideation whilst improving insight and quality of life. This study found that MCT participants (relative to TAU controls) exhibited significant decreases in delusional severity and conviction on a variety of measures (e.g. SAPS: $d = 1.63$), and significant improvements in clinical insight ($d = 1.09$), and performance on the cognitive bias tasks (e.g. illusion of control task: $d = 1.44$). Moreover, performance improvements on the cognitive bias tasks significantly correlated with the observed reductions in overall positive symptomology, and participants evaluated the training positively. Although interpretations of these results are limited due to the lack of an optimally designed randomized controlled trial and a small sample size, the results point to the potential effectiveness of even minimal exposure to MCT (Balzan, Delfabbro, Galletly, & Woodward, 2014).

One randomized controlled trial tested the efficacy of individualized metacognitive therapy (MCT+), where 24 subjects were assigned to a hybrid of group MCT and individualized MCT+, or cognitive remediation as the control condition (Moritz, Vitzthum, Randjbara, Veckenstedt, & Woodward, 2011). Pre- and post-assessments were separated by four weeks. Participants in the MCT/MCT+ arm showed significantly greater improvement on delusion severity ($d = 0.68$), delusion conviction ($d = 0.63$), as well as on a measure of JTC ($d = 0.59$). Similar results have been recently reported by Favrod *et al.* (2013), where 52 patients receiving MCT significantly improved on a number of positive symptoms (e.g., PSYRATS delusion scores) at both 8-week and 6-months follow-up ($d = .56$ and .64, respectively), relative to treatment-as-usual controls. Building on these preliminary results, a large assessor-blind randomized-controlled trial involving a clinical sample 150 people with schizophrenia spectrum disorders was carried out, with MCT being compared to cognitive remediation using 16 sessions each, with assessments at baseline, 4 weeks, 6 months, and 3 years later (Moritz *et al.*, in press; Moritz, Veckenstedt, *et al.*, 2014). Relative to the active controls receiving cognitive remediation, MCT participants significantly reduced delusions on multiple scales at all post-treatment time points, including 3 years post treatment (4 weeks and 6 months, $d = .41$ and $.51$, respectively; 3 years, $d = .48$). Importantly, significant group differences at the 3-year follow-up were also found on measures of self-esteem and quality of life, which did not distinguish groups at earlier assessment points. Taken together, these results suggest that MCT exerts *sustained* effects on the reduction of delusions over and above the effects of antipsychotic medication.

Conclusion

Over the last two decades, increasing support has been accumulating for psychological models of schizophrenia, indicating that cognitive and social biases may play an important role in the formation and maintenance of delusions. These include attribution biases, jumping to conclusions, belief inflexibility, overconfidence in errors, theory of mind deficits, and depressive cognitive schemata. The goal of the MCT is to sharpen clients' (metacognitive) awareness of these biases, and to carry over the learning aims to their daily life and experiences. Awareness of the role of these cognitive biases in daily situations is increased, and thinking tools are developed that promote linking this awareness to personalized delusional content. An understanding that the cognitive biases affect all people (not only those experiencing delusions) contributes to a reduction of the stigmatization associated with mental illness. Although originally a group-led intervention, MCT can now also be administered to individuals (MCT+). Given mounting evidence for beneficial effects of cognitive intervention in schizophrenia, and considering the high rates of relapse, there is a strong argument for integrating these cognitive interventions into treatment programmes.

References

Aghotor, J., Pfueller, U., Moritz, S., Weisbrod, M., & Roesch-Ely, D. (2010). Metacognitive training for patients with schizophrenia (MCT): Feasibility and preliminary evidence for its efficacy. *Journal of Behavior Therapy and Experimental Psychiatry, 41*, 207–211.

Andreou, C., Moritz, S., Veith, K., Veckenstedt, R., & Naber, D. (2014). Dopaminergic modulation of probabilistic reasoning and overconfidence in errors: A double-blind study. *Schizophrenia Bulletin, 40*, 558–565.

Balzan, R. P., Delfabbro, P. H., Galletly, C. A., & Woodward, T. S. (2014). Metacognitive training for patients with schizophrenia: Preliminary evidence for a targeted, single-module programme. *Australian and New Zealand Journal of Psychiatry*, doi: 10.1177/0004867413 508451.

Barrowclough, C., Haddock, G., Lobbab, F., Jones, S., Siddle, R., Roberts, C., & Gregg,

L. (2006). Group cognitive–behavioural therapy for schizophrenia. *The British Journal of Psychiatry, 189*(6), 527–532.

Bechdolf, A., Knost, B., Nelson, B., Schneider, N., Veith, V., Yung, A. R., & Pukrop, R. (2010). Randomized comparison of group cognitive behaviour therapy and group psychoeducation in acute patients with schizophrenia: Effects on subjective quality of life. *The Australian and New Zealand Journal of Psychiatry, 44*, 144–150.

Bell, V., Halligan, P. W., & Ellis, H. D. (2006). Explaining delusions: A cognitive perspective. *Trends in Cognitive Sciences, 10*(5), 219–226.

Bentall, R. P. (1994). Cognitive biases and abnormal beliefs: Towards a model of persecutory delusions. In A. S. David & J. C. Cutting (Eds.), *The Neuropsychology of Schizophrenia* (pp. 337–361). Hillside, NJ: Erlbaum.

Blackwood, N. J., Howard, R. J., Bentall, R. P., & Murray, R. M. (2001). Cognitive neuropsychiatric models of persecutory delusions. *American Journal of Psychiatry, 158*(4), 527–539.

Brune, M. (2005). "Theory of mind" in schizophrenia: A review of the literature. *Schizophrenia Bulletin, 31*, 21–42.

Buckley, P. F., Miller, B. J., Lehrer, D. S., & Castle, D. J. (2009). Psychiatric comorbidities and schizophrenia. *Schizophrenia Bulletin, 35*(2), 383–402.

Combs, D. R., Adams, S. D., Penn, D. L., Roberts, D., Tiegreen, J., & Stem, P. (2007). Social Cognition and Interaction Training (SCIT) for inpatients with schizophrenia spectrum disorders: Preliminary findings. *Schizophrenia Research, 91*(1–3), 112–116.

Corcoran, R., Mercer, G., & Frith, C. (1995). Schizophrenia, symptomology and social inference: Investigating "theory of mind" in people with schizophrenia. *Schizophrenia Research, 17*, 5–13.

Diez-Alegria, C., Vazquez, C., Nieto-Moreno, M., Valiente, C., & Fuentenebro, F. (2006). Personalizing and externalizing biases in deluded and depressed patients: Are attributional biases a stable and specific characteristic of delusions? *British Journal of Clinical Psychology, 45*, 531–544.

Doody, G. A., Gotz, M., Johnstone, E. C., Frith, C. D., & Owens, D. G. (1998). Theory of mind and psychoses. *Psychological Medicine, 28*(2), 397–405.

Elkis, H. (2007). Treatment resistant schizophrenia. *Psychiatric Clinics of North America, 30*, 511–533.

Favrod, J., Rexhaj, S., Bardy, S., Ferrari, P., Hayoz, C., Moritz, S., Conus, P., & Bonsack, C. (2013). Sustained antipsychotic effect of metacognitive training in psychosis: A randomized-controlled study. *European Psychiatry*, doi: 10:1016/j.eurpsy.2013.08.003.

Fine, C., Gardner, M., Craigie, J., & Gold, I. (2007). Hopping, skipping or jumping to conclusions? Clarifying the role of the JTC bias in delusions. *Cognitive Neuropsychiatry, 12*, 46–77.

Fioravanti, M., Bianchi, V., & Cinti, M. (2012). Cognitive deficits in schizophrenia: An updated metanalysis of the scientific evidence. *BMC Psychiatry, 12*(1), 64.

Freeman, D., Garety, P. A., Kuipers, E., Fowler, D., & Bebbington, P. E. (2002). A cognitive model of persecutory delusions. *British Journal of Clinical Psychology, 41*(Pt 4), 331–347.

Frith, C. D., & Corcoran, R. (1996). Exploring "theory of mind" in people with schizophrenia. *Psychological Medicine, 26*, 521–530.

Garety, P. A., & Freeman, D. (1999). Cognitive approaches to delusions: A critical review of the evidence. *British Journal of Clinical Psychology, 38*, 113–154.

Garety, P. A., Kuipers, E., Fowler, D., Chamberlain, F., & Dunn, G. (1994). Cognitive behavioural therapy for drug-resistant psychosis. *British Journal of Medical Psychology, 67*, 259–271.

Garety, P. A., Kuipers, E., Fowler, D., Freeman, D., & Bebbington, P. E. (2001). A cognitive model of the positive symptoms of psychosis. *Psychological Medicine, 31*(2), 189–195.

Gaweda, L., Moritz, S., & Kokoszka, A. (2009). The metacognitive training for schizophrenia patients: Description of method and experiences from clinical practice. *Psychiatria Polska, 43,* 683–692.

Granholm, E., Auslander, L. A., Gottlieb, J. D., McQuaid, J. R., & McClure, F. S. (2006). Therapeutic factors contributing to change in cognitive-behavioral group therapy for older persons with schizophrenia. *Journal of Contemporary Psychotherapy 36,* 31–41.

Keefe, R. S. E., Poe, M. P., Walker, T. M., Kang, J. W., & Harvey, P. D. (2006). The Schizophrenia Cognition Rating Scale: An interview-based assessment and its relationship to cognition, real-world functioning, and functional capacity. *American Journal of Psychiatry, 163,* 426–432.

Kinderman, P., & Bentall, R. P. (1997). Causal attributions in paranoia and depression: Internal, personal, and situational attributions for negative events. *Journal of Abnormal Psychology, 106,* 341–345.

Köther, U., Veckenstedt, R., Vitzthum, F., Roesch-Ely, D., Pfueller, U., Scheu, F., & Moritz, S. (2012). "Don't give me that look" – Overconfidence in false mental state perception in schizophrenia. *Psychiatry Research, 196,* 1–8.

Landa, Y., Silverstein, S., Schwartz, F., & Savitz, A. (2006). Group cognitive behavioral therapy for delusions: Helping patients improve reality testing. *Journal of Contemporary Psychotherapy, 36*(1), 9–17.

Lecomte, T., Leclerc, C., Corbiere, M., Wykes, T., Wallace, C., & Spidel, A. (2008). Group cognitive behavior therapy or social skills training for individuals with a recent onset of psychosis? Results of a randomized controlled trial. *The Journal of Nervous and Mental Disease, 196,* 866–875.

Leucht, S., Komossa, K., Rummel-Kluge, C., Corves, C., Hunger, H., Schmid, F., Asenjo Lobos, C., Schwarz, S., & Davis, J. M. (2009). A meta-analysis of head-to-head comparisons of second-generation antipsychotics in the treatment of schizophrenia. *The American Journal Psychiatry 166*(2), 152–163.

Lieberman, J. A., Stroup, T. S., McEvoy, J. P., Swartz, M. S., Rosenheck, R. A., Perkins, D. O., . . . Hsiao, J. K. (2005). Effectiveness of antipsychotic drugs in patients with chronic schizophrenia. *New England Journal of Medicine, 353,* 1209–1223.

Medalia, A., & Thysen, J. (2010). A comparison of insight into clinical symptoms versus insight into neuro-cognitive symptoms in schizophrenia. *Schizophrenia Research, 118*(1–3), 134–139.

Moritz, S., Andreou, C., Schneider, B. C., Wittekind, C. E., Menon, M., Balzan, R. P., & Woodward, T. S. (2014). Sowing the seeds of doubt: A narrative review on metacognitive training in schizophrenia. *Clinical Psychology Review.* doi: 10.1016/j.cpr.2014.04.004

Moritz, S., Kerstan, A., Veckenstedt, R., Randjbar, S., Vitzthum, F., Schmidt, C., Heise, M., & Woodward, T. S. (2011). Further evidence for the efficacy of a metacognitive group training in schizophrenia. *Behaviour Research and Therapy, 49*(3), 151–157.

Moritz, S., Veckenstedt, R., Andreou, C., Bohn, F., Hottenrott, B., Andreou, C., Leighton, L., . . . Köther, U., Woodward, T. S., Treszl, A., Menon, M., Viertel, B. Pfueller, U., & Roesch-Ely, D. (in press). Delayed and "sleeper" effects of metacognitive group training (MCT) in schizophrenia. *JAMA Psychiatry, 151,* 619–69.

Moritz, S., Veckenstedt, R., Bohn, F., Hottenrott, B., Scheu, F., Randjbar, S., Aghotor, J., Köther, U., Woodward, T. S., Treszl, A., Andreou, C., Pfueller, U., & Roesch-Ely, D. (2013). Complementary group metacognitive training (MCT) reduces delusional ideation in schizophrenia. *Schizophrenia Research, 151,* 61–69.

Moritz, S., Veckenstedt, R., Randjbar, S., Vitzthum, F., & Woodward, T. S. (2011). Antipsychotic treatment beyond antipsychotics: Metacognitive intervention for schizophrenia patients improves delusional symptoms in schizophrenia patients. *Psychological Medicine, 41*, 1823–1832.

Moritz, S., Vitzthum, F., Randjbar, S., Veckenstedt, R., & Woodward, T. S. (2010). Detecting and defusing cognitive traps: Metacognitive intervention in schizophrenia. *Current Opinion in Psychiatry, 23*, 561–569.

Moritz, S., Vitzthum, F., Veckenstedt, R., Randjbar, S., & Woodward, T. S. (2010). Metacognitive training in schizophrenia: From basic research to intervention. In J. H. Stone & M. Blouin (Eds.), *International Encyclopedia of Rehabilitation.* Buffalo, New York: Center for International Rehabilitation Research Information and Exchange (CIRRIE). Available online: http://cirrie.buffalo.edu/encyclopedia/en/article/149/

Moritz, S., & Woodward, T. S. (2006). A generalized bias against disconfirmatory evidence in schizophrenia. *Psychiatry Research, 142*(2–3), 157–165.

Moritz, S., & Woodward, T. S. (2007a). Metacognitive training for schizophrenia patients (MCT): A pilot study on feasibility, treatment adherence, and subjective efficacy. *German Journal of Psychiatry, 10*, 69–78.

Moritz, S., & Woodward, T. S. (2007b). Metacognitive training in schizophrenia: From basic research to knowledge translation and intervention. *Current Opinion in Psychiatry, 20*, 619–625.

Moritz, S., Woodward, T. S., & Chen, E. Y. H. (2006). Investigation of metamemory dysfunctions in first-episode schizophrenia. *Schizophrenia Research, 81*, 247–252.

Moritz, S., Woodward, T. S., Cuttler, C., Whitman, J. C., & Watson, J. M. (2004). False memories in schizophrenia. *Neuropsychology, 18*, 276–283.

Moritz, S., Woodward, T. S., Jelinek, L., & Klinge, R. (2008). Memory and metamemory in schizophrenia: A liberal acceptance account of psychosis. *Psychological Medicine, 38*(06), 825–832.

Moritz, S., Woodward, T. S., & Rodriguez-Raecke, R. (2006). Patients with schizophrenia do not produce more false memories than controls but are more confident in them. *Psychological Medicine, 36*(05), 659–667.

Moritz, S., Woodward, T. S., Whitman, J., & Cuttler, C. (2005). Confidence in errors as a possible basis for delusions in schizophrenia. *Journal of Nervous and Mental Disease, 193*, 9–16.

Moritz, S., Woznica, A., Andreou, C., & Köther, U. (2012). Response confidence for emotion perception in schizophrenia using a Continuous Facial Sequence Task. *Psychiatry Research, 200*, 202–207.

Muench, J., & Hamer, A. (2010). Adverse effects of antipsychotic medications. *American Family Physician, 81*, 617–622.

Pickup, G. J., & Frith, C. D. (2001). Theory of mind impairments in schizophrenia: Symptomatology, severity and specificity. *Psychological Medicine, 31*(2), 207–220.

Poletti, S., Anselmetti, S., Riccaboni, R., Bosia, M., Buonocore, M., Smeraldi, E., & Cavallaro, R. (2012). Self-awareness of cognitive functioning in schizophrenia: Patients and their relatives. *Psychiatry Research, 198*, 207–211.

Randjbar, S., Veckenstedt, R., Vitzthum, F., Hottenrott, B., & Moritz, S. (2011). Attributional biases in paranoid schizophrenia: Further evidence for a decreased sense of self-causation in paranoia. *Psychosis, 3*, 74–85.

Roberts, D. L., & Penn, D. L. (2009). Social cognition and interaction training (SCIT) for outpatients with schizophrenia: A preliminary study. *Psychiatry Research, 166*(2–3), 141–147.

Ross, K., Freeman, D., Dunn, G., & Garety, P. (2011). A randomized experimental investigation of reasoning training for people with delusions. *Schizophrenia Bulletin, 37*(2), 324–333.

Sanford, N., Veckenstedt, R., Moritz, S., Balzan, R. P., & Woodward, T. S. (in revision). Impaired integration of disambiguating evidence in delusional schizophrenia patients. *Psychological Medicine.*

Speechley, W. J., Ngan, E. T. C., Moritz, S., & Woodward, T. S. (2012). Impaired evidence integration and delusions in schizophrenia. *Journal of Experimental Psychopathology, 3*, 688–701.

Spidel, A., Lecomte, T., & LeClerc, C. (2006). Community implementation successes and challenges of a cognitive-behavior therapy group for individuals with a first episode of psychosis. *Journal of Contemporary Psychotherapy, 36*, 51–58.

Steel, C. (Ed.). (2013). *CBT for Schizophrenia: Evidence-Based Interventions and Future Directions.* West Sussex, UK: Wiley-Blackwell.

Waller, H., Freeman, D., Jolley, S., Dunn, G., & Garety, P. A. (2011). Targeting reasoning biases in delusions: A pilot study of the Maudsley Review Training Programme for individuals with persistent, high conviction delusions. *Journal of Behavior Therapy and Experimental Psychiatry, 42*, 414–421.

Woodward, T. S., Moritz, S., & Chen, E. Y. H. (2006). The contribution of a cognitive bias against disconfirmatory evidence (BADE) to delusions: A study in an Asian sample with first episode schizophrenia spectrum disorders. *Schizophrenia Research, 83*, 297–298.

Woodward, T. S., Moritz, S., Cuttler, C., & Whitman, J. C. (2006). The contribution of a cognitive bias against disconfirmatory evidence (BADE) to delusions in schizophrenia. *Journal of Clinical and Experimental Neuropsychology, 28*, 605–617.

Woodward, T. S., Moritz, S., Menon, M., & Klinge, R. (2008). Belief inflexibility in schizophrenia. *Cognitive Neuropsychiatry, 13*(3), 267–277.

Wykes, T., Steel, C., Everitt, B., & Tarrier, N. (2008). Cognitive behavior therapy for schizophrenia: Effect sizes, clinical models, and methodological rigor. *Schizophrenia Bulletin, 34*(3), 523–537.

Zimmermann, G., Favrod, J., Trieu, V. H., & Pomini, V. (2005). The effect of cognitive behavioral treatment on the positive symptoms of schizophrenia spectrum disorders: A meta-analysis. *Schizophrenia Research, 77*, 1–9.

INDEX

aberrant beliefs, defined 1
abnormal experience: and delusion
    formation 35–6; term 52n.2
accentuated emotional modulation process
    (AEM), DSMF model 21
affect, and delusional reasoning 21–2, 23
affective disturbances, dysfunctional coping
    strategies 163
affective prediction error: and Capgras
    delusion 41–2, 51–2; and ventromedial
    prefrontal cortex (VMPFC) 42, 50
Affective Simon Task 139
affect-laden content, and delusional
    people 19 *see also* emotional
    content/materials
affirmation of the consequent (AC) 134
agency 125
algorithmic conception of sociality 109
alternative thinking strategies 155
ambiguity, aversion to 15 *see also*
    uncertainty
analytical thinking 17–19, 25, 92
Andreou *et al.* 65, 69
anomalous perceptions theory 23, 25
anorexia nervosa 62
antipsychotics 65, 154, 160 *see also*
    medication
anxiety: and avoidance behaviour 139;
    and beads task 71; and Better Safe
    Than Sorry strategy 148; and cognitive
    biases 149; cognitive theory of 1;
    and danger-relevant information
    processing 132; and data-gathering 70,

71; and decision-making 67; and
    delusions 9, 92; and emotion-based
    reasoning (ER) 135; and experiential
    reasoning 92; and fear 134–5; health
    anxiety 140; and hyper-vigilance
    for threat 10; and intrusions 137–8;
    and JTC bias 70–2, 86–7, 92; and
    maladaptive cognitive structures in
    memory 132; measurement of 71; and
    negative schemas 9; and reasoning 70,
    108, 149; schema-based cognitive model
    of 9; vulnerability 132, 133, 149
apophenia 125
Arieti, A. 102
Arntz *et al.* 137
arousal, and JTC bias 70–2
Asperger syndrome 64
associative system: and danger signals 134;
    fear responses generated by 132–3
attention allocation, and prediction
    error 51
attention deficit hyperactivity disorder
    (ADHD) 64
attributional bias: and misinterpretation of
    events 23; and schizophrenia 156
attributional styles: and MCT 156–7; social
    consequences of 156
Autism-Psychosis Model 63
autistic spectrum disorder (ASD) 63, 72
automatic associations, and phobic
    fears 139–40
automatic 'unconscious' system, of
    reasoning 91

avoidance behaviour: and anxiety
disorders 139; and phobic fears 138–9

BADE 16–17; and delusions 23, 67; future
research needs 26; and JTC bias 163;
and liberal acceptance bias 16–17; and
MCT 158–60; and schizophrenia 159;
and selection of evidence 24; and
ToM 162; and two-factor account 20
Balzan *et al.* 4
Bayesian model 24
beads task: and anxiety 71; Asperger
syndrome 64; autistic spectrum disorder
(ASD) 63; criticisms of 57; and
Empathising/Systemising scores 63;
explained 105; and JTC bias 11–12,
15, 16; and liberal acceptance bias 15;
methodological considerations 86;
people with delusions 13–14, 17,
19, 22, 56–7, 105–6; people with
OCD 62; role of emotional saliency 60;
schizophrenia 65, 86; variations in
results 59; and working memory/
executive processes 68–9
Beck, A. T. 1, 9
behavioural intervention, MCT as 155
behaviour, of participants/decision-making
tasks 86
belief bias 141, 142, 143, 144, 145–6,
146–7
belief bias modification training, as
cognitive vaccine 147
belief-confirming reasoning strategies, and
delayed extinction 147
belief evaluation system, abnormality
in 37, 38
belief flexibility, and schizophrenia 3–4
belief revision 2, 20, 110
belief(s) *see also* delusions: changing/
MCT 158–60; conviction of
truthfulness of 81; and cultures/
subcultures 81; delusions as multi-
dimensional 83; false 81; formation 25,
48; inflexibility/disadvantages
of 159; and JTC bias 25; as kind of
memory 43; mood-congruent 25; and
negative emotions 142; notion of 47;
peculiar/and intuitive thinking/negative
affect 92; and perception 45, 47–8;
phobogenic 133; sensitivity/and human
reasoning 108; and two-factor theory/
prediction-error theory 44–8; universal
danger beliefs 142–4 *see also* danger
beliefs; unsound 11
Bensi *et al.* 14

Bentall *et al.* 10, 62, 69, 105
Bentall, R. P. and Swarbrick, R. 15
Bermudez, J. L. 109, 110
Better Safe Than Sorry strategy 106, 144,
148
bias against disconfirmatory evidence
(BADE) *see* BADE
bias, term 11
Binswanger, L. 104, 108
bipolar disorder, and induced positive
mood 22
bizarre stranger hypothesis 20
Blackmore, S. J. and Trościanko, T. 115,
116, 117, 123, 125
Blagrove *et al.* 119, 120
blaming others, and persecutory
delusions 10
Blankenburg *et al.* 109
Bleuler, E. 101
Boden *et al.* 92
bodily fear response 135
body dysmorphic disorder (BDD) 63, 72
Bouhuys *et al.* 89
Brennan, J. H. and Hemsley, D. R. 2
Bressan, P. 117, 118, 119
Broome *et al.* 68
Brugger *et al.* 116, 117
Brugger, P. and Taylor, K. I. 125

Capgras delusion 3, 20, 35, 36, 37, 38–9,
41–2, 45, 46, 48, 49–51, 84
categorical syllogisms, and belief bias 142
causal attribution, and paranormal
believers 125
CBT 55, 66, 149
CBTp 56, 154, 164
chance effect, and paranormal
believers 116, 119, 123, 125
clairvoyance 126n.2
cognitive behavioural therapy (CBT) *see*
CBT
cognitive behavioural therapy for psychosis
(CBTp) *see* CBTp
cognitive biases: and anxiety disorders 149;
and CBT 149; and delusions 166; and
MCT 155, 164
cognitive deficits, and JTC bias 68
cognitive dissonance, and delusional
beliefs 25
Cognitive-Experiential Self Theory of
Personality (CEST) 90–1
cognitive impairment, and delusions 84
cognitive models, of anxiety
vulnerability 132
cognitive style, and memory 106

cognitive system, and threat detection 134
cognitive theories, of delusions 12
cognitive theory, of anxiety/depression 1
cognitive vaccine: belief-biased reasoning/
    socially anxious people 145–6; belief
    bias modification training as 147
Colbert et al. 59
Colbert, S. M. and Peters, E. R. 15
Coltheart et al. 2, 3, 20, 24, 25, 37, 38, 42,
    46, 48, 50
Coltheart, M. 45, 48, 49, 51
common sense, and schizophrenia 103
component–conjunction relationship,
    paranormal beliefs 122
conditional reasoning, schizophrenia
    104–5, 108
confirmation bias 115
conflict modulation failure, delusional
    people 18–19
conjunction errors, and paranormal
    belief 121, 122
conjunction fallacy, and paranormal
    belief 120, 122–3, 124
conservatism bias, phobic
    danger-beliefs 144
contamination fear 136–7, 138
control, illusion of/paranormal
    believers 117, 120
Conway et al. 106
coping strategies, dysfunctional/affective
    disturbances 163
Corcoran et al. 61
Corlett et al. 34, 41, 42, 43, 44, 46, 47,
    49, 51
Cotard delusion 3, 36
counter-evidence/counter argument,
    downplaying of/delusional
    people 158–9
cultures, and beliefs 81

Dagnall et al. 119, 120
Daley, K. 71
danger, and fear 134
danger associations 133, 139
danger beliefs 4, 133–4, 136, 138–9, 141,
    142–6, 148–9, 150 see also threat
danger-confirming reasoning 133, 139,
    148
danger-confirming strategy 21
danger-confirming vicious circle 134
danger-related associations 133, 139
danger-relevant belief bias, and linear
    syllogisms 142–3
danger-relevant information processing,
    and anxiety 132

danger signals, and reflexive (associative)
    system 134
data-gathering: and anxiety 70, 71;
    and arousal 71; and ASD 72;
    and BDD 72; biased 10, 12–14,
    57–8, 61; biased/predating psychosis
    onset 59; and domain-specific
    factors 87; and emotionally loaded
    content 60–1; and impulsivity/
    ADHD 64; and medication 73;
    and need for closure (NFC) 67; and
    non-clinical population 62; people
    with delusions 105; prevalence of
    reduced 58–60; and psychosis 58,
    59; with realistic tasks 13–14;
    schizophrenia 58, 69; and training in
    reasoning 12; and working memory/
    executive processes 64
decision-making: and anxiety 67;
    and arousal 70; and behaviour of
    participants 88; intuitive style 91;
    irrational 115; JTC bias/and
    MCT 157–8; and liberal acceptance
    bias 88; and OCD 62–3; people with
    delusions 19, 56–7; rational style 91, 92
deductive reasoning: performance/and
    emotional content 141–2; problems/
    and delusional people 20; syllogistic
    reasoning 102–4
de Jong, Peter 4
deliberation, preference for/positive
    affect 92
delusional beliefs see delusions
delusional conviction, reducing 12
delusional disorder see paranoia
delusional experiences/beliefs 83
delusional people: and BADE 16; beads
    task 13–14, 17, 19, 22, 56–7, 105–6;
    conflict modulation failure 18–19;
    data-gathering 105; emotional creativity
    of 89; MCT programmes 85; and
    negative schemas/affect 23; over-
    adjustment 18; recognition memory 14;
    and unusual scenarios 89; urgency to
    decide 19
delusional reasoning 2, 3, 4, 11–22, 22–5,
    56, 72, 84
delusional theme, paranormal beliefs as 4
delusional thinking, as DMSF 18–19
delusions 7–8 see also belief(s); and aberrant
    perceptions 9; as abnormal perceptual
    experiences 35–6, 84; affect and
    schemas 9–10; of alien control 36;
    and anomalous perceptions 23, 25; and
    anxiety 9, 92; and BADE 23, 67;

delusions (*cont.*):
  Capgras *see* Capgras delusion; and
  CBTp 56; and cognitive biases 166;
  and cognitive dissonance 25; and
  cognitive impairment 84; cognitive
  theories of 12; consideration/
  tentative acceptance of delusional
  hypothesis 24; continuity in 83;
  of control/passivity 81; of control/
  thought insertion 52; and data-
  gathering bias 12–14, 58–60, 61;
  and decision-making/evidence 19,
  56–7; defined 55, 80–1, 101, 110;
  dichotomous or continuous? 82–4; and
  draws to decision 62; emergence of
  delusional idea 23; and emotions 104;
  and epistemic rationality 110; as
  evaluations 84; example of 99–
  100; as fixed/resistant to counter
  evidence 55–6; formation/and
  abnormal experience 35–6; formation/
  maintenance 8, 34–5, 38–9, 49 *see also*
  delusions; maintenance of; four stages
  of 22–5; in general population 55,
  82, 83; grandiose 10, 22, 55, 57,
  61–2; and hallucinations 9; and hearing
  impairment 9; and hypersalience 67;
  incidence 80; and JTC bias 2, 11–12,
  23, 58–9, 64, 85, 105–6; maintenance
  of 25, 42–3, 46–7, 110; MCT
  programme for 4; and medication 73;
  monothematic 3, 35, 37, 44, 45–6;
  as multi-dimensional beliefs 83; and
  need for closure (NFC) 15–16, 67;
  non-clinical population 55, 82, 83;
  not always firmly sustained 81; and
  paranormal beliefs 1, 4; and perceptual
  experiences 9, 84; of persecution/
  reference/misidentification 10;
  persecutory 10, 55, 57, 61–2, 92,
  106–7; polythematic 37, 45–6;
  and probalistic reasoning 13, 107;
  psychological theories of 9–11; and
  reasoning 2, 3, 4, 11–22, 22–5, 56, 72,
  84; and schizophrenia 7, 80; selection
  of evidence/full acceptance of the
  delusional hypothesis 24–5; and social
  biases 166; specificity to 61–4; and
  talking therapies 56; theories of 3,
  22–5; and ToM 10–11; traits/
  vulnerability factors 59; two-factor
  theory 2–3, 9, 20, 23, 34–9; and
  ventromedial prefrontal cortex
  (VMPFC) 36, 37
Delusions Inventory (PDI) 83

depersonalisation disorder 36
depression 1, 10, 61, 62, 163
depressive cognitive biases 163
Diaconis, P. and Mosteller, F. 115
disgust, and phobias 136–7
disorganization, term 101
dissociability argument, Capgras
  delusion 36
dopaminergic agonist (l-dopa), and JTC
  bias 69
dopaminergic antagonist (haloperidol), and
  JTC bias 69
dopamine transmission, in
  schizophrenia 40
draws to certainty (DTC) 12
draws to decision (DTD) 17, 59, 61, 62, 66
DSMF 18–19, 21
DSM-IV/V: and delusional beliefs 7, 42,
  56, 80, 81, 82, 110; schizophrenia 101
dual process theories, of reasoning 18, 90
dual stream modulation failure (DSMF)
  see DSMF
dual system models, anxiety
  vulnerability 133, 149
dual system perspective, and correction/
  persistence of beliefs 133
Dudley *et al.* 12, 13, 19, 59, 60, 66, 85
Dudley, R. E. J. and Over, D. E. 21, 24
Dudley, Rob 2, 3

egocentric bias 115
Ellett *et al.* 70
Ellis, H. and Young, A. 35, 41
emotion: attempts to induce 21–2;
  heightened/and hypersalience effect 24;
  and testing 89
emotional content/materials: and data-
  gathering 60–1; and delusional
  reasoning 21; and JTC bias 21, 60; and
  reasoning 22, 90, 141–2
emotional creativity, of delusional
  people 89
emotion-based reasoning (ER): and anxiety
  disorder 135; and fear 137; and phobic
  beliefs 136
emotions: and delusions 104; and
  reasoning style preferences 91–2
Empathising/Systemising scores, and
  psychosis/evidence 63
empathizing, and MCT 161–3
epistemic rationality 109–10
epistemic utility 21–2
Epstein, Seymour 90, 91
erroneous responding, delusional
  people 20

errors, overconfidence in/and MCT 160–1
Evans *et al.* 69
Evans, J. St. B. T. and Over, D. E. 21
evidence: belief-confirming/-
disconfirming 115; contradictory 25;
and Empathising/Systemising
scores 63; and liberal acceptance
bias 24; mood-congruent 24; quality
of gathered/delusional people 24;
quantity of/JTC bias 25, 56; seeking
alternative/MCT 161
excitement, and holding unusual beliefs 89
executive processes: and bead task 69; and
data-gathering 64; and impulsivity/
ADHD 64; and probabilistic
reasoning 106
experiential reasoning 91, 92
experimental parapsychology 114
external events, and delusional ideas/
misinterpretation of 23
externalising attribution bias, two-factor
theory 38
extrasensory perception (ESP) 81, 114,
116, 122, 124, 125, 126; defined 126n.2

facial expressions, over-relying on/people
with schizophrenia 162
false memories 160
fear: and anxiety 134–5; bodily fear
response 135; of contamination 136–7,
138; and danger 134; and emotion-
based reasoning (ER) 137; phobic/and
automatic associations 139–40; phobic/
and avoidance behaviour 138–9;
responses/generated by associative
system 132–3
Fear, C. F. and Healy, D. 62
feelings, of participants/decision-making
tasks 86
Fine *et al.* 12, 21, 60, 73
Fisk, J. E. 121
Fletcher, P. and Frith, C. 34, 44, 45
Foulds Delusions-Symptoms-State
Inventory 83
fragmentation exercise, MCT 158
Freeman, D. 2, 23
Freeman, D. and Garety, P. A. 92
Freeman *et al.* 9, 10, 15, 18, 55, 58, 70,
85, 105
Freud, Sigmund 90
Frith, C. 10

gambling task, reasoning 106
Ganzfeld test, telepathy 124, 127n.9
Garety *et al.* 58, 59, 61, 62, 66, 69, 81, 105

Garety, P. A. and Freeman, D. 12, 64, 84
Garety, P. A. and Hemsley, D. R. 84
Garety, Philippa 2
gestures, over-relying on/people with
schizophrenia 162
goal sensitivity, and human reasoning 108
Goel *et al.* 102
Gottesman, L. and Chapman, L. J. 102
grandiose delusions 10, 22, 55, 57, 61–2

Hadlaczky, G. and Westerlund, J. 125
hallucinations 9, 10, 101
haloperidol, and JTC bias 69
health anxiety 140
hearing impairment: and delusions 9; and
paranoia 84
Helmholtz, H. 48
Hemsley, D. R. 13
heuristics, and paranormal believers 115
Hohwy, J. and Rajan, V. 45, 47
human reasoning *see* reasoning
Huq *et al.* 2, 11, 58, 59
hypersalience: and heightened emotion 24;
people with delusions/psychosis 18, 67
hyper-vigilance for threat 10, 23, 24
hypothesis-testing tasks 13

illusory correlations, of paranoid patients 2
Implicit Association Test 139
imposter hypothesis, and ventromedial
prefrontal cortex (VMPFC) 53n.3
impulsivity, and data-gathering 64
infectious disease, avoidance of/and
disgust 136
intolerance of uncertainty (IOU), and JTC
bias 67, 68
intrusion-based reasoning (IR), and
PTSD 137–8
intrusions, and anxiety disorders 137–8
intuitive scaling rule 115
intuitive style 91, 92
intuitive thinking 17–19, 23, 25, 92
IQ, and JTC bias 68

Jacobsen *et al.* 63
Jänsch, C. and Hare, D. J. 64
Jaspers, K. 80
John, C. H. and Dodgson, G. 13
JTC bias 11–12; and anorexia
nervosa 62; and anxiety 70–2, 86–7,
92; and arousal 70–2; and Asperger
syndrome 64; and attention deficit
hyperactivity disorder (ADHD) 64; and
autistic spectrum disorder (ASD) 63;
and BADE 163; and bead task 11–12,

JTC bias (*cont.*):
  15, 16; and body dysmorphic disorder
    (BDD) 63; and cognitive deficits 68;
    defined 58; and delusions 2,
    11–12, 23, 58–9, 64, 85, 105–6; and
    depression 62; and dopaminergic
    agonist (l-dopa) 69; and dopaminergic
    antagonist (haloperidol) 69; and
    emotional materials 21, 60; first-
    episode population 70; future research
    needs 26; in general population 59–60,
    85; and grandiose delusions 61–2; and
    intolerance of uncertainty (IOU) 67,
    68; and intuitive judgements 17; and
    IQ 68; and ketamine 69; and liberal
    acceptance bias 25, 88–90; longitudinal/
    intervention studies 64–6; manipulating
    stress/relaxation in 22; as marker
    of poor response/psychosis 66; and
    MCT 157–8; and medication 65,
    69; and memory 68–9, 72, 108;
    monothematic/and two-factor
    theory 44; motivational account of
    67–8; and need for closure (NFC) 15–16,
    67; or pushed to conclusions 84–5;
    over time 65–6; and paranoia 61–2,
    106; and persecutory delusions 61–2,
    106–7; and positive affect 92; as positive
    response 106; prefrontal groups 64;
    and probabilistic reasoning 108;
    and psychosis 85; and quantity of
    evidence 25, 56; and reasoning style
    preferences 92; schizophrenia 61, 62,
    66, 106; and stress 22, 86–7; as trait/
    state-like variable 64–5; two-factor
    theory 38; why do people? 66–72
jump to conclusions (JTC) bias *see* JTC
  bias

Kahneman, D. and Tversky, A. 117, 118
Kaliuzhna *et al.* 110
Kaney *et al.* 107
Kapur, S. 40
Kemp *et al.* 103, 104, 107
ketamine, and JTC bias 69
King, L. A. and Hicks, J. A. 92
knowledge translation programme, MCT
  as 155

lake/fish task 17
Langdon *et al.* 23, 105
LaRocco, V. A. and Warman, D. M. 88
Law of Truly Large Numbers (LTLN) 115
l-dopa, and JTC bias 69
Lee *et al.* 22

left visual field/right hemisphere (LVF/
  RH), and randomness perception 125
letter task 15
liberal acceptance bias 14–15; and
  BADE 16–17; and decision-making
  tasks 88; and delusional ideas 23; future
  research needs 26; and JTC bias 25,
  88–90; and plausibility 24, 88, 89; and
  quality of evidence 24
life after death 81, 127n.8
Lincoln *et al.* 22, 61, 62, 70
linear syllogisms: and danger-relevant
  belief bias 142–3; and social anxiety
  disorder 144–5
Linney *et al.* 13
logical reasoning: and general
  population 108; impaired/in delusional
  people 19; and schizophrenia 3–4, 103,
  104, 105, 108–9, 110; testing of 148;
  and WST 148
Lommen *et al.* 149
Lunt *et al.* 64

Magical Ideation Scale 83
Maher, B. A. 9, 20, 23, 25, 36, 81
Manktelow, Ken 3
Martha Mitchell Effect 81
McGuire *et al.* 88
McKay *et al.* 15, 37, 38
McKay, R. 39, 45, 49
medication *see also* antipsychotics: and
  data-gathering/delusions 73; and JTC
  bias 65, 69; schizophrenia 154
Mellet *et al.* 104
memory: and anxiety 132; belief as a kind
  of 43; confidence 160; fallibility 161;
  false memories 160; and JTC bias 68–9,
  72, 108; metamemory/MCT 160–1;
  and probabilistic reasoning 106;
  recognition/delusional people 14;
  reconsolidation/and maintainenance of
  delusions 46–7; schizophrenia/objective
  deficits 160; working memory 20, 64,
  68–9, 72, 139
Menon *et al.* 106
mental disorders, rationality in 109
metacognitive therapy (MCT+) 163–6
metacognitive training (MCT) 4, 66, 85,
  155–66
metamemory, and MCT 160–1
mind-over-matter 126n.2
Minkowski, E. 104
Mirian *et al.* 102, 103
mirrored-self misidentification 36
misattribution hypothesis 116

misidentification, delusions of 10
misinterpretation, of external events 23
Miyazono *et al.* 3
monothematic delusions: and dissociability
    argument 36; and polythematic
    delusions 45–6; and two-factor
    theory 3, 35, 37, 44
mood: manipulating positive 22; and
    MCT 163
mood-congruent: belief 25; evidence 24
mood disorders, reasoning in 108
mood induction, and testing 89–90
morbid rationalism 104
Moritz *et al.* 14, 15, 16, 22, 89
Moritz, S. and Woodward, T. S. 14, 58,
    88
Moritz, S. 2
Mortimer *et al.* 58, 62
motivational account, of JTC bias 67–8
motivationally formed delusions, two-
    factor theory 37, 38
multidimensional personality trait,
    schizotypy as 8
Muris *et al.* 135
Myin-Germeys *et al.* 81

need for closure (NFC): and data-
    gathering 67; delusion prone
    people 15–16, 67; and JTC bias 15–16,
    67
Need for Closure Scale (NFCS) 15
negative affect 23, 92
negative emotions, and beliefs 142
negative events, and people with
    delusions/schizophrenia 107
negative-other schemas, and grandiose
    beliefs 10
negative recency 115
negative schemas 9, 10, 23
neuropsychological delusions, and non-
    neuropsychological delusions 46
neuropsychological impairment, and bizarre
    perceptual anomalies 20
non-neuropsychological delusions, and
    neuropsychological delusions 46
normality, and psychosis 82

objective memory deficits, and
    schizophrenia 160
observational adequacy, and delusion
    formation 49
observational adequacy bias, two-factor
    theory 38
obsessive compulsive disorder (OCD)
    62–3, 138

Ormrod *et al.* 65
over-adjustment, delusional people 18
overconfidence in errors, and MCT
    160–1
Owen *et al.* 103, 110
Oxford-Liverpool Inventory of Feelings
    and Experiences (O-LIFE) 83

paleological thought 102
paranoia: and data-gathering bias 61; and
    depression 61; and draws to decision
    (DTD) 61; example of 99–100;
    and hearing impairment 84; and
    intuitive/rational thinking 18; and JTC
    bias 61–2, 106; and negative schemas 9;
    and self-esteem/depression 10; threat
    anticipation model of 2; and ToM 11
paranoid patients, illusory correlations of 2
paranormal beliefs: and causal
    attribution 125; and chance effect 116,
    119, 123, 125; component–conjunction
    relationship 122; and conjunction
    errors 121, 122; and conjunction
    fallacy 120, 122–3, 124; as a delusional
    theme 4; held in UK 81; and illusion
    of control 117, 120; and lack of
    analytical thinking 92; and probabilistic
    reasoning 4, 114, 115–24, 126; and
    psychological disorders 1; randomness
    misperception hypothesis (RMH)
    of 115, 116–17, 118–19, 123, 124,
    125, 126; and reasoning style 4; and
    uncertainty 115
patternicity 124
Pelissier, M. C. and O'Connor, K. P. 63
perceived utility, and reasoning 148
perception(s): and belief 45, 47–8;
    faulty/tainting reasoning process 9;
    formation of 48; and two-factor theory/
    prediction-error theory 44–8
perceptual experience(s): delusions as
    abnormal 9, 84; pre-potent doxastic
    responses to 38
persecutory delusions: and blaming others
    for negative events 10; and data-
    gathering bias 61; and experiential/
    rational reasoning 92; and JTC bias
    61–2, 106–7; and likelihood of negative
    events 107; and a person's worth 57;
    schizophrenia 55
Peters, E. and Garety, P. 59, 65, 84
Peters *et al.* 65, 83
pharmaceutical interventions,
    schizophrenia 154 *see also* medication
Phillips, L. D. and Edwards, W. 11, 86

phobic beliefs: and automatic associations 139–40; and avoidance behaviour 138–9; as conditional propositions 147; danger beliefs 4, 133–4, 136, 138–9, 141, 142–6, 148–9, 150; and disgust 136–7; and emotion-based reasoning (ER) 136; and reasoning 144, 149; refractoriness of 140; and rule-based system 4, 132–3
phobic stimuli, as signals of impending danger 132
phobogenic beliefs 133
Plato 90
plausibility, and liberal acceptance bias 24, 88, 89
polythematic delusions 37, 45–6
positive affect 10, 92
post-traumatic stress disorder (PTSD) 137–8
precognition 126n.2
prediction-error theory: delusion formation 34–5, 40–3; delusion maintenance 42–3; and hallucinations/delusions 3; problems with 41–3; target phenomena 44; v. two-factor theory 43–52
prefrontal groups, JTC bias 64
premonition, belief in power of 81
pre-potent doxastic responses, to perceptual experience 38
prior (danger) beliefs 141
probabilistic reasoning: beads task 17–18; and delusions 13, 107; and JTC bias 108; and memory 106; and paranormal beliefs 4, 114, 115–24, 126; schizophrenia 105–7
procedural rationality 109, 110
prosopagnosia (face blindness) 36
psychiatric phenomenology 108
psychokinesis (PK) 114, 122, 123, 124, 126n.2
psychological disorders, and paranormal beliefs 1
psychological models, of schizophrenia 166
psychological theories, of delusions 9–11
psychosis: and CBT 55; on a continuum 82; data-gathering bias predating onset 59; draws to decision (DTD) in 66; and Empathising/ Systemising scores 63; first-episode/JTC stability 65–6; and hypersalience 67; and JTC bias 85; and MCT 155; and normality 82; proneness measures 83; questionnaires/measuring liability to 83; and rationality 104; and reduced data

gathering 58; and schizotypy 8; targeted treatments 73; and ToM 11
Psychoticism Scale 83

questionnaires, measuring liability to psychosis 83

randomness, defined 126n.3
randomness misperception, and paranormal believers 115, 116–17, 118–19
randomness misperception hypothesis (RMH), of paranormal belief 119, 123, 124, 125, 126
randomness perception, and left visual field/right hemisphere (LVF/RH) 125
rational Bayesian analysis, using abductive inference 20
rational decision-making style 91, 92
Rational Experiential Inventory (REI) 18, 91
rational-experiential processing, and System 1/and 2 models 90–1
rationalism, morbid 104
rationality: epistemic/procedural 109–10; in mental disorders 109; notion of 108, 109; and psychosis 104; in schizophrenia 101
rational reasoning 18, 91, 92, 100, 103–4
realistic tasks, data-gathering with 13–14
reality testing, MCT+ 164
reasoning: and aberrant beliefs 1; and anxiety 70, 108, 149; automatic 'unconscious' system of 91; belief-biased/and syllogisms 141; and belief/goal sensitivity 108; biases/future research needs 26; danger-confirming fallacy 133, 139, 148; deficit/childhood/adolescence 26; delusional 2, 3, 4, 11–22, 22–5, 56, 72, 84; disgust based/and danger beliefs 136; dual process theories of 18, 90; effects of emotional material 21, 22, 90, 141–2; and emotions 91; experiential system of 91, 92; faulty perceptions tainting 9; and formal logic 2, 108; gambling task 106; with heart/head 90–1; human 108; and logic 148 *see also* logical reasoning; models 141; in mood disorders 108; and paranormal beliefs 4, 114, 115–24, 126; and perceived utility 148; and phobic beliefs 144, 149; and phobic danger beliefs 149, 150; and positive mood 22; probabilistic 69, 115–24; rational 18, 91, 92, 100, 103–4; in

schizophrenia 11, 85, 101, 102, 105, 107–10; self-referent 10; styles 4, 66, 91–2, 146; tasks/with emotive content 22; theories of 22; and training in data-gathering 12
recognition memory, delusional people 14
Reese *et al.* 63
reference, delusions of 10
reflexive (associative) system, and danger signals 134
reflexive responses, to impending threat 133–4
relapse, prevention/and MCT 155
representativeness heuristic 115
Reverse Othello syndrome 37, 38
Rhodes *et al.* 87
right hemispheric functioning, and ESP believers 125
Rogers *et al.* 120, 121, 122
Rominger *et al.* 125
rule-based system: and anxiety disorders 137; and danger associations 139; and phobic beliefs 4, 132–3

safety behaviours 138–9
salient experience, and prediction errors 40–1
scenarios, unusual/and delusion-prone individuals 89
schema-based cognitive model, of anxiety 9
schemas, negative 9–10, 23
schizophrenia: and antipsychotics 154; and attribution bias 156; and BADE 159; and bead task 65, 86; and belief flexibility 3–4; and belief revision 110; and CBTp 154; and common sense 103; and complex social events 156–7; conditional reasoning 104–5, 108; continuity in condition 82–3; data-gathering 58, 69; and delusions 7, 80; and depression 163; and dopamine transmission 40; and epistemic rationality 110; and global affective flattening 36; incidence 80; JTC bias 61, 62, 66, 106; and liberal acceptance bias 14; and likelihood of negative events 107; and logical reasoning 3–4, 103, 104, 105, 108–9, 110; medication 154; and memory confidence 160; meta-cognitive training (MCT) programme 66; and objective memory deficits 160; and persecutory/grandiose delusions 55;

and prediction-error theory 44; predictors of remission 65; probabilistic reasoning 105–7; procedural rationality 110; psychological models of 166; reasoning in 11, 85, 100, 101, 102, 103–4, 105, 107–10; reduced data-gathering 58, 69; and self-esteem 163; social cognition in 161–2; and social relationships 109; syllogistic reasoning 102–4, 108; and two-factor theory 44
Schizotypal Personality Scale 83
schizotypy 8, 16, 26
self-esteem: fragile/and persecutory delusions 10; low social 146; and MCT 163; and paranoia 10; people with schizophrenia 163; and self-serving bias 156
self-generated physical behaviour/mental events, and delusions 52
self-referent reasoning 10
self-serving bias, and self-esteem 156
sequential information, and delusional people 13
Shermer, M. 124, 125
Signal Detection Theory (SDT) 124
social anxiety disorder (SAD) 135, 144–6
social biases: and delusions 166; and MCT 155
Social Cognition and Interaction Training (SCIT) programme 155
social cognition, in schizophrenia 161–2
social comparison, and social anxiety disorder 144
social consequences, of attributional styles 156
social events, complex/and people with schizophrenia 156–7
social relationships, and schizophrenia 109
Socratic discussion, MCT+ 164
So *et al.* 62, 70
Speechley *et al.* 17–18, 19, 21, 24, 25
spider phobia 144
split-mind speculations 90
Stanghellini, G. and Ballerini, M. 109
Stanovich, K. E. 91
statistical theory 126n.4
Stone, T. and Young, A. 49
stress: induced 22; and JTC bias 86–7
supernatural phenomena 114 *see also* paranormal beliefs
syllogisms: and belief-biased reasoning 141; categorical/and belief bias 142; linear/and danger-relevant belief bias 142–3; linear/and social anxiety disorder 144–5

syllogistic reasoning, in schizophrenia
102–4, 108
System I/System II mental systems 90
see also analytical thinking; intuitive
thinking

talking therapies, and delusions 56
telepathy 126n.2
temporal bias 115
testing: and emotion 89; and mood
induction 89–90
Thematic Aperception Test (TAT) 14, 88
theory of mind (ToM) 10–11, 23,
161–3
therapeutic interventions, targeting
delusions 81
therapy goals, establishing/MCT+ 164
threat *see also* danger beliefs: and cognitive
system 134; hyper-vigilance for 10,
23, 24; potential/and JTC bias 106;
reflexive responses as input 133–4
threat anticipation model 2, 9–10, 23
threat-confirming belief bias 148, 149
traits: and emergence of psychosis/
delusional beliefs 59; JTC bias 64–5
trauma-related intrusions 137
treatments, targeted/psychosis 73
Twenty Questions Game 13
two-factor theory: and BADE 20;
of delusions 2–3, 9, 20, 23, 34–9;
incorporating elements of prediction-
error theory 48–52; and monothematic
delusions 3, 35, 37, 44; problems
with 37–9; target phenomena 44; v.
prediction-error theory 43–52

Type 2 belief bias effects 141

uncertainty: inability to tolerate/JTC 67,
68; and paranormal believers 115

validation, and threat-biased
conclusions 148
ventromedial prefrontal cortex (VMPFC):
and affective prediction error 42, 50;
and Capgras delusion 46; damage
to/and delusions 36, 37; and imposter
hypothesis 53n.3
visual discrimination tasks 13
Volans, P. J. 62
von Domarus, E. 2, 11, 102
von Domarus principle 102
vulnerability factors, and emergence of
psychosis/delusional beliefs 59

Warman, D. M. and Martin, J. M. 21,
60
Warman *et al.* 62, 66
Wason Selection Task (WST) 13, 19,
147–8
White *et al.* 149
White, L. O. and Mansell, W. 14, 15, 19
Williams, E. B. 11
Wittorf *et al.* 62
Woodward *et al.* 65
Woodward, Todd 2
working memory 20, 64, 68–9, 72, 139

Young, H. F. and Bentall, R. P. 13, 14

Ziegler *et al.* 13, 15